DATE DUE

MAY 0 3 2008			
GAYLORD			PRINTED IN U.S.A.

Schools and Religions
Imagining the Real

Also available from Continuum

Is Religious Education Possible? – Michael Hand

Education and Community – Dianne Gereluk

Philosophy of Education – Richard Pring

Theory of Education – David Turner

Analysing Underachievement in Schools – Emma Smith

Key Ideas in Educational Research – David Scott and Marlene Morrison

Private Education – Geoffrey Walford

Markets and Equity in Education – Geoffrey Walford

Schools and Religions

Imagining the Real

Julian Stern

continuum

Continuum International Publishing Group

The Tower Building
11 York Road
London
SE1 7NX

80 Maiden Lane
Suite 704
New York
NY 10038

www.continuumbooks.com

British Library Cataloguing-in-Publication Data
A catalogue record for this book is available from the British Library.

ISBN-10: 0826485049 (hardback)
ISBN-13: 9780826485045 (hardback)

Library of Congress Cataloging-in-Publication Data
A catalog record for this book is available from the Library of Congress.

Typeset by BookEns Ltd, Royston, Herts.
Printed and bound in Great Britain by Biddles Ltd, King's Lynn, Norfolk

Contents

Acknowledgements

Wanting to meet an author because you like his work is like wanting to meet a duck because you like pâté.

(Atwood 2003, p. 30)

The Westhill Trust sponsored the series of seminars on which much of Chapters 5 to 10 and parts of Chapter 14 are based. Many thanks should go to all the trustees, especially Colin Johnson who attended most of the seminars, both for sponsoring and for helping to organize the series. Lat Blaylock of *RE Today Services* was the chief organizer of the seminars and of the arrangements for the publication of this book and its companion (Stern 2006b): his wisdom and knowledge of the world of religious education is invaluable. Lat is also a member of the CE Research Committee which supported both the seminar series and the two books derived from it, and the whole of this group, including its chair Ian Birnie, should be thanked. All of the presenters and participants in the seminars will, I hope, find themselves in the book. Pupils in a number of schools contributed to the book, especially those quoted in Chapter 7 (largely from Ipgrave's research), Chapter 8 (largely from my own research), and in some of the chapter headings (largely from the PCfRE religious education festival database, www.pcfre.org.uk/db/). The researchers in those schools agreed not to name pupils, but I hope they recognize themselves: readers will recognize their insight and authority, and thank them for that. As the 8 year old is quoted in Chapter 7 as saying, 'we're sort of teaching the grown ups'. Indeed.

Those who helped at other stages of the writing include Lat, once more, and Mike Bottery, Steve Burwood, Nick Owen, Pam Rauchwerger, Peter Ryley, Chris Sink, Marie Stern and Gary Wilkinson. Many other colleagues and friends in various organizations have been supportive, providing time, encouragement, audiences and much more. These include those at the University of Hull, the European Forum for Teachers of Religious Education (EFTRE), the Hull and East Riding Standing Advisory Councils for Religious Education (SACREs), Lincolnshire SACRE, the Westhill Trust, the CE Research Committee, the Association of University Lecturers in Religion and Education (AULRE), the Hong Kong Institute of Education, and Seattle Pacific University. Alexandra Webster and Continuum Books have been imaginatively supportive of this whole project. All the faults in the book remain my own.

The book is dedicated to Marie: no one stands alone.

Foreword

If the world is to be harmonious and secure, we must understand and welcome the diversity of peoples that make up the pluralism which is typical of many modern nations. Sometimes, however, the demand for national identity with clear boundaries seems to lead away from the community integration which alone can create the security that is compatible with diversity. How can various communities live together, whether within a nation or between nations? How can they understand and accept each other?

Education must play a key role in this, and there is a fact about the educational system described in this book which is highly relevant to the problems that face the world today. The fact is that in the schools of England and Wales the vast majority of pupils receive a basic introduction into the lofty ideals and the daily practices of Islam. In some countries this is not yet possible. Either the law does not permit it, the churches may not encourage it or the public (and sometimes the Muslim communities themselves) will not tolerate it. In England and Wales, however, this has been achieved, not without some opposition and some misunderstanding, and has become a regular feature of the curriculum in both primary and secondary schools, often including church related schools. Islam, of course, is not the only religion taught to children; learning about and from Christian faith is even more widespread, while Judaism, Hinduism, Buddhism and Sikhism are not neglected.

Religious education in England and Wales is remarkable in that children and young people of all religions are taught in one classroom, not divided along religious lines, and learn from a professionally trained teacher who does not necessarily represent any of the religions included in the curriculum. In some countries, only one religion is taught in the schools; in others, many religions are taught, but separately. In England and Wales, religious education is not based on the religious identity which children may or may not possess, but on what they have in common, their role as learners.

This feature of the educational system, although supported by government and indeed required by law has flowed from a deep sense of the value of the human person. Modern religious education affirms the right of every boy and girl to make educational contact with the spiritual inheritance of humanity and also the right of every pupil to develop there own life values in dialogue with other people and with the various traditions and commitments of their families and communities.

These values and their educational expressions are explained and defended by

Julian Stern in this book. Religious education, he argues, must be based upon a philosophy of the person. He shows how this influences religious education and enables the subject to offer so much to pupils with all kinds of special needs and interests. At every stage, the discussion is supported by references to relevant and influential research. Julian Stern makes a notable contribution to the quest for peace and justice through education and his book will inspire and inform those who have this concern at heart.

John M. Hull
The Queen's Foundation
Birmingham, August 2006

Preface

Each book is a tactic

(Benjamin 1997, p. 19)

This book presents and analyses research on religion and schools (including on religious education in schools) generating a philosophy of schooling that puts schools at the centre of debates on education, social inclusion and politics. It is a contribution to dialogue, dialogue much needed in a world full of fundamental divisions – divisions recognized in, and often overcome in, classrooms across the world.

The idea for the book started back in 2001, with a seminar held in London funded by the St Gabriel's Trust on research in religious education and its relationship to broader educational research (with one key presentation adapted from Jackson 1999 and later published in Jackson 2004, ch. 9). At the same time, the present author completed research on learning communities (Stern 2001a, 2001b) and on religious education and school effectiveness (Stern 2000b, 2001c, 2001d, 2001e, also related to Lenga and Ogden 2000, Lovelace 2001, Lowndes 2001), and came to a position, in the University of Hull, where he could bring together these research themes in his work. Following the St Gabriel's Trust seminar, the RE Today Research Committee decided to bring together UK religious education professionals and researchers in a series of meetings, to exchange ideas on what was happening in religious education classrooms and what was being covered in religious education research. Over a year was spent, working out what areas of research were going on in religious education, and how to divide up the meetings, geographically and by topic. Thanks to the generosity of the Westhill Trust, a series of six meetings subsequently took place during 2004 and 2005, the *Westhill Trust Seminars*. A total of 73 people attended one or more of those meetings, over 30 of whom were practising classroom teachers. The topics were religious education and sacred text, dialogue, inclusion, pedagogy, human rights and citizenship, and ethnography. Presenters included Fatma Amer, Lat Blaylock, Terence Copley, Liam Gearon, James Holt, Julia Ipgrave, Bob Jackson, Eleanor Nesbitt, Linda Rudge, Sarah Smalley, Julian Stern and Geoff Teece.

All the meetings included presentations by key researchers, and contributions by, and discussions with, all the participants. A number of articles have been published (such as Johnson and Stern 2005), and in addition to those articles, two books would be published. One book (Stern 2006b) would be a guide for all religious education teachers about how research and practice in religious education come together. A second book, the current book, would provide more scholarly work on all the themes of the Westhill Seminars, set in a context of a much wider debate on education, connecting schooling and religion, fulfilling, it is hoped, the suggestion of Jackson of setting research in religious education in the mainstream of education research debates.

Chapter 1

Introduction: the philosophy of schooling

the space between

(Salmon 2004, p. 1)

Action philosophy

Schooling is taken for granted, despite being a rather modern invention; religion is often ignored, despite its longevity. Time to take stock of schooling and religion, then. Those who take schooling for granted tend to assume that schooling and learning are synonyms. Yet learning is a universal: everyone learns and learning has been going on throughout history. If schooling is worth retaining, it must prove its connection to learning, and it must do much more. It must show what it is for, and why the alternatives are insufficient. No other organization is quite like a school, and no other organization could replace a school: that is what must be demonstrated. Those who ignore religion tend to treat it as old-fashioned, false, irrelevant and dangerous. Perhaps it is all these things, perhaps not, but it is here: it has not gone away. Religion must at the very least be taken account of, when studying how people live: the need to understand religion is what must be demonstrated.

Research on the nature and purpose of schooling has in recent years increasingly focused on schools as learning communities. This brings together learning theories of 'communities of practice', looking at apprenticeship models of learning, with theories of dialogue and community, looking at the character of human relationships. Looking inwards, schooling must be understood in terms of the nature of its pupils and staff and their relationships. Looking outwards, schooling must be understood in terms of its relationships with communities beyond the school, and the national and global social, cultural and political context beyond that. In a world in which variety within and between religious and non-religious ways of living underpins personal, communal, national and international identity, schooling can be at the hub of dialogue between people, young and old, dialogue within and between religions, past and present, dialogue between religious and non-religious ways of living, and dialogue between nations.

This book therefore investigates what schooling is for. Drawing on research from sociological, psychological, religious and policy studies disciplines, it is most of all a book of philosophy. The connection to more empirical research disciplines makes it tempting to say this is a book of 'applied philosophy', but that phrase begs the question of what its opposite might be: 'pure philosophy', 'philosophy unconnected to the world', 'useless philosophy'? All are inappropriate. Instead, a lead is taken from the use of 'action research' to describe a type of research that is set in a cycle of being informed by, informing, then being informed by (at a more advanced level), the professional activity of the researcher. 'Action philosophy' is therefore the description given to an attempt to understand, where that understanding informs and is informed by professional activity – in this case, work in schools and other learning communities. To be philosophy, it is not enough simply to be an attempt to understand and to inform and be informed by activity; there must also be what Pring requires of action research: 'a context of openness, public scrutiny and criticism' (Pring 2000, p. 138). The embeddedness of this philosophical approach (in activity and in public scrutiny) is therefore able to recognize what Cherry (1995) memorably refers to as the 'stubborn particulars' of the world, those particulars that research of all kinds ignores at its peril.

The first stubborn particular is the person. Section A of the book starts from being human (in Chapter 2), and the book moves on to consider the place of people in the world and the nature of reality, explaining the subtitle of the book as 'imagining the real'. These are the foundations of any philosophical study of humanity, and the foundations of much of the study of religion. There is a more narrow focus on the nature of community, in Chapter 3, which investigates how a community (the second stubborn particular) can exist when the people within it have contrasting and apparently incompatible ways of living and believing. Living with plurality is a characteristic of modern communities and societies, most especially because the connections and communication in the smallest of communities is likely, *inter alia*, to involve the whole world: true privacy is barely possible, yet true intimacy as well as social-political engagement are still absolutely necessary. Nowhere is this more significant than in schools. Schools themselves are therefore the third of the stubborn particulars, and their purposes and activities are explored in Chapter 4, with the nature of school-based research – a very specific form of learning – explored, in turn, in Chapter 5.

People, community and schools are brought together, philosophically speaking, in ways that are recognized by those studying and involved with religion. The fourth and most stubborn of particulars is religion itself, as all the powers of rationalism and late modernity have, despite widespread predictions to the contrary, left the world full of religious people, religious battles, religious fundamentals and fundamentalisms. In the absence, at times, of recognition of the positive value of religion, it is religions' destructive powers that have caught the world's attention in recent years. Section B therefore looks at how religion and schools interact, based around common research themes and common teaching themes in school religious education. Chapter 6 investigates uses of sacred texts in classrooms, and the ways in which they may be misused, sometimes out of a concern for their 'storybook' qualities at the expense of their religious significance, sometimes out of a concern about their status as religious artefacts at the expense of their meaning. The relationship between text and context is initially considered as a concern for teachers of religious education, but it is clearly a concern for all subjects dealing with texts, especially language and literature lessons, and history lessons. Similarly widely used across all subjects, yet with a particular resonance for teachers of religious education, are techniques for the effective use of dialogue in classrooms, addressed in Chapter 7. Dialogue has personal, existential, significance. Dialogue is also the basis for national and international politics, and not simply because, in Churchill's phrase, 'to jaw-jaw is always better than to war-war'. In politics, dialogue continues even through war. The point is, to engage in real dialogue, not 'monologue disguised as dialogue' (Buber 2002a, p. 22), alongside fighting and peace-making and working and living.

Making dialogue central to education does not in itself determine who will be dialoguing. The principles of inclusive education are needed, to affirm the need for dialogic communities to be of particular kinds. Inclusion can be peculiarly difficult to achieve within religion and religious education, and it is therefore all the more important to consider inclusion in these areas. Chapter 8 looks at ways of achieving inclusion in religious education across the range of pupil needs, and ways of achieving an inclusiveness with respect to religious traditions. Given those complex, overlapping, needs and traditions, the relationship between teachers and pupils is in need of careful study. It is therefore the nature of religion and religious education itself that is addressed by Chapter 9, in considering how pupils and teachers work together in classrooms. However, just as dialogue has broad political implications and influences, the teaching–learning relationship in the classroom has a political side. This is captured in Chapter 10 by a consideration of religious education, human rights, values and citizenships. Children's rights to, and need of, learning are complemented by rights to safety and self-respect. How this is achieved when dealing with religious education is a challenge: a challenge met by some by ignoring or refusing to countenance any religious education. Religious education really is seen as dangerous: why else would it be excluded from most schools in France and the USA?

Having looked at how religion and schools come together in various forms of religious education, Section C reviews the theorizing of the first part of the book, in the light of religious education. Chapter 11 traces links between dialogue and creativity, to develop a model of imaginative learning that builds on the work from Chapters 2 and 7. Chapter 12 draws together the community political implications of earlier work, especially in Chapters 3 and 10, into a model of leading and following in learning communities. The boundaries between school and non-school, raised first in Chapter 4 and addressed throughout the chapters on religious education (notably Chapter 9 on pedagogy), are concluded in Chapter 13 on learning beyond school. Finally, the research themes, especially from Chapters 5 to 10, are brought together in Chapter 14, which is a celebration of sincerity, research and people. Of course, life is going on, with or without religious education, and the detailed study of life, especially studies using ethnographic techniques, can help pupils and teachers alike come to understand religion – and all ways of living – without necessarily searching specifically for the religious. It is that discovery of how people think about life and death that has stimulated much interest in religious education from those without a theological background. Schools and religions have in common various community characteristics, contested approaches to truth, and boundary disputes, all making them hard to research and understand. To the extent that schools and religious communities are themselves striving towards truths, that striving can in itself both link them to each other and provide a basis for enlightening research. The philosophy of schooling is therefore tested by school engagement with religion, illuminated by characteristics of religions, and best understood through research reflecting that engagement and those characteristics.

Philosophers and more

Throughout the book, there are engagements with philosophers and others who have written about people, schooling, community and religion. An introduction to the book's structure should therefore be complemented by an introduction to some of these key authors. At the centre of things is a pair of philosophers active in the middle years of the twentieth century, John Macmurray and Martin Buber. John Macmurray lived from 1891 to 1976. Brought up in the Scottish Calvinist tradition, as a youth he became an evangelical Christian preacher, but withdrew from all institutional religion during World War I in response to the reception churchgoers gave his views on war. His reasons for withdrawal are interesting, and illuminate his views on human nature and the making of community. Life in the trenches, facing death all the time, appeared to him to allow people to make more 'real' connections, and therefore be more 'real' in a spiritual sense. He describes how, on a brief period of leave from the war, during which time he was preaching,

> [b]efore twenty-four hours had passed I wanted to get back to the trenches, where for all the misery and destruction, the spiritual atmosphere was relatively clean. It was, I think, the ignorant and superstitious hatred of the Germans, and the equally ignorant and unreal glorification of us, in the trenches, as heroes that had this effect. (Macmurray 1995a, p. 20)

He joined the Society of Friends late in his life, but despite spending most of his life outside organized religion, he always considered himself a Christian, and wrote extensively about religion in his work as a professional philosopher. That academic career started in Balliol College, Oxford, becoming a professor at University College London, and then settling in Edinburgh University where he eventually became Dean of the Faculty of Arts and retired in 1955. As a philosopher, he did not follow the mainstream (see for example Hodgkin 1997), avoiding the language philosophy of Ayer and colleagues, but was a popular writer and radio broadcaster on moral, social, political and religious issues, as a 'public intellectual'. His work on education is less well-known than that on religion. Indeed, Macmurray's papers on education were rejected for publication by two publishers, and remain unpublished (Costello 2002, p. 320 and p. 417, with one of the rejection letters in Macmurray 1968). However, his philosophical reputation rose in the 1990s, two decades after his death, as academic philosophy and psychology returned to the personal, relational and applied ethical topics that had dominated Macmurray's work. His views on community also gained fame through the high-profile admiration shown by UK prime minister Tony Blair, who wrote the foreword to a new selection of Macmurray's works (Macmurray 1996, and see Brittan 1997). Blair praised the philosopher for his views on the relationship of people to society and on spirituality, as Macmurray 'places the individual firmly within a social setting – we are what we are, in part, because of the other' (Blair in Macmurray 1996, p. 9), and 'spirituality was based in this world; it was not an abstraction from it' (Blair in Macmurray 1996, p. 10). In a characteristic phrase, Blair reportedly said that

> if you really want to understand what I'm all about, you have to take a look at a guy called John Macmurray. It's all there. (Kirkpatrick 2005, p. 157)

Blair was following in the tradition of a previous leader of the Labour Party, Hugh Gaitskell, who was a student of Macmurray's at Oxford before becoming a political philosopher at University College and then a politician. Of course, the extent to which Gaitskell's Labour Party or Blair's government followed Macmurray's principles is a separate issue.

As a philosopher, Macmurray not only rejected narrowly linguistic philosophy, but also the bulk of the philosophical tradition from Descartes. It is Descartes' dualism, often seen as the starting point of modern European philosophy, to which Macmurray objects, as it 'led inevitably to atheism' (Conford in Macmurray 1996, p. 21). The division between mind and matter led to the division of the 'spiritual' and the 'secular', and in the end, religion 'if not rejected outright as illusory, becomes a question of pure subjectivity, while the organization of everyday life is surrendered to scientists, managers and technocrats' (Conford in Macmurray 1996, p. 21). Philosophical systems based on dualism, and approaches to education based on these systems, therefore fall into an atheistical materialism or an idealism based on false views of the 'spiritual'. Spinoza, incidentally, had a similar view of Descartes, and in one of the surprisingly robust parts of the *Ethics* says: 'Such is the doctrine of this illustrious philosopher (in so far as I gather it from his own words); it is one which, had it been less ingenious, I could hardly believe to have proceeded from so great a man' (Spinoza 1955, p. 246).

Martin Buber (1878–1965) met Macmurray, and Buber is quoted as saying 'I see no difference between us ... [i]t is simply that you are the metaphysician and I am the poet' (Costello 2002, p. 322). Buber was far more than a poet, but his was not a traditional academic career. He was born in Vienna, and grew up in Lemberg/Lvov. He first worked as an editor in a publishing house, living in Berlin, then near Frankfurt, and continued freelance writing. In 1923, in his mid-40s, he became a lecturer in the Study of Jewish

Religion and Ethics at the University of Frankfurt, and was later – through the Nazi period until 1938 – director of the Centre for Jewish Adult Education. In 1938 he took up a post of professor of sociology in the Hebrew University in Jerusalem, after religious objections to a post in religious studies, and stayed there through his retirement until his death in 1965 (see Schaeder's biographical sketch in Glatzer and Mendes-Flohr 1991, and www.buber.de/en/). He is described by Friedman as taught by Dilthey, inflenced by Simmel, and having a philosophy that 'went back to Ferdinand Tönnies's distinction between *Gemeinschaft* (community) and *Gesellschaft* (association) and to that stream of "utopian socialism" that flowed from Proudhon and Lassalle through ... Kropotkin and Gustav Landauer' (Friedman 1999, p. 403). However, Buber's sense of community 'was not the natural community of the family or the village commune ... [but] a community of choice around a common centre, the voluntary coming together of human beings in direct relationship' (Friedman 1999, p. 406).

Buber's philosophy and life were both dominated by dialogue or meetings between people, an approach to life he upheld through the fires of Nazi Germany and the conflicts creating and straining the state of Israel. It is with considerable feeling that Friedman can therefore say of Buber that '[t]here is no human situation which is so rotten and God-forsaken that the meeting with otherness cannot take place within it' (Friedman 2002, p. 101). The attempt to *engage* was not an attempt to incorporate or create a single organic whole. Central Europe and Jerusalem in the twentieth century were not places for such thin utopianism. As Hölderlin (Buber's favourite poet, according to Schaeder in Glatzer and Mendes-Flohr 1991, p. 10–11), said in the poem *The Root of All Evil*:

> Being at one is god-like and good, but human, too human, the mania
> Which insists there is only the One, one country, one truth and one way.
> (Hölderlin 1990, p. 139)

Just as Macmurray had high-profile political supporters, so did Buber, who was put forward for a Nobel Prize by the Secretary General of the United Nations, Dag Hammarskjöld (Buber 2002a, p. xi). When Hammarskjöld said he wanted to translate some of Buber's work into Swedish, Buber suggested he start with *I and Thou*. The project was never completed, but the original text and twelve pages of translation were found with his papers and his body in the plane crash that killed him in 1961 (Glatzer and Mendes-Flohr 1991, pp. 641–2). Four years later, Buber's own death has Israel's President Shazar leading the mourners, with the principal funeral oration delivered by Premier Levi Eshkol (Schaeder in Glatzer and Mendes-Flohr 1991, p. 61).

At the start of this section, reference is made to 'philosophers and others' who have influenced the book. The 'other' to be introduced here is the personal construct psychologist Phillida (Phil) Salmon (1933–2005), who worked on education and psychology in distinctive and enormously important ways (for example Salmon 1988, 1998). For every teacher excited by teaching and loving learning, there is a cynic and a fact-monger. For every enthusiastic and creative child, there is a disruptive and bored pupil. Amongst many of Salmon's insights, is that each of these opposites exists in the same person. She explored how people can understand and live with both, and how people can change. A simple description of the research tool carrying her name starts with drawing a straight line, and putting contrasting words at each end. Happy and sad, successful and unsuccessful, cooperative and uncooperative, good teacher and bad teacher: anything. That is the start, the Salmon Line (Salmon 1994, also used in Chapter 8, below, to analyse religious education). Where are you on the line, now? Where would you like to be in the future? Mark these points on the line. Now write, or better still talk, about how you think you will get from one point to the other. In the talk is the learning, an insight complementing Buber on dialogue.

Personal construct psychology, developed by George Kelly (1905–66) (Kelly 1955), was the tradition within which Salmon worked, and as the name suggests, it is concerned with how people construe or construct themselves – part of the broader social constructivist tradition in psychology from Vygotsky (1896–1934). For Salmon, 'we should think of construing not as something that is the property of separate individuals ... [as] it is a process that occupies the space between them' (Salmon 2004, p. 1). This interpersonal view of personal construing is supported by a study of thought-disordered schizophrenia, following the work of Don Bannister. According to Salmon and Bannister, 'it is not to the cognitive sphere that we should be looking [for the construing of thought-disordered schizophrenics], rather the discursive sphere within which personhood becomes established and sustained' (Salmon 2004, p. 5), as successful work has concentrated on dialogue, where 'the goal has been to establish respectful, non-intrusive yet empathic relations with people labelled schizophrenic' (Salmon 2004, p. 5). Salmon's work illuminates personhood for everyone, recognizing difference and 'otherness': '[i]t is the refusal to allow children their otherness in over-intrusive, symbiotic early relationships which evidently forestalls the development of personhood' (Salmon 2004, p. 6). Learning is how people live and change, and learning is not always a happy experience, even when it is necessary. This is illustrated by the biblical accounts of Adam and Eve: coming to know does not lead to a peaceful enlightenment, a happy-ever-after of wisdom (or, in the more restricted modern view, employment), but in responsibility and work and perhaps pain (Salmon 1995, pp. 18–20). And with that encouragement, may the rest of the book begin.

Section A: Dialogue, community, society and learning

The fact is that the creation of common purposes presupposes a unity of persons already achieved; not through purpose.

(Macmurray 1968)

This section starts from being human and moves on to consider the place of people in the world and the nature of reality. People in dialogue make community. Schools are public organizations that 'mediate between the family and the larger world of adult life' (Macmurray 1968, p. 35), often expected to fulfil national and international political expectations. How do people come to understand how schools might function in the modern, plural, increasingly globalized, world? Can schools be inclusive community schools? What possible roles does research have in such schools?

The movement is from self through transcendence of self, without the loss of self: 'the capacity for self-transcendence ... is the defining character of the personal' (Macmurray 1993, p. 58). It is an imaginative movement, imagining the real, a reality of the personal and communal. Politics comes later – in Sections B and C – as even politics must start from the personal. Havel describes it well when he says that '[p]oliticians at international forums may reiterate a thousand times that the basis of the new world order must be universal respect for human rights, but it ... must be rooted in self-transcendence: transcendence as a hand reaching out to those close to us, to foreigners, to the human community, to all living creatures, to nature, to the universe; ... transcendence as the only real alternative to extinction' (Václav Havel quoted in Sacks 2003, p. 45). Surprisingly, educational policy-makers have come to a similar conclusion, with UK statutory curriculum guidance recommending '[r]ecognising and valuing the worth of each individual; developing a sense of community; the ability to build up relationships with others ... [and] recognising the existence of others as independent from oneself' (SCAA 1995, pp. 3–4). Perhaps it is too much to suggest, with Brighouse, that '[i]n the end, teachers are the bedrock of social justice and political freedom and the enemies of mental and economic slavery' (Brighouse 2004), but it is at least worth agreeing with Kelly, that 'learning is not something that happens to a person on occasion; it is what makes him [*sic*] a person in the first place' (George Kelly, quoted in Dryden 1984, p. 144, and quoted again in Chapter 4 below).

People as learners, schools as learning communities, and research as a special form of learning – systematic, imbued with theory, publicly reviewed – together form the foundation for the later consideration of religious education, citizenship, creativity and much more.

Chapter 2

The self and inclusion: imagining the real

the individual as such ... is a mighty abstraction

(Buber 2002a, p. 240)

Introduction

Being human is the subject of this chapter. It is the humanity of Buber and Macmurray, of constructivist psychologists such as Phillida Salmon, Jean Lave and Etienne Wenger, and of educationists such as David Hay and Richard Pring. It is not a separated humanity of 'possessive individualism' (Macpherson 1962), and is not an essentialist, idealized, humanity to which few can aspire. The three key concepts that can be drawn from all the authors mentioned are *learning, connection* and *dialogue*. Describing being human in terms of learning suggests a journey, a search for truth or for greater reality. It is multisensory learning, not simply in terms of sight or touch, but also, in Hay's terms, including awareness-sensing, mystery-sensing and value-sensing (Hay and Nye 1998, *passim*). It is also a creative learning, creating meaning and not simply accumulating information. Such learning will involve connection, and connection itself is, in this model, part of being human. Connection may be with other people or objects, or with otherness or 'the Other'. It therefore suggests both an embodied self and a transcendence of self, along with an inclusion of the other through the overcoming of transcendence. There are various kinds of connection, amongst which are friendship, trust and love. What learning and connection have in common is the need for dialogue – the third key concept. Dialogue is the means by which learning and connection take place. This dialogue, the dialogue of Buber and Bakhtin, requires imagination. It is not restricted to the imagining of fantastical things or, in Rosengren's chilling description of magic and religion 'imagining the impossible' (Rosengren *et al.* 2000). It is the dialogue described by Friedman as 'experiencing the other side' of the relationship, 'or, as Buber later calls it, *"imagining the real,"* [which] goes hand in hand with remaining on one's own side of the relationship' (Friedman in Buber 2002a, pp. xiii–xiv, and see also Friedman 1999).

The self described in this chapter is a person, and personhood has a long, complex, history. Personhood was arguably attributed to Adam, in biblical texts; only once Adam was connected to Eve by a 'thou', according to Sacks. The concept of the isolated, atomic, self was undermined in the twentieth century by sociologists and philosophers such as

Mead or Wittgenstein. Long before that, the same point was made in the Bible. When the first man sees the first woman, he says: 'This is now bone of my bone, flesh of my flesh; she shall be called woman [*ishah*] because she was taken from man [*ish*]' (Sacks 2003, p. 150). Whereas *Adam*, taken from the earth, signifies the biological species, *Ish* is closer in meaning to 'person', and Adam is said to utter that word only when he sees another: he 'must pronounce the name of his wife before he can pronounce his own' or '[h]e must say "Thou" before he can say "I"' (Sacks 2003, p. 151).

The learning person

It is helpful to continue with Adam and Eve, to illustrate further the nature of humanity. According to Salmon, the founder of personal contruct psychology, George Kelly, helped clients understand that they could not go back to an 'Eden' of childhood, as by 'eating the forbidden fruit' Adam and Eve came to know good and evil or see moral possibilities. Education does not end with a simple reward, but with knowledge that changes a person's responsibilities (Salmon 1995, p. 19). The happy, simple and entirely incorrect view that a person can learn all that is needed, is illustrated by the account given by Buber of a 'stupid' man who represents each of us. That man found it so hard finding his clothes in the morning that he wrote down the previous evening where he had put each item. The next morning, pleased with himself, he found every piece of clothing, following the list, until he was dressed:

> 'That's all very well, but now where am I myself?' he asked in great consternation. 'Where in the world am I?' He looked and looked, but it was a vain search; he could not find himself. 'And that is how it is with us,' said the rabbi. (Buber 1965, pp. 22–3)

Learning is continuing, as '[o]ne does not know the truth about oneself, one seeks it, and to the end of one's life the search remains unsatisfied' (Mitscherlich 1993, p. 13). Learning is at the core of humanity, and though we may be born human, we still 'have to learn to be human': a hard lesson, and 'very few of us learn more than a smattering of it; our own reality lies always beyond us, and we reach after it but never grasp it' (Macmurray 1968, p. 143). It is as though people are 'apprentice' people (as, etymologically, an apprentice is simply a learner), and apprenticeship models have come to dominate a number of theories of learning, notably those associated with Lave and Wenger (Lave and Wenger 1991, Wenger 1998). Prior to the development of specialized, formalized, education systems, there was little distinction between an apprenticeship as a person and as a worker, as both were likely to be family-based. Gradually, with the growth in regulation in trades, then industrialization of work, then mass schooling, various separate forms of learning emerged. The learning that took place in family homes still happened, with a somewhat reduced role yet still dominating the life of each person; the learning that took place at work could be formally described in an apprenticeship contract or could be less formally described in terms of 'staff development'; the learning that took place in formal educational institutions such as schools seemed to be of a different type, formalized and abstract, often with tenuous links to either the home or the workplace. One of the tasks of this book is to bridge the various forms of learning described here, recognizing that there is a long and not always successful tradition of such attempts.

Perhaps learning in school should become more work-related, a tradition including Proudhon who insisted that all teaching should be in the form of work-related apprenticeship. For example, '[i]f the school of mines is anything else than the actual work in the mines, accompanied by the studies suitable for the mining industry, the school will have for its object, to make, not miners, but chiefs of miners, aristocrats' (Proudhon 2004, p. 275). Perhaps, instead, the emphasis should be on school learning as home- and community-related, a tradition including Macmurray for whom '[t]his school community stands between family and the wider community and looks back to the first and forward to the second' (Macmurray 1968, p. 35, quoted more fully in Chapter 4 below). Learning is nevertheless, in all these situations, 'essential to becoming fully a person' (Pring 2000, p. 19). It is also multi-faceted: learning to be human could not be restricted to one kind of learning alone, any more than it could be restricted to one context or set of relationships. As Kelly describes it, '[t]he burden of our assumption is that learning is not a special class of psychological process; it is synonymous with any and all psychological processes' (Kelly, quoted in Dryden 1984, p. 144).

A vital aspect of learning and the self, is that self-understanding is dependent in a very distinctive way on others. One of Salmon's discoveries emerged from how people recognize themselves in photographs (Salmon 1980). Working with alcoholics, Salmon presented a set of photographic portraits. A person was asked which photograph he or she most resembled. Then others who knew that person were asked which photograph that person most resembled. Typically, the choices were different. However, when the first person was asked which photograph they would most like to resemble, who was their ideal, they often chose the photographs originally identified by others as most resembling them: '[t]heir perceived real self did not generally look like them; their perceived ideal self almost always did' (Salmon 1980, p. 3). The inner voice that Salmon herself was aware of, commenting on and criticizing her, had been rejected as 'other', but as a result of this research she realized that the ideal, striving, voice was 'every bit as much as me as – the rest of me' (Salmon 1980, p. 4). This was a liberating experience as '[i]t became possible to feel a personal ownership of things that had always seemed outside and beyond me' (Salmon 1980, p. 4). Each person has a real self and an ideal self; the surprise is that the ideal self, the self that looks down its nose at everyday follies, is every bit a part of the person as what is thought of as the real self. This is realized through others, and learning therefore depends on connection. It is connection that is addressed next.

Connection

Learning is at times portrayed as a wholly individual activity, with images of learners typically including people working alone in a room or shielding their writing from prying eyes. The learning described by Macmurray or Salmon, however, is social, and can be associated with the tradition of social constructivism of Vygotsky (Veer and Valsiner 1994, Daniels 1993, 1996, 2001). Connection may be realized in a moment of great crisis, or in an apparently trivial moment. The latter seems to be the case for Buber when he pressed his walking stick against a trunk of an oak tree.

> Then I felt in twofold fashion my contact with being: here, where I held the stick, and there, where it touched the bark. Apparently only where I was, I nonetheless found myself there too where I found the tree. (Buber 2002b, p. 49)

Buber cites that moment as the origin of his idea of dialogue, '[f]or the speech of man [*sic*] is like that stick wherever it is genuine speech, and that means: truly directed address' (Buber 2002b, pp. 49–50).

> Here, where I am, where ganglia and organs of speech help me to form and to send forth the word, here I "mean" him to whom I send it, I intend him, this one unexchangeable man. But also there, where he is, something of me is delegated, something that is not at all substantial in nature like that being here, rather pure vibration and incomprehensible; that remains there, with him, the man meant by me, and takes part in the receiving of my word. I encompass him to whom I turn. (Buber 2002b, p. 50)

It is the connection that distinguishes this account: people exist in connection, in relation. Those writing about humanity must go beyond a contrast between the individual and the aggregate.

> The fundamental fact of human existence is neither the individual as such nor the aggregate as such. Each, considered by itself, is a mighty abstraction. The individual is a fact of existence in so far as he steps into a living relation with other individuals. The aggregate is a fact of existence in so far as it is built up of living units of relation. The fundamental fact of human existence is man with man. (Buber 2002a, p. 240)

The way in which people exist in connection is through dialogue: a conversation, a lesson, or an embrace. Each must be 'real': for conversation, this means 'not one whose individual parts have been preconcerted, but one which is completely spontaneous, in which each speaks directly to his partner and call forth his unpredictable reply', for a lesson it is one that 'develops in mutual surprises', for an embrace it is 'not one of mere habit' (Buber 2002a, p. 241). It is all too common for writing about humanity to contrast isolated individuals and social aggregates – communities or societies – with the individuals having their own understanding (as in Descartes) and their own appetites (as in Hobbes). The connectedness of Buber and Macmurray brings together the individual and the aggregate precisely by describing both in terms of the 'between'. This approach is used in religious traditions, with a quotation from Macmurray from 1967 being included in the Society of Friends (Quaker) book of texts for use in meetings, which contrasts the sense of the 'pathetic littleness of our ephemeral existence' with the sense of connection to 'something eternal and infinite in which our existence ... is grounded' (The Yearly Meeting of the Religious Society of Friends (Quakers) in Britain 1999, item 26.11).

The nature of connection is divided by Buber into two kinds, characterized as *I–It* and *I–Thou* connections. This is well illustrated by his account of some of the central problems with the modern (in his case, twentieth-century) world. There are problems with how modern institutions, and how modern private lives, are organized.

> Institutions are 'outside,' where all sorts of aims are pursued, where a man [*sic*] works, negotiates, bears influence, undertakes, concurs, organises, conducts business, officiates, preaches. They are the tolerably well-ordered and to some extent harmonious structures, in which, with the manifold help of men's brains and hands, the process of affairs is fulfilled.
>
> Feelings are 'within,' where life is lived and man recovers from institutions. Here the spectrum of the emotions dances before the interested glance. Here a man's liking and hate and pleasure are indulged, and his pain if it is not too severe. Here he is at home, and stretches himself out in his rocking-chair. ... But the separated *It* of institutions is an animated clod without soul, and the separated *I* of feelings an uneasily-fluttering soul-bird. Neither of them knows man: institutions know only the specimen, feelings only the 'object'; neither knows the person, or mutual life. (Buber 1958, p. 63)

People must go beyond the safety of institutions (as described here) and of private lives (as described here), and walk instead through a world of meeting, of inclusion. Otherwise people will be less 'I' or 'Thou' and more 'It'. Buber describes such a person as 'self-willed', a term often used – similarly critically – in Sikh, Buddhist and Hindu religious traditions. Such a person 'does not believe and does not meet', and 'does not know the solidarity of connexion, but only the feverish world outside and his feverish desire to use it' (Buber 1958, p. 82). To see connection as that which makes us human, to see the individual as a 'mighty abstraction', is what makes this approach so significant. It is supported equally by Macmurray, for whom '[w]e are not individuals in our own right; and in ourselves we have no value at all, since we are meaningless', continuing that '[o]ur human Being *is* our relations to other human beings and our value lies in the quality of these relations' (Macmurray 1995a, p. 72).

What is required, for both of these philosophers, is the retention of self in the connection with other. This is variously described as *inclusion*, or experiencing the other side of the relationship, as in Friedman's account of Buber in the introduction to this chapter. Levinas referred to this a 'one of the most original notions of [Buber's] philosophy' (Levinas 1989, p. 67), describing Buber's account of dialogue, in terms of inclusion (*Umfassung,* also translated as *embrace* and *enclosure*) as distinct from empathy (*Einfühlung*) 'where the subject puts itself completely in the other's place, thus forgetting itself' (Levinas 1989, p. 68). Such a personal process is also described in terms of erotic love (as in Yaron 1993, p. 3), familial love (as in Wenger 1998, p. 277, on 'the life-giving power of mutuality ... in the miracle of parent-hood'), and in terms of friendship (again in Wenger 1998, p. 277 on how 'we can open our practices and communities to others ... newcomers, outsiders'). The connection through friendship is of particular relevance here, as it can stretch beyond families and lovers, and has the self at its centre. For Macmurray, '[t]o be a friend is to be yourself for another person', such that 'pretence ... and sentimentality ... [constitute] the grossest sin of all against friendship' (Macmurray 1979, p. 5). Friendship has a great significance for Macmurray, as '[a]ll meaningful knowledge is for the sake of action, and all meaningful action for the sake of friendship' (Macurray 1991a, p. 15). There is an irreplaceability that is commonly applied to family members, that Macmurray also applies to friends and thereby to pupils and teachers: '[a]s husbands or wives, as parents, as brothers, or as friends, we are related as persons in our own right: and we are not replaceable' (Macmurray 2004, p. 169, addressed in more detail in Chapter 4 below). Connection through friendship enables the self to become more real, therefore, and 'expressing our own reality in word and action ... is freedom, and the secret of it lies in our capacity for friendship' (Macmurray 1992, p. 150).

It is in that sense that the poet Spender could write that 'An "I" can never be Great Man' (Yeats 1936), whilst Jacobi, more forcefully, could say 'The I is impossible without the Thou' (quoted in Buber 2002a, p. 250). The connection indicated by all these accounts is an active connection, not a passive one. This is well illustrated by Macmurray's interpretation and use of the biblical account of the Good Samaritan. Members of the same national or religious group might be regarded as having a connection with a person. However, the account of the Samaritan – a member of another group altogether – was given in response to the question 'who is my neighbour?' It therefore indicated that it is through action that connection is made, with active connection more significant than passive membership. '[T]he Samaritan shared his material possessions with the Jew in his need, while the priest and the Levite made their natural community as members of the same nation and the same faith an ideal matter which did not express itself in action' (Macmurray 1996, p. 111). Hence '[t]he parable of the Good Samaritan is a definite assertion that the basis of human relationship is common humanity' (Macmurray 1993, p. 68). For Macmurray, this is part of a claim for religion as well as community to be described in active rather than ideal terms, as '[r]eligion is about action' (Macmurray 1995a, p. 65), and idealism or 'the purely spiritual' 'is the purely imaginary, a ghost world without substance or shadow' (Macmurray 1995a, p. 59).

Both learning and connection as activities are characterized by Macmurray in terms of the relational, and more specifically by Buber in terms of dialogue, so this also needs further explanation.

Dialogue

As dialogue has already been addressed in various ways, here there will be a clarification of Buber's position and how that is developed by the literary theorist Bakhtin, and more indirectly by the psychologist Salmon and the educationist Hay. Buber's concern with dialogue clearly reflects personal commitment. Schaeder says that 'Buber's truest form of expression was conversation' as he 'needed confrontation with the Thou for his own spontaneity to kindle, for the spark to leap out of the unpredictability of dialogue' (Schaeder in Glatzer and Mendes-Flohr 1991, p. 1). Buber himself takes up the same issues:

> Just as the most eager speaking at one another does not make a conversation (this is most clearly shown in that curious sport, aptly termed discussion, that is, 'breaking apart', which is indulged in by men who are to some extent gifted with the ability to think), so for a conversation no sound is necessary, not even a gesture. Speech can renounce all the media of sense, and it is still speech. (Buber 2002a, p. 3)

Indeed, of the 'three ways in which we are able to perceive a man [*sic*] who is living before our eyes', that is, observing, looking on and becoming aware, the last can also be of an animal, a plant or a stone (Buber 2002a, p. 10). There are also three forms of dialogue: genuine dialogue, technical dialogue and 'monologue disguised as dialogue' (Buber 2002a, p. 22). Being aware, and taking part in genuine dialogue, is how people *are*. To live in dialogue involves a sense of reciprocity, whilst living in monologue 'will not, even in the tenderest intimacy, grope out over the outlines of the self' (Buber 2002a, p. 24). Reciprocity is not the 'altruism' described by individualists, as altrusim implies a complete separation prior to the 'altruistic' act. Buber also distinguishes dialogue from love, as a person can be in dialogue with any other person, but cannot love any person, suggesting that '[e]ven Jesus obviously loved of "sinners" only the loose, lovable sinners, sinners against the Law; not those who were settled and loyal to their inheritance and sinned against him and his message', although with the latter he remained in dialogue (Buber 2002a, p. 24).

Dialogue is of the greatest importance, yet can be completed without words and with mere looks and touches, even 'glances which strangers exchange in a busy street as they pass one another with unchanging pace' (Buber 2002a, p. 5). As with awareness, dialogue for Buber can also exist beyond humanity, as in his perhaps optimistic view of a person and a machine, describing a compositer experiencing a relationship with a machine as 'one of dialogue' with the machine's humming being interpreted as 'a merry and grateful smile at me for helping it to set aside the difficulties and obstructions which disturbed and bruised and pained it, so that now it could run free' (Buber 2002a, p. 43). In this, Buber disagrees with Macmurray, who rejects dialogue with non-human animals and objects, and rejects even the idea of a person as an animal – a distinction that Salmon, very briefly a student of Macmurray's in Edinburgh, found distasteful in the first lecture she attended of his, and never returned. Macmurray's position is derived from the idea that being 'human' is not 'natural' (i.e. 'biological') but communal and social. Hence, for people, 'to live by nature is to live by custom', and, quoting Aristotle, 'Man is a political (i.e. a social) animal': '[t]he generic definition of man as an animal we must totally reject' (Macmurray 1991b, p. 128). Perhaps the positions of Buber and Macmurray are not so far apart, if Macmurray is simply avoiding the biological determinism rejected by Aristotle.

Whoever might be in dialogue, though, the 'I' of dialogue is a more complete person. The 'separated I' is 'degraded', whilst 'the I of enless dialogue' is 'lively and impressive' (Buber 1958, p. 89). Of the various people who have developed Buber's work on dialogue, one of the most distinctive is Bakhtin (1895–1975). Friedman describes Bakhtin as someone who thought Martin Buber 'the greatest philosopher of the twentieth century, and perhaps in this philosophically puny century, perhaps the sole philosopher on the scene' (Friedman 2002, p. 353). Bakhtin, like Buber, contrasts the dialogic and the monologic, with the literary form of the novel being most characterized by dialogue. 'The novel can be defined as a diversity of social speech types (sometimes even diversity of languages) and a diversity of individual voices, artistically organized', with the various voices being the 'fundamental compositional unities with whose help heteroglossia [*raznorečie*] can enter the novel; each of them permits a multiplicity of social voices and a wide variety of their links and interrelationships (all more or less dialogized)' (Bakhtin 1981, p. 263). The novel is made up of interrelationships between voices, made into dialogue by being dispersed into 'the rivulets and droplets of social heteroglossia' (Bakhtin 1981, p. 263). This is far from just a literary theory, as for Bakhtin 'all language – indeed, all thought – appeared dialogic' (en.wikipedia.org/wiki/ Dialogic). The quotation from the Wikipedia peer-written encyclopedia itself illustrates Bakhtin's influence, as it is 'an intensely dialogic phenomenon, doing away with the idea of knowledge as emanating from single, authoritative, closed (what Bakhtin would call "monologic") sources and instead embracing the idea of knowledge as collective, relational and dynamic' (en.wikipedia.org/wiki/Dialogic and see also c2.com/cgi/ wiki?WelcomeVisitors).

Whereas Bakhtin might be said to have propelled literary theory into psychology, Salmon, meanwhile, used literary techniques, especially story-telling, in her work as a psychologist (as in Salmon 2001). She described living as creating a life story, and '[t]o create a life story which is credible, which allows development as well as continuity, which tells a tale worth telling – this is the task that, as human beings, we must all attempt' (Salmon 1985, quoted in Frances 2005). This is clearly a task requiring imagination, as '[i]t is only through our imaginative construction that we shall be able to own the full heritage of the experience we have acquired through living in time' (Salmon 1985, in Frances 2005). As has been described in Chapter 1 above, Salmon sees personal 'construing' as taking place 'between', in and through a creative dialogue. This takes the description of dialogue back to the philosophy of Macmurray and what Jung calls 'the sanctity of "interbeing"' (Jung in Fergusson and Dower 2002, p. 174). Jung identifies the

Judeo-Christian root of the philosophies of Macmurray and Levinas, in contrast to what is referred to as the Greek and Platonic root of Cartesian philosophy.

It is in the study of religions that a considerable amount of insight into dialogue is held. Hay writes of children's spirituality, and tells of his late appreciation of Macmurray's relational view of personhood. Hay says that he came across Macmurray's writing towards the end of his own research into how children talked about spirituality, and found considerable pleasure in seeing how his research 'pointed overwhelmingly in the communal direction expounded by Macmurray' (Hay 1998, pp. 10–11). The research to which Hay refers here was published in the same year (Hay with Nye 1998), and there, as a result of the analysis of children's talk about spiritual issues, a framework is created of 'categories of spiritual sensitivity'. A relational view of personhood, in this model, is co-dependent on a relational view of spirituality. The categories of spiritual sensitivity then appear as the modes or senses of spirituality, complementing the 'relationships' which are the subjects and objects of those senses. Hay's categories of spiritual sensitivity are awareness-sensing (here-and-now, tuning, flow, focusing), mystery-sensing (wonder and awe, imagination) and value-sensing (delight and despair, ultimate goodness, meaning). The relationships described by Hay and others include a person's relationship with self, with the 'other', with others, with groups, and with the world or the whole. It is these categories of spiritual sensitivity and types of relationship that inform this book (as also in Stern and James 2006, www.hull.ac.uk/php/isg/ and en.wikipedia.org/wiki/Spirituality_studies). Here, though, the account of central elements of humanity ends, as learning, connection and dialogue are all interrelated, and consideration must be given to community.

Chapter 3

Community and society: fundamentals and fundamentalism

Just as our singularity is grounded in our belonging, so individual autonomy is linked inescapably with participation in the wider community.

(Cooper 2001)

Introduction

If the book's first 'stubborn particular' is being human, this necessarily leads to the second stubborn particular, of community. Although it is possible to think of a community as a single organic entity, denying the individuality of its members, this is not a form of community that is attractive – philosophically, politically or personally. The model of community as organic unity is attributed to Hegel (for example by Hawkesworth in Alperson 2002, p. 323), although Hegel himself refers explicitly only to communities of this kind as 'churches', as '[t]he real community is what we generally call the *church*' (Hegel 1988, p. 475). It is, in any event, more interesting, challenging and valuable to investigate how a community can exist when people within it exist in their own right, and come together with contrasting and apparently incompatible ways of living and believing. A diverse or many-voiced community might be termed *heteroglot*, in Bakhtin's description (Bakhtin 1981, p. 411). Whilst recognizing the challenges of disagreement and conflict in diverse groups, this account is based on the possibility of communities being heteroglot and more human – as in Salmon's discovery, when in hospital for surgery, that a lack of homogeneity helped members be 'related to each other in a ... low-key, friendly way' (Salmon 2000, p. 5). This chapter starts from a consideration of community and its contrast with society. It goes on to investigate one of the great modern, and anti-modernist, 'tests' of community and society: the existence of what is called fundamentalism. Reactions to fundamentalism test, in turn, the definitions of community, society and citizenship. The chapter therefore ends with a framework for considering a variety of responses to modernism, in order to capture the significance of fundamentalism for theories of society and, in particular, community.

Communities and societies

Macmurray's philosophy centres on the nature of personhood in community, and the nature of actual communities such as families, religious groups and schools. Macmurrian communities are organizations that are positive and personal, in contrast to what he refers to as societies – that are negative and impersonal. Both are unavoidable and are to be positively engaged with: it is certainly not that Macmurray thought social and broad political issues were to be ignored. He was engaged in political debate throughout his life, and was particularly concerned with international issues of war and peace. What was to be avoided, however, was a confusion of community and society. When societies attempt to unify themselves by having community characteristics, this is an 'error'. Macmurray pulls together issues of community, religion, society, power and politics in a remarkable analysis.

> 'Liberty, equality and fraternity' do, as we have recognized, constitute community. For this very reason they cannot be achieved by organization [i.e. society]; yet the democratic revolutions proclaimed them as the goal of politics. To create community is to make friendship the form of all personal relations. This is a religious task, which can only be performed through the transformation of the motives of our behaviour. . . . Law . . . is a technological device, and the State is a set of technical devices for the development and maintenance of law. Now the value of any device lies wholly in its efficiency. To personalize the State, to assign it the religious function of creating community, to make it an end in itself and ascribe to it an intrinsic value, is, in fact, to value efficiency for its own sake. It is to make power the supreme good, and personal life a struggle for power. This is the height of unreason. For power is merely a general term for the means of action. To make power an end is to invert the logical relation between means and end. (Macmurray 1991b, pp. 198–9)

It should be noted that the distinction between community and society is not a matter of scale, and not a practical matter of what is achievable. It is about the intentions of the members of the group: whether they treat each other as people in their own right, rather than as a means to an end. In society, there is nothing inappropriate about treating people as a means to an end, such as treating a taxi driver as a means to facilitate travel from one place to another. In community, in contrast, such a way of treating people is wrong, as in the frequent complaint of parents about their children treating them like taxi drivers. Both communities and societies (that is, all 'functional' groups, including the state and international organizations) can be unified, but they will exhibit different kinds of unity. In some ways, Macmurray, like Buber, continues the tradition of Tönnies' contrast between community and society (i.e. *Gemeinschaft* and *Gesellschaft*), as Tönnies contrasts '[a]ll intimate, private, and exclusive living together . . . undertood as life in Gemeinschaft' with 'Gesellschaft [which] is conceived as mere coexistence of people independent of each other' (Tönnies in Searle-Chatterjee *et al.* 2000, pp. 29–30). However, Tönnies says that

[i]n contrast to Gemeinschaft, Gesellschaft is transitory and superficial. Accordingly, Gemeinschaft should be stood as a living organism, Gesellschaft as a mechanical aggregate and artifact. (Tönnies in Searle-Chatterjee *et al.* 2000, p. 30)

Macmurray would object to the analogy of the 'living organism' for community, in the same way that Durkheim objected to this, and would agree with Durkheim in attributing some 'organic' characteristics to society instead (describing society in terms of 'organic solidarity', Durkheim 1973, p. 63, and 1982, p. 59). Macmurray would also object to Tönnies regarding society as necessarily 'transitory and superficial'. Both can be substantial and unified. However, the unity characteristic of community is different to the unity characteristic of societies. He suggests that 'we should use the term "society" to refer to those forms of human association in which the bond of unity is negative or impersonal; and to reserve for the contrasted forms of association which have a positive personal relation as their bond, the term "community"' (Macmurray 1991b, p. 147). A community is 'personal, not an impersonal unity of persons' (Macmurray 1991b, p. 147), and '[l]ike a society, a community is a group which acts together; but unlike a mere society its members are in communion with one another; they constitute a fellowship' (Macmurray 1996, p. 166). Hence, whereas a society 'is an organization of functions', a community 'is a unity of persons as persons' (Macmurray 1996, p. 166).

The similarity with Durkheim, however, should not be exaggerated, as for Macmurray, although there is an apparently 'organic' division of labour in society, there is no organic unity. Instead, what unifies a society, for Macmurray, is intention:

Its continuity is a continuity of action, not of process. Any human society, however primitive, is maintained by the intention of its members to maintain it. Short of the extermination of its members, it can be destroyed only by destroying this intention. The history of the Poles or the Czechs, or, above all, of the Jews, should be sufficient evidence of this. (Macmurray 1991b, p. 128)

Durkheim may have had 'a deep respect for the dignity of the individual' (Bellah in Durkheim 1973, p. lv), but this was socially not communally determined, as '[s]ociety has consecrated the individual and made him pre-eminently worthy of respect' (Durkheim in Durkheim 1973, p. xxiv). This contrasts with Macmurray's focus on communal relationships, such that 'the state is for the community and not the community for the state', even if 'the community is through the state' (Macmurray 2004, p. 154). This view of the significance of community is shared with Buber, and is closer to some of Tönnies' formulations, as *Gemeinschaft* typically existed alongside *Gesellschaft*. Macmurray and Buber, however, saw the future, not the past, in community. Buber, for example, recognized the functional unity of social groups, as 'the only important thing in groups, in the present as in history, is what they aim at and what they accomplish' (Buber 2002a, p. 35), '[b]ut community, growing community (which is all we have known so far) is the being no longer side by side but *with* one another of a multitude of persons' (Buber 2002a, p. 37). 'Collectivity', for Buber, 'is based on an organized atrophy of personal existence, community on its increase and confirmation in life lived towards one other' (Buber 2002a, p. 37). The *I–Thou* nature of life in community is described by Macmurray in terms of the possibility of friendship, as '[f]riendship ... is the condition of freedom in community' (Macmurray 1968, p. 34). These are moral terms: it would be impossible for Buber or Macmurray to conceive of a 'society of many virtuous but isolated individuals' (Putnam 2000, p. 19), as virtue is not possible in isolation.

Given the account of personhood in community and society, including the essential role of the possibility of friendship, provided in this and the previous chapters, the challenge to this account is not simply an intellectual one. There are substantive challenges to the possibility of community in modern society. Communitarians may 'receiv[e] a sympathetic ear from leading British politicians', such as Blair's support for Macmurray noted above in Chapter 1,

> but cynics point to the naïvety of the approach. Can the Protestants and Catholics in Northern Ireland really be reconciled, or the Israelis and Palestinians? Is persuasion rather than battle really likely to lead men into shared childcare? ... Sociologically minded thinkers (just as much as religious and philosophical ones), struggle with the contradictoriness of believing both in social (or divine) causation and in the power of individuals and groups to produce change; in structure and agency, to put it another way. Yet revolutions have occurred and dreamers may be powerful. Without a dream, the oppressed and dispirited cannot activate a new consciousness: perhaps there is still a place for the idea of community. (Searle-Chatterjee *et al.* 2000, p. 234)

The *ad hominem* response to accusations of naïvety and 'dreaminess' might point, in Macmurray's case, to being socially and politically active through two world wars and the Cold War, and in Buber's case, to being socially and politically active not only through wars but also as a Jewish activist in Nazi Germany until 1938 and for decades working on overcoming Jewish-Palestinian conflict. However, a more substantial response is needed, not least in the light of contemporary forms of fundamentalism that engage not only at the national and international level, but also with individuals and communities.

Testing community and society: fundamentalism and modernism

One of the most striking challenges to community and society is the challenge of fundamentalism. How can communities and societies involve people who might be called fundamentalists? It is a political challenge as well as a personal challenge, and one that has grown in significance throughout the twentieth and early twenty-first centuries. Various forms of fundamentalism are all, in different ways, religious reactions to rationalist, secularist, materialist, modernity, and to relativist, liberal, post-modernism. They are reactions of religious truth in the contemporary world: they are not anachronisms or pockets of past, preserved. They are modern (that is, recent, contemporary) even when they object to modernism. As Armstrong says, 'it is important to realize that these movements are not an archaic throwback to the past; they are modern, innovative, and modernizing' (Armstrong 2000, p. 369). She continues that the emergence of fundamentalism surprised those who thought secularism was 'an irreversible trend', and who 'assumed that as human beings became more rational, they either would have no further need for religion or would be content to confine it to the immediately personal and private areas of their lives' (Armstrong 2000, pp. ix–x). This modern fundamentalism is difficult to define, and any single definition will be contested, but Ruthven suggests that 'at its broadest, it may be described as a "religious way of being" that manifests itself in a strategy by which beleaguered believers attempt to preserve their distinctive identity as a people or group in the face of modernity and secularization' (Ruthven 2004, p. 8). That is hardly, in itself, a reason for shock, and in that form would deserve to be treated seriously and engaged with in an intelligent way: fundamentalism may be regarded as *making sense*. Ruthven refers to common liberal responses to fundamentalism being one of outright rejection, regarding fundamentalists as 'anti-intellectual, bigoted, and intolerant' and therefore unacceptable (Ruthven 2004, p. 7).

> The term fundamentalism is reserved for those who have the temerity to attempt to project their world-view onto others. Against such people we lash out with a label that immediately deligitimates them, that immediately says these people are out of the mainstream and therefore deserve to be given *ad hominem* dismissal. 'We' immediately know that 'they' are not like us, or even worthy of our time, since clearly 'we' cannot deal with 'them'. Further 'we' would like very much to believe that we would never behave as they do and that we have never done so. (Ruthven 2004, p. 7, quoting Jay M. Harris)

Such anti-intellectual dismissal, and a rejection of 'them', is complemented by those who write about fundamentalism and reactions against fundamentalism in terms of fear. Armstrong says that 'it is important to recognize that these [fundamentalist] theologies and ideologies are rooted in fear' (Armstrong 2000, p. 368), and the fundamentalists and secularists 'gaze ... at the other with horror' (Armstrong 2000, p. 354, and see also Ali 2002).

Both the dismissal as 'them', and the fear on both sides that might underpin such dismissal, can generate an apparently more benign yet considerably more invidious response of embarrassment. A world dominated by embarrassment does not want to deal head-on with difficult topics, does not want to challenge falsehoods, does not want to seem too definite about morality. The characteristic principle of the embarrassed is a particular kind of tolerance, a tolerance that is tolerant of all 'nice' things, that treats all world religions, for example, as being about the golden rule (do unto others ...), and there are no real differences except for the names of the buildings and the dates of the holidays. The politics of embarrassment pushes all questions of truth into the personal and private worlds of individuals, leaving public spaces free of truth but implacably tolerant. Tolerant, that is, unless truths 'rear up and bite', unless bombs start falling, including the bombs of the tolerant falling on those deemed beyond the pale, even if the pale moves from year to year. Giddens promotes 'cosmopolitan tolerance', but is criticized by Bottery for ignoring the difficulty of developing any such tolerance, as 'fundamentalism is already in some respects with us', so 'Giddens' world of cosmopolitan tolerance needs to be developed not just by looking outwards, but by looking inwards as well, and particularly to the nurturing of educational institutions as a primary base' (Bottery 2004, p. 98).

Working through periods of history involving war and genocide, and hypocrisy, on a grand scale, Macmurray was not one for embarrassment, but tackled truths head-on and even 'wanted to get back to the trenches, where for all the misery and destruction, the spiritual atmosphere was relatively clean' (Macmurray 1995a, p. 20, quoted above in Chapter 1). It is useful to consider his views on fear, here. For Macmurray, all religion 'is grappling with fear', but convincing people that there 'is nothing to be afraid of' may mean that nothing bad will happen (the principle of false religion), or may instead mean that 'there is no reason to fear [what might happen] even if they do [happen]' (Macmurray 1996, p. 202, and see also for example the lyrics to the song *I Ain't Afraid*, Klezmatics 2003). There is a moment in 1937 when Macmurray had an opportunity to meet with Nazi leaders in Berlin, with a church delegation. He refuses, and sets out his rejection carefully, rejecting a 'romantic liberal attitude' just as he rejects Nazism:

> I wish that good people in this country could manage to escape from the fog of liberal attitudes. It is a kind of moral blindness. I know what you feel about it. 'Such a visit shows a readiness to be friendly. Does not Christ teach us to love our enemies?' Precisely: but that is the very reason why this visit is compromising to Christianity. For what it says is: 'You and we are not enemies. We are really friends.' Or do you propose to say to the Nazi leaders, 'You and we are enemies. Yet, as Christians, we love you in spite of that. Until you set free your pacifists and stop your anti-Jew activities, and repeal the laws under which they suffer, there can be no peace between us, but only a sword'? Of course you do not intend to say that. On those terms the discussion would come to an end before it started. (Macmurray, in a letter of 26 November 1937, quoted in Costello 2002, p. 273, with the referernce to 'a romantic liberal attitude' on p. 274)

Macmurray, like Buber, was religious and reacted to rationalist, secularist, materialist, modernity, as to relativist, liberal, post-modernism. These things are held in common with fundamentalists. One of the ways in which they differ, is in seeing the possibility of difference within communities. In that way, Macmurray and Buber also reject the positions of both Tönnies and Durkheim, who saw, in different ways, communities as being bound together simply by the similarity of the views and activities of their members.

Heteroglot communities in a world with fundamentalism

To be a community, for Macmurray and Buber, a group of people must be *inclusive*. All the people of the group must be members of the community. Fundamentalisms raise the question of how communities should react, and requires the answer: not with fear or embarrassment, such as that expressed in some policies of 'tolerance'. Inclusive communities include people living contrasting ways of life. They are – in an older terminology applied to schools in the UK – 'comprehensive' (as in Hargreaves 1982, Benn and Chitty 1996), with Macmurray promoting similar views through supporting co-educational schools whose pupils would be drawn from all classes and if possible from different cultures and races (Macmurray 1968, pp. 42–4). This is a requirement of inclusivity, and means that a policy of promoting inclusivity is limited by – though not necessarily negated by – the existence of sectionalism. Sectional communities are those that on principle (rather than as a matter of geographical chance) do not include the whole range of ways of life: single-sex communities, communities that require members to come from a particular religious position, or communities that select from those able to pay. It would be absurd to say that such communities are all in a quite different category to non-sectional communities, and cannot be as inclusive. Clearly, there are countless limitations to inclusion in all communites, and a sectional community may be more inclusive in other ways than a non-sectional community. Indeed a sectional community may derive a large part of its inclusivity precisely from what makes it sectional: from, for example, an inclusivist interpretation of a religious tradition – as might also have been implied by Hegel's association of community with church (Hegel 1988, p. 475). Yet sectionalism will always, in its sectionalism, limit inclusion.

What Macmurray therefore has in common with fundamentalisms is his having a religious reaction to rationalist, secularist, materialist, modernity, and to relativist, liberal, post-modernism. He crosses boundaries by attempting 'to integrate private and public ethics' (Costello 2002, p. 9), and refuses to succumb to embarrassment. Complementing this view, Buber describes the modernist problem in terms of the 'the separated *It* of institutions [being] an animated clod without soul, and the separated *I* of feelings an uneasily-fluttering soul-bird', quoted above in Chapter 2. Fundamentalists also reject such modernism, and embarrass modernists precisely by refusing to let private lives to be cut off from public concerns. As Macmurray says

> We are all more or less unreal. Our business is to make ourselves a little more real than we are. (Macmurray 1992, p. 143)

Communities must be places where people learn to make community: they are places of 'immanence' (or 'emergence' for Hoyle and Wallace 2005), places where self and community emerge. More 'real' communities could be contrasted with more 'unreal' communities, according to the nature of the relationships within the community. The unity is not a transcendent unity, an 'aggregation', but an intentional immanent unity, from different positions, that not only allows but requires objection to that unity at the same time as membership. The poet Larkin, famous for his misanthropy, illuminates some of the challenges of communities. In the poem *Dockery and Son*, Larkin writes of the difference between himself and a friend from university who had a child at nineteen, saying 'how / Convinced he was he should be added to! / Why did he think adding meant increase? / To me it was dilution' (Larkin 1988). The answer is, families, like other forms of community, can indeed mean 'increase'.

It is the expectation of change, the need for variety and opposition, and most of all the developing or immanent nature of communities, in Macmurray and in Buber, that pushes them beyond fundamentalism. The immanence is a characteristic of a number of community and social philosophers, with the tradition well described by Yovel for Spinoza and others (Yovel 1989a, 1989b), the variety or heteroglossia a characteristic of fewer authors, but well captured by Bakhtin, and by psychologists such as Salmon (quoted above, on greater friendliness in diverse groups, from Salmon 2000, p. 5) and others from the personal construct theory perspective (such as Ravenette 1999), and Mitscherlich (1993, on the need for diversity and opposition within families and societies) from the Freudian perspective. The sociologist Ball describes the need for variety and conflict, unrecognized by 'systems theorists', in a way that links well with the concern with schools of the following chapter. For him, systems theorists allow for some conflict in the system but treat it as 'aberrant and pathological' and harmful to the organization, and they therefore 'provide only a limited and naive account of the possibilities of change and have no real capability for explaining or describing intra-organizational conflict or contradiction' (Ball 1987, p. 4). It is precisely the same rejection of goal-orientation, for a community (such as a school) that most links Ball's approach to that of Macmurray. Ball continues that '[o]ne of the major distortions imposed by the use of social systems analysis is the over-emphasis on organizational goals and goal attainment', whilst in fact schools, specifically, 'are typically lacking in ... consensus' and 'allow ... for and reproduce ... dissensus and goal diversity' (Ball 1987, pp. 11–12). Indeed, Ball continues that he 'take[s] schools, in common with virtually all other social organizations, to be *arenas of struggle*; to be riven with actual or potential conflict between members; to be poorly co-ordinated; to be ideologically diverse' (Ball 1987, p. 19), with this not necessarily being problematic.

Conclusion: modelling diversity and religion

The different approaches to diversity are matched by different approaches to religion: fundamentalism is characteristically a religious position that rejects diversity, just as modernism and some forms of post-modernism are characteristically secular or non-religious and embrace diversity. However, this is not a simple contrast or even a continuum with fundamentalism and modernism at either end of the scale. Both modernism and post-modernism may 'tolerate' religion, unlike some of the secularist traditions (including numerous versions of state communism), even if this is somewhat problematic, as Ruthven notes for post-modernism. 'The compliment post-modernism pays to religion is back-handed and treacherous', as 'post-modernism opens up public space for religion – but at the price of relativizing its claims to absolute truth' (Ruthven 2004, p. 198). Instead, it is possible to look at approaches to the nature of community and society, in terms of two dimensions: more or less religious, and more or less open to diversity. In such a model, fundamentalism might be said to share with various 'illiberal' and modernist social theories a rejection of substantial diversity (beyond narrow limits), whilst differing in an attitude to religion. Fundamentalism might however share with writers such as Buber or Macmurray a deep concern for religion in all areas of life, whilst differing in its attitude to diversity. This is outlined in Figure 3.1.

Figure 3.1: Modelling diversity and religion

Chapter 4

Schooling and learning: to live human lives properly

learning is a way of being in the social world, not a way of coming to know about it.
(William F. Hanks, in Lave and Wenger 1991, p. 24)

Introduction: learning school or learning community?

Following accounts of the person and of community, in Chapters 2 and 3, this chapter tackles the third of the book's stubborn particulars: schools. Schools are peculiar modern constructions: peculiar in their very unusual place in the history of learning, and peculiar in being all too often taken for granted. Although the argument of this chapter will be for schools as learning communities, it is not until the peculiarities of schooling are described that the non-trivial nature of this argument will become clear. As Lave and Wenger say, ' "[l]ocating" learning in classroom interaction is not an adequate substitute for a theory about what schooling as an activity has to do with learning' (Lave and Wenger 1991, p. 54). Carr helpfully describes the possible associations between a number of key terms, saying that 'there is a clear enough relationship between education and *learning*', and 'any learning surely presupposes *learners*' (Carr 2003, p. 4). In addition, 'there are apparent links between education, learning and *teaching*: learning is often assumed (rightly or wrongly) to be a causal or other consequence of teaching', and finally, 'there is a fairly common association between education and *schooling* ... though the very idea of schools as sites of education has also been seriously questioned in recent times (in my view, coherently if not necessarily justifiably)' (Carr 2003, p. 4).

Carr's list raises the question of what is *educational* about schools. Those attacking the very idea of schooling, such as Illich who said that for most people 'the right to learn is curtailed by the obligation to attend school' (Illich 1971, p. vii), also remind others of the need to justify the existence of schools, and not just of education or learning. Although perhaps more sympathetic to schooling than Illich, Lave and Wenger in their immensely influential work on learning communities avoid talking about 'the problem of school learning', even if this 'was not always easy to adhere to as the issue kept creeping into our discussions' (Lave and Wenger 1991, p. 39). The problems as they saw them were that '[i]ssues of learning and schooling seemed to have become too deeply interrelated in our culture in general, both for purposes of our own exploration and the exposition of our ideas', and that, contrary to their suppositions, 'the organization of schooling as an educational form is predicated on claims that knowledge can be decontextualized' – even though schools are clearly 'contexts' in their own right (Lave and Wenger 1991, pp. 39–40). Lave and Wenger more specifically separate the two concepts of learning and teaching: 'this viewpoint makes a fundamental distinction between learning and intentional instruction', which 'does not deny that learning can take place where there is teaching, but does not take intentional instruction to be in itself the source or cause of learning' (Lave and Wenger 1991, pp. 40–1). They go on to set an agenda (in part fulfilled by Wenger 1998), concerning 'the relation of school practices to those of the communities in which the knowledge that schools are meant to "impart" is located, as well as issues concerning relations between the world of schooling and the world of adults more generally' (Lave and Wenger 1991, p. 41).

It is clear therefore that Lave and Wenger see schools as places for 'imparting knowledge' from other communities of practice, as '[s]choolchildren are legitimately peripheral, but kept from participation in the social world more generally' (Lave and Wenger 1991, p. 104). They have a concern that physics teaching, for example, does not take place in the community of physicists, but in the community of teachers who are 'schooled adults', as '[t]he reproduction cycles of the physicists' community start much later, possibly only in graduate school' (Lave and Wenger 1991, pp. 99–100). What links Lave and Wenger to the philosophies of Macmurray and Buber is the concern with learning and personhood. For them, 'learning is not merely situated in practice – as if it were some independently reifiable process that just happened to be located somewhere; learning is an integral part of generative social practice in the lived-in world' (Lave and Wenger 1991, p. 35). Or as Hanks says in his introduction, 'learning is a way of being in the social world, not a way of coming to know about it' (Lave and Wenger, p. 24), echoing Kelly, quoted above, for whom learning 'is not something that happens to a person on occasion; it is what makes him a person in the first place' (George Kelly, quoted in Dryden 1984, p. 144). Schooling should therefore not have a monopoly on learning, any more than toys labelled 'educational' are the only toys from which children learn (Stern 1999, p. 4). For Wenger, 'we belong to several communities of practice at any given time' (Wenger 1998, p. 6), yet for many pupils '[s]chool learning is just learning school' (Wenger 1998, p. 267). For that author, the most significant learning additional to 'learning school' takes place outwith the curriculum 'in the classroom as well as on the playground, officially or in the cracks'. Hence, 'in spite of curriculum, discipline, and exhortation, the learning that is most personally transformative turns out to be the learning that involves membership in these communities of practice' (Wenger 1998, p. 6).

Referring to teachers as 'didactic caretakers' who are responsible for '[t]he commoditization of learning' for example through tests and the creation of an 'exchange value of knowledge' (Lave and Wenger 1991, p. 112), it is possible to see the influence of satirists such as L. Frank Baum, whose attitude to the commoditization of learning was made clear to the Straw Man towards the end of the film *The Wizard of Oz*:

Why, anybody can have a brain. That's a very mediocre commodity. Every pusillanimous creature that crawls on the Earth or slinks through slimy seas has a brain. Back where I come from, we have universities, seats of great learning, where men go to become great thinkers. And when they come out, they think deep thoughts and with no more brains than you have. But they have one thing you haven't got: a diploma. (Baum *et al.* 1939)

Having, in the language of Lave and Wenger, 'decoupled' schooling and learning, and noted, in Carr's terms, the contingency of the relationship between learning, teaching and schooling, the task remains to create a positive description of schooling that includes but does not monopolize learning.

What are schools?

Macmurray takes up the challenge of describing schools positively by striking at the heart of the curriculum. For him, schools are communities and are there in order to make people more human through living in community. Subjects have a distinctly subsidiary role. In a phrase that pre-empts much more recent work on citizenship, he says, for example, that '[t]o be educated today means to have learned to be human – not Scottish, not British, not even West-European – but human' (Macmurray 1968, p. 145). 'The school is a community; and we learn to live in community only by living in a community' (Macmurray 1968, pp. 149–50), and a school's 'first principle is that it must be a real community' (Macmurray 1968, p. 35). This is '[n]ot because community is a good thing – I would underline this – but because this is the condition of success in its educational function' (Macmurray 1968, p. 35). Hence

> when we try to teach, we must deal with living human beings. We, the teachers, are persons. Those whom we would teach are persons. We must meet them face to face, in a personal intercourse. This is the primary fact about education. It is one of the forms of personal relationship. It is a continuing personal exchange between two generations. To assert this is by no means to define an ideal, but to state a fact. It declares not what education ought to be, but what it is – and is inescapably. We may ignore this fact; we may imagine that our task is of a different order; but this will make no difference to what is actually taking place. We may act as though we were teaching arithmetic or history. In fact we are teaching *people*. The arithmetic or the history is merely a medium through which a personal intercourse is established and maintained. (Macmurray 1968, p. 5)

In these ways, Macmurray seems to distance himself from the formal school curriculum of subjects, for the sake of schools as communities. Teachers 'are not training children to be mathematicians or accountants or teachers or linguists; ... [they] are training them to be men and women, to live human lives properly' (Macmurray 1968, p. 112). And 'a good education is one which succeeds in training a child to live well, to live his whole life as life should be lived' (Macmurray 1968, p. 111). 'The golden aim of education [is] to teach the children how to live', and this should not be 'crowded out by a multiplicity of little aims' (Macmurray 1968, p. 114).

Despite the impression given here that Macmurray was not concerned with the specifics of subjects, it is, rather, that he was avoiding subjects or 'subject communities' (such as the community of physicists, historians, mathematicians) being the principal aims of schooling. The schools with which he worked were still committed to teaching identifiable subjects, and Macmurray spent his professional career teaching subjects and leading subject specialists as Dean of the Faculty of Arts at Edinburgh University. In the latter capacity, he was seen as something of a curriculum innovator, founding the first university-based nurse education in the UK (see Costello 2002, p. 347, Tilley 2005, and the article *Nurses in an Expanded Health Service* in Macmurray 1968). Perhaps the best way to illustrate the way in which Macmurray could regard something as important and yet inappropriate as a principal aim, would be with respect to examinations. As has been described above, Lave and Wenger regard tests as enormously problematic, leading to the commoditization of learning (Lave and Wenger 1991, p. 112). Macmurray has a similar problem with examinations, saying that if 'the examination system frustrates your efforts to educate your pupils ... [t]hen let's get rid of it' (Macmurray, 1979, p. 13), and even that 'the major alteration required to make our method of education truly effective ... [is] the abolition of the examination system' (Macmurray, 1968, p. 2). However, that is not to say he did not care about examinations. The apparent view expressed in the last quotation (probably written in 1941) was not borne out in his subsequent management of courses at Edinburgh University as Professor of Philosophy and then as Dean. He was renowned in the university for the meticulous care with which he would mark and monitor examination scripts whilst at Edinburgh, and his annoyance at what he saw as the undermining of the examination system when a junior lecturer in Macmurray's department completed an exam paper in order to see what mark he would achieve (Somerville 1999, Rauchwerger 1999, and Costello in the presentation of Costello 1998). In other words, examinations may be important, but they should not be the main *aim* of education.

On the curriculum, there are for Macmurray three types of knowledge reflected in the curriculum (from a lecture given in 1965 on 'the Notion of an Educated Man') 'technological' or 'knowing how to do what we choose' (Macmurray 1968, p. 233b), 'valuational' or 'knowing why we choose to do this rather than that' (Macmurray 1968, p. 233b), and 'communal' with 'its roots in the mutuality of intersubjective experience' (p 235). 'Knowing how' gives rise to science, 'knowing why' to the arts, and '[t]he third kind of knowledge ... [i.e.] of community [,] ... arises in and from the problematic of personal relations' (Macmurray 1968, p. 239). Macmurray wants to 'reinstate the concept of the educated man [*sic*] as our objective in education', covering the three kinds of knowledge, and noting that '[a]ll are important, but not equally so', and that '[w]e have listed them, indeed, in the inverse order of their importance' (Macmurray 1968, p. 245). It is not so important, here, to critique these divisions of knowledge. What is important is to realize the significance of the priorities. The person who is the teacher interacts with the pupils, and the teacher comes with 'subject matter'. A developing relationship between teacher, subject and pupils is described by the present author for teachers of history (Stern 1999, p. 26), where the movement of a teacher is from history as the 'object' of study, through to the teacher representing history for the pupils and therefore becoming the pupils' 'object'. That view complements Macmurray's position on the curriculum, and is even closer to that of Buber, as described by Friedman. 'The teacher makes himself [*sic*] the living selection of the world, which comes in his person to meet, draw out, and form the pupil'. which in turn is only possible with real mutuality that 'can only come into existence if the child trusts the teacher and knows that he is really there for him' (Friedman 2002, p. 207).

There would be a loss of curriculum, if teachers simply 'gave themselves up' to pupils. and let the pupils determine what was to be studied.

> The old, authoritarian theory of education does not understand the need for freedom and spontaneity. But the new, freedom-centred educational theory misunderstands the meaning of freedom, which is indispensable but not in itself sufficient for true education. The opposite of compulsion is not freedom but communion, says Buber, and this communion comes about through the child's first being free to venture on his own and then encountering the real values of the teacher. The teacher presents these values ... and the pupil learns from this encounter because he has first experimented himself. (Friedman 2002 pp. 208–9, emphasis added)

It is a generational encounter: an encounter across the generations (as quoted from Macmurray above as 'a continuing personal exchange between two generations') and one that generates community, that generates people. That this is an exchange between generations, not a mastery of one over the other, is also noted by Benjamin who asks 'who would trust a cane wielder who proclaimed the mastery of children by adults to be the purpose of education?' (Benjamin 1997, p. 104). Rather than mastery, Benjamin sees schooling as an exchange between generations. The exchange can – indeed, must – include 'subject matter', as well described by Pring, even if this is not itself the prime aim of the exchange. The exchange 'respects the learning needs of the learner, on the one hand, and, on the other, mediates the aspects of the culture which meet those needs' (Pring 2000, p. 28). Teachers of subjects may 'speak from a love of their subject' and believe themselves custodians of a tradition in a subject. 'They believe that the understanding enshrined within that tradition, of which they are the custodians, is important to the young people as they seek a deeper appreciation and knowledge of their lives and of the challenges within them' (Pring 2000, p. 28), so the subject is in need of no external 'goal' or 'end'. 'One might refer to it as an element within a particular form of life, a way of thinking, a mode of valuing, into which the learner is being invited or even seduced' (Pring 2000, pp. 28–9, and see also Pring 2004, ch. 5).

A Macmurrian view of humanity allows that schools are concerned with making communities, and a concern for human relationships within school is central to its aim, not an additional, perhaps unnecessary or merely functional, quality. Learning a subject (any subject) in school is then simply an example of learning to be human, justified in terms of the subject's ability to help pupils become human. In the terms of Lave and Wenger, school pupils are not trying but failing to be attached to the communities of practice of physicists, mathematicians and historians. They are properly members of the community of practice of human community itself, in a community including adults who are themselves interested in physics, mathematics or history. School pupils are not 'learning school', as the formulations of school – the specialized language, the subjects, the tests – are not in themselves the aim of schooling. They are however learning to be human in the school, itself a community of and for learning, filled with dialogue (for which, see also Alexander 2004, 2006).

It is not, then, that schools simply 'might' be communities, but rather that they 'must' be communities. That is, they are required to be communities, as schools: this is central to their educational role, with education broadening the spirit of families – which themselves are small communities. Hence '[t]his school community stands between family and the wider community and looks back to the first and forward to the second ... [and] is able to do this, and to combine in miniature the conditions of each of these, because unlike either of them it has one concern to which everything else is directed – the education of young persons who are entrusted to it' (Macmurray, 1968, pp. 35–6). It could be noted, too, that the legal position of teachers in the UK as being *in loco parentis* strengthens the idea of the school being a 'broadened' family (University of Bristol 1998, and see also Stern 2003 and the more critical Myers 2005). This leaves schools in an ambiguous position. They are broadened families, but are not families; they teach subjects, but are not fully engaged with the technical or professional communities of those subjects; they are learning communities bound together by personal relations, but personal relationships amongst members of the community are necessarily professionally restricted. These and other schooling ambiguities are worth exploring in some more detail.

Ambiguities of schools

Ambiguity as a concept comes from a long literary and philosophical tradition. It is seen by writers such as Empson as the foundation of all literature, all art. The ambiguities of schooling are therefore not necessarily problems: they may be the source of the school's very richness. A number of writers on ambiguity refer back to Keats' description of the characteristic shared by literary and other people who are high achievers. He describes a discussion when

> it struck me what quality went to form a Man [*sic*] of Achievement, especially in Literature, and which Shakespeare possessed so enormously – I mean *Negative Capability*, that is, when a man is capable of being in uncertainties, mysteries, doubts, without any irritable reaching after fact and reason. (Keats 1947, p. 72)

Keats is not referring to apathy or a lack of care about facts and reason. Rather, he is referring to the possibility of 'achieving' with and through the presence of unresolved multiple meanings. Shakespeare continued to be 'negatively capable' through the twentieth century, a 'hero' of the left (for example with Brecht), of the right (for example with Hitler), and all points in between (for example with Churchill). It is not that Shakespeare was seen as 'beyond' politics: he was and continues to be interpreted as being of *every* politics. Similarly, Spinoza demonstrated his negative capability by being positively interpreted as both 'God-obsessed' and as an atheist (as in Yovel 1989a, p. 127): remarkable for anyone, and even more so for a religious philosopher. This is surely an approach to achievement and negative capability that could also be applied to schools. The ambiguities within schools are of similar kinds to those described by Keats, with pupils, teachers, families, and the voices within the 'content' of the curriculum all being full of uncertainties, mysteries and doubts, without the expectation or need for all of these to be definitively resolved.

For Empson, ambiguity means 'any verbal nuance, however slight, which gives room for alternative reactions' (Empson 1961, p. 19). More recently, Atwood takes Keats' more romantic theme up in her account of the writer's life, by describing the 'duplicity' of all writing and all writers (in a chapter referring to 'the slippery double: Why there are always two', Atwood 2003, p. 25). Ambiguity for Empson is seen as representing a surfeit of meaning, dividing and joining, forcing interpretation, rather than merely a presence of confusion or uncertainty. This suits also the 'plenitude of meanings' of Bakhtin (Holquist in Bakhtin 1981, p. 26). Bakhtin's novel could be compared with the classroom, both places of many voices coming together in a kind of unity, as '[a] language is revealed in all its distinctiveness only when it is brought into relationship with other languages, entering with them into one single heteroglot unity of societal becoming' (Bakhtin 1981, p. 411). Reference to unity also indicates that ambiguity can sit alongside *singularity*, as in literary theorists such as Attridge (2004). This is related in turn to irreplaceability as described by Macmurray, who says that '[o]ur personal relations ... are unique ... [and] not replaceable ... [such that i]f I lose a friend I lose part of my own life' (Macmurray 2004, p. 169). People connected through social relationships need not be friends, and are therefore 'replaceable'; friends and family are irreplaceable. If a colleague moves on, it is appropriate to say 'well, there will be someone else taking their place'; if a friend or family member is lost, such a statement would be insulting. It is the uniqueness and irreplaceability of friends, including for Macmurray teachers and pupils, that means they must be fully personal relationships, and a personal relationship is one that can live with mysteries and uncertainties and multiple meanings. The singularity of friends and therefore communities requires the possibility of rich ambiguities and diverse voices. Elsewhere in philosophy, ambiguity can be seen in (or created by) the 'puzzles' of Zen koans (such as 'What is the sound of one hand clapping?', or 'If you meet the Buddha on the road, kill him', as in Olson 2005, p. 310 and pp. 356–7), in the Marrano-like tradition from which came Spinoza (as described in Yovel 1989a), in the dialectics of Hegel and his successors (as described in Yovel 1989b), and in the almost cabalistic ambiguity of Walter Benjamin and his 49 levels of meaning (as described by Sontag in Benjamin 1997, p. 19).

The ambiguity of schools as learning communities therefore needs exploring. Some work on organizations suggests a slightly 'thinner' version of ambiguity. Meyerson and Martin write of ambiguous paradigms of organizational cultures, which are 'most likely to be adopted in settings where creativity and constant experimentation are valued (classrooms, research laboratories, innovative industries, etc.); in contexts where ambiguity is unavoidably salient . . .; in occupations where technology is unclear (social work and book publishing); and in work where ideological and cognitive openness is required (such as cross-cultural business and inter-organizational negotiations)' (Meyerson and Martin, in Harris *et al.* 1997, p. 40). Hoyle and Wallace (2005) write of ambiguity in terms of 'uncertainty of meaning', with consequent opportunities for both situational irony (the unintended consequences of well-intentioned actions), and semantic irony (the intended or unintended gap between meaning and language used, such as conscious wordplay or the unwitting use of hype). Conditions for irony are endemic ambiguity or 'uncertainty of meaning'. However, there are richer nuances of ambiguity (or, in Empson's terms, the types of ambiguity with higher numbers, of the seven): people must look for schools' 'astonishing, sophisticated ambiguity' (as used by Gifford of Hogg's *Confessions of a Justified Sinner*, Hogg 1978, p. 10). This ambiguity helps determine the nature and purpose of schooling, underpinned as it is by the philosophies of Macmurray and Buber.

The three ambiguities mentioned in the previous section of this chapter were that schools are broadened families, but are not families; they teach subjects, but are not fully engaged with the technical or professional communities of those subjects; and they are learning communities bound together by personal relations, but personal relationships amongst members of the community are necessarily professionally restricted. Such ambiguities are not needing to be resolved, but clarified and as appropriate celebrated. The first, about the familial nature of schooling, is clarified by research on the role of parents, such as Munn (1993) and Vincent (2000). It might be expected that parental involvement in schools would enhance the familial nature of schooling, but some suggest that '[f]ar from enabling inclusion, the constructs used to frame parents' place in education often in fact marginalize and exclude' (Thomas and O'Hanlon, in Vincent 2000, p. x). It is the framing of the relationship between parents and schools that is most important, rather than a simple description of schools or of families and a statement that there should be a connection. Taken from these and other examples of family research, the following four principles are an attempt to frame the relationship. Firstly, school is about the whole of life, and teachers need to draw on the outside world, including the world of pupils' families. Secondly, the curriculum should be applicable to the rest of pupils' lives. The curriculum is not for the benefit of the subjects, it is for the benefit of the pupils – it should help them understand, grow, take hold of the world, become more 'real'. Thirdly, teachers should recognize that parents know more than teachers about their children, and are likely to have taught them more, too. Fourthly and finally, parents are not to be seen as cheap substitutes for teachers: teachers are, at best, quite expensive substitutes for parents (see also Stern 2003, p. 3). In these ways, schools can indeed 'broaden' families, by drawing on family worlds and exploiting family knowledge, and at best 'substituting' for (that is, consciously adding to the work of) parents, without attempting to replace families by ignoring, excluding or downplaying their significance.

The subjects taught in school have interesting relationships to academic and working communities. As part of an argument for 'curriculum integration', breaking down barriers between school subjects, Beane makes a powerful positive case for dissociating school subjects from academic 'disciplines of knowledge', just as Lave and Wenger talk negatively about school subjects being dissociated from professional and work-based communities. 'Though school-based subject areas, like disciplines of knowledge, partition knowledge into differentiated categories, they are not the same thing as disciplines ... since they deal with a limited selection of what is already known within the field ... [or] their presence in schools really has to do with economic, social, or academic aspirations' (Beane 1995, p. 617). A discipline of knowledge and a school subject 'serve quite different purposes, offer quite different experiences for those who encounter them, and have quite different notions about the fluidity of the boundaries that presumably set one area of inquiry off from others' (Beane 1995, p. 617). The purpose of Beane's work is to defend a view of the curriculum as 'integrated' and as related to the 'problems, issues, and concerns posed by life itself ... [including] self- or personal concerns and ... issues and problems posed by the larger world' (Beane 1995, p. 616). Whether or not that end-point is supported, the importance of the argument for the ambiguity of school subjects is worth repeating. Each school subject is not and cannot be a part of the community of scholars or practitioners who carry the same or a similar name. Schools teach subjects, but are not fully engaged with the technical or professional or academic communities associated with those subjects. Any subjects taught cannot claim to be ends in themselves, through their association with those other communities. '[T]he separate-subject approach, as a selective representation of disciplines of knowledge, has incorrectly portrayed the latter as "ends" rather than "means" of education ... [so y]oung people and adults have been led to believe that the purpose of education is to master or "collect" facts, principles, and skills that have been selected for inclusion in one or another subject area instead of learning how those isolated elements might be used to inform larger, real-life purposes' (Beane 1995, p. 618). Subjects must therefore be justified in other ways, as for example the English and Welsh national curriculum (DFEE and QCA 1999) which justifies the curriculum in terms of purposes such as the development of pupils' social, moral, spiritual and cultural development.

It is not just the existence and purpose of subjects that are ambiguous. There is an ambiguity created by the contrasting demands of epistemological egalitarianism and epistemological hierarchy. Schools have a need for epistemological egalitarianism, as the beliefs and understanding of all in the school need to be recognized and included. Each lesson, to be 'real', must be one which 'develops in mutual surprises' (Buber 2002a, p. 242, quoted above in Chapter 2). This is essential in plural, heteroglot communities, if the school is to be inclusive, and is essential in those school subjects which are contentious and contended. That is, all school subjects. However, schools also have a need for hierarchy. Teachers are appointed to have what is often called 'subject knowledge', and it is proper that they are and are seen as 'experts' (as in aspects of the apprenticeship model of Lave and Wenger 1991). Bringing these two positions together is dialogue. There must be dialogue – a clash of truths – in classrooms (as exemplified by Ipgrave 2001, 2003): it must happen that when people meet, and when 'belief systems' meet, there will be a conflict, a clash of beliefs about what is true. School teaching as 'a continuing personal exchange between two generations' (Macmurray 1968, p. 5) means that it is not enough that teachers are in dialogue with each other or external subject-related communities; teachers must be in dialogue with pupils as an *exchange*. Pupils should not be treated as 'empty vessels' or as foolish: teachers should be modest enough to allow for a real exchange. In the terms of Lave and Wenger, teachers can be considered experts who are creating their own successors and replacements, just as parents are experts who are creating the next generation of parents. Wenger asks 'How can we enable transformative experiences that change students' understanding of themselves as learners and thus their ability to move among practices and learn whatever they need to learn where they are?' (Wenger 1998, p. 269). He replies by referring to 'the life-giving power of mutuality' (Wenger 1998, p. 277, as quoted above in Chapter 2).

This view is dependent on a view of truth emerging, rather than being already-discovered and to be transmitted. As Salmon says of personal construct psychology, it is based on the assumption, uncommon amongst psychologies, that 'knowledge is provisional', and 'is ultimately governed by constructive alternativism; everything can always be reconstrued' (Salmon 1995, p. 22). For her,

> [r]eality is not to be pinned down forever in a standardized curriculum. The understanding which teachers offer is necessarily provisional – for the time being only. And for all that school knowledge has high social consensus and is grounded in the whole cultural heritage, it is also indelibly personal. It takes its significance from within the construct system of any particular teacher. Since each person inhabits a distinctive world of meaning, the curriculum of education is constructed afresh, and individually, by every teacher who offers it. (Salmon 1995, p. 22)

The third of the ambiguities of schooling, that schools are learning communities bound together by personal relations, but personal relationships amongst members of the community are necessarily professionally restricted, is the one that could be most challenging, as there are considerable sensitivities in how relationships should work in professional organizations. As Macmurrian communities, schools are necessarily *personal*, yet schools are full of quite specific, institutionally and legally promoted, personal taboos, hierarchies and restrictions. This includes the separation of pupils by age and in many ways by gender (though these are more contested), and various forms of separation between pupils and adults and amongst adults. Many of those 'separations' are represented by toilet arrangements, such as the separate toilets for male and female pupils, and for staff and perhaps also for the headteacher. Along with toilets, other taboo-related hierarchies include expectations of no sexual or sexually-related contact between pupils and teachers, some restrictions of such contact amongst staff (see Myers 2005, and Lind in Fergusson and Dower 2002 for a study of the clergy), and no exchange of 'bad language' between pupils and teachers (despite each group using such language amongst its own). To deal with those ambiguities, Macmurray uses the concept of friendship.

There is a requirement, derived from Macmurray – and to an extent disagreed with by Buber – for schools to be places of possible friendship. The nature of friendship is not necessarily sexual (in contrast to the privatized and romanticized view of friendship largely created in the nineteenth century), but is more 'Aristotelian'. As MacIntyre says, in an account that, interestingly, underplays the possibility of modern schools dealing with 'the whole of life', Aristotle's 'notion of the political community as a common project is alien to the modern liberal individualist world'. Though it may be 'how we sometimes at least think of schools, hospitals or philanthropic organizations ... we have no conception of such a form of community concerned, as Aristotle says the *polis* is concerned, with the whole of life, not with this or that good, but with man's good as such' (MacIntyre 1985, p. 156). He continues that '[i]t is no wonder that friendship has been relegated to private life and thereby weakened in comparison to what it once was' (MacIntyre 1985, p. 156). The researcher of social policy, Roseneil (2004), writes of the need to understand how significant friendship is in the 'post-heteronormative' twenty-first century. She and other researchers have returned to Aristotle, whose writing on friendship had been somewhat neglected. For Aristotle, the personal relations in a state should be such that friendship is possible, as 'in a tyranny there is little or no friendship ... just as there is no justice' (Aristotle 1976, p. 278). In that sense, Macmurray's 'community' is the same: a place where friendship must be possible. Friendship is in this sense a full relationship of person to person, where neither is treated as a means to a further end. It is therefore possible for people to be friends, and necessary that this be possible in a school, as the most likely barrier to this would be inappropriate attitudes to other people. The restrictions on sexual contact between people in a school community is itself, significantly, based on problems associated with the misuse of sexuality. That is, the possibility of harassment or the inappropriate use of power relations within the school, is what makes sexual contact inappropriate, not the possibility of friendship-leading-to-sexual-contact itself. Teachers having sexual contact with pupils or students of any age is likely to be restricted, informally or by rules or laws of professional conduct, for precisely this reason: it is likely to be exploitative, with one of the people involved treating the other as a means to an end. This is well described by Myers (2005, p. 14 and throughout), and the possibility of exploitation being itself ambiguous and contested is well described for school pupils by Epstein (2002) and in a fictional university setting by Mamet in the play *Oleanna* (Mamet 1992).

The difference between Buber and Macmurray on friendship in schools is based on Buber's concern that schooling – and also healing – relationships should not be fully mutual. For Buber, 'however much depends upon [the teacher] awakening the *I–Thou* relationship in the pupil ... – and however much depends upon the pupil, too, meaning and affirming him as the particular person he is – the special educative relation could not persist if the pupil for his part practised "inclusion", that is, if he lived the teacher's part in the common situation' (Buber 1958, p. 165). A teacher and pupil may become friends, but not *as* teacher and pupil: 'it is plain that the specifically educative relation as such is denied full mutuality' (Buber 1958, p. 165). That is, 'however intense the mutuality of giving and taking with which he is bound to his pupil, inclusion cannot be mutual in this case ... [and i]n the moment when the pupil is able to throw himself across and experience from over there, the educative relation would be burst asunder, or change into friendship' (Buber 2002a, p. 119). This position may be based on Buber's narrower, perhaps even a romanticized, view of friendship, when compared to that of Macmurray. However, it also reflects Buber's view that '[a] great and full relation between man and man can only exist between unified and responsible persons' (Buber 2002a, p. 138), and in that sense, school pupils are not seen by him as yet as entirely 'unified and responsible'. Buber was a specialist in adult education, having set up and run the Centre for Jewish Adult Education in Germany until 1938, and the Seminar (later Center) for Teachers of Adult Education in Jerusalem from 1949 (Schaeder in Glatzer and Mendes-Flohr 1991, p. 3, and Smith 2000). As Smith describes it, Buber 'contrasted the education of children with that of adults – the latter involved full mutuality, the former on a more asymmetrical relationship' (Smith 2000).

To the extent that schools for children are *not* based on 'real questions', and are involved only in 'preparation for examinations', Buber and Macmurray would agree that there is not true mutuality in schools. This is, indeed, the position of Schutz on the 'stranger': his model of joining a group – a family or social group or community – is applied to adults, with 'children and primitives' having a different position (Schutz 1976, pp. 91–3). Macmurray, of course, would disagree with Buber's description of schooling, and it may be that the adult educator – Buber – had a view of the distinctiveness of adult education contrasted with school education, in terms of 'real questions', that down-played the possibilities of school education. This is a theme expressed elsewhere by adult educators, such as the distinctiveness of 'relevance' in adult education as described by Knowles (1984). Perhaps the difference could also be resolved through the use of Lave and Wenger (1991) on 'legitimate peripheral participation'. Children in schools may be further out on the 'periphery' of community life than adults, so there is a greater distance between them and those at the 'centre' of community life, than there is between adults joining a community and those at the 'centre' of the community being joined. Yet they may still be on the same trajectory towards the centre. It is in the formulations of later writers such as Noddings (1984, 1993, 2003) on education, and Stern-Gillet (1995) or Roseneil (2004) on Aristotle's conception of friendship, that support the more Macmurrian approach.

Conclusion: the fictive school

A fourth, as yet unstated, ambiguity of schooling can serve both as a conclusion to this chapter and a preparation for the following chapter. This is the ambiguity represented by the need for school-based research, in order for those outside as well as within the schools to have an evidence base for making policy, with the problems associated with school-based research, including problems of access (for outsiders, as in McDonald 1989) and bias (for insiders, as described in all standard research methods books, as well as texts such as McDonald 1989). These are similar to research problems encountered by those studying other forms of community such as the family (as described by Oakley 1992 and numerous other family researchers) and religion (as described by several contributors to McCutcheon 1999). To approach this ambiguity requires consideration of schools not just as communities, but as learning communities. Schools, unlike families or religious groups, are peculiarly dedicated to learning, which means that school research not only can be, but must be, school-centred yet going beyond the school. This is the basis for research such as that of MacBeath (1999), Rudduck *et al.* (1996), and Flutter and Rudduck (2004). All attempt to give voice to pupils and teachers and outsiders (as with parents, in Stern 2003), and to use both 'insiders' and 'outsiders' to analyse and critique those voices. Schools are complex learning communities, rich with meanings and meaning-making: hence one might refer to the fictive school. In order to understand schools, research is needed, and research is of the character of schooling itself. It is therefore the subject both of the following chapter and of Chapter 14.

Chapter 5

Inclusive research: voicing and learning

Research is more than intelligent action or reflective practice. . . . It requires a context of openness, public scrutiny and criticism.

(Pring 2000, p. 138, also quoted in O'Hanlon 2003, p. 113)

Introducing inclusive research

The book has attempted to develop an *action philosophy* of schooling, recognizing the 'stubborn particulars' of the world (Cherry 1995). Those particulars addressed in Chapter 2 are related to being human, whilst it is the nature of community that is addressed by Chapter 3, and Chapter 4 addresses schools as the third of the stubborn particulars. People are described as more-or-less existing in and through relationships: the 'more-or-less' indicating the possibility of becoming more real through relationships. Relational activity itself is described as dialogue, and community is the description of a set of people related to each other in a particular way – related as people in themselves, and not for any external purpose. Dialogue typically involves acts of inclusion, and communities can therefore be inclusive in distinctive ways. Schools can be – must be – communities, places full of dialogue such that people are treating each other as people in themselves, with no dominating extrinsic purposes. The possibility of becoming more real, in schools as inclusive communities, can itself be described as a process of learning.

There are countless social structures for learning, with learning typically involving a movement from the periphery to the centre of a group of practitioners (as described by Lave and Wenger 1991). For Lave and Wenger, learning is 'situated' as it involves participation in a 'community of practice'. These are not necessarily communities in Macmurray's sense, as the term refers to any group, such as midwives, butchers, tailors, quartermasters, or recovering alcoholics, which has a characteristic quasi-apprenticeship structure of movement from the periphery to the centre. It is worth noting, again, that the structure is not dyadic but cyclical: the essence of learning is to replace the current learnèd. How schools as Macmurrian communities can also be communities of practice in the way described by Lave and Wenger is dependent on the 'practice' of schools being that of being human, rather than it being the practice of mathematics, history, or science. Those subject-based or job-based practices may be part of but not the central purpose of schooling, as may other external purposes such as the economic success of the country or rising exam results.

As learning is central to schooling, and as schools are Macmurrian communities, research as a distinctive form of learning has a particular role in schools, and has particular challenges. The current chapter therefore investigates the nature of school-based research, and the possibility of inclusive research linking school communities to wider communities. How research 'voices' members of learning communities is the first part of the investigation, and how research methodology can through engagement with communal philosophy avoid some of its own problems is the second part of the investigation. The 'inclusion' in the chapter title is therefore both a personal inclusion (voicing pupils and other members of the school community) and a methodological inclusion (avoiding a narrow view of research, and instead seeing research as a distinctive form of learning). Research, in this sense, is connected to the search for truth, and is identified as searching for truth in particular ways. It has been defined (by Pring, from Stenhouse) as 'any "systematic, critical and self-critical enquiry which aims to contribute to the advancement of knowledge" ... [which] is broad enough to encompass not only empirical research, but also historical, documentary and philosophical research' (Pring 2000, p. 7). Developing that definition, the Higher Education Funding Council for England (Hefce, the largest funders of UK research) says that 'research [in terms of their Research Assessment Exercise] is original investigation undertaken in order to gain knowledge and understanding ... [and] excludes routine testing and analysis [and] the development of teaching materials that do not embody original research' (Hefce 2005). Research involves originality, as is already implied by the 'advancement' of knowledge; it also involves a particular way of using theories. 'Laypeople base [theories] on haphazard events and use them in a loose and uncritical manner [, whilst s]cientists, by contrast, construct their theories carefully and systematically' (Cohen *et al.* 2000, p. 2). For Pring, similarly, theories and theorizing are characteristic of research, forming a 'framework of ideas and beliefs' that 'we bring to our observations of the world' and that 'shape ... the observations we make' (Pring 2000, p. 76). He goes on to say that making these assumptions explicit could 'reveal' theory, although this would depend on its 'level of reflection and articulation' (Pring 2000, p. 76).

If someone is 'finding out' in a way that is original, careful and systematic, and that is placed in a systematically-constructed 'theory', then that person may well be completing research. However, despite all that complex description, it is worth saying that research is something quite ordinary. It could well be something with which teachers are regularly involved, and it may even be something expected of school pupils, as it is difficult for teachers to develop professionally, and difficult for pupils to learn, without their being researchers in some sense. The only professional development and learning that could not be covered by the description of research given above, would be learning that is wholly unoriginal or routine, or that does not fit in any 'theory' or systematic understanding of how things or ideas fit together. Teachers are unlikely to be satisfied with education that did not involve their pupils in something like research, or that did not involve them in research of this kind.

An element missing from the definition to this point is the process of peer review. Within the academic community, complex and significant systems of peer review have been developed, and these are systematically in place within publishing (chiefly with respect to academic journals) and within research audits such as the UK's Research Assessment Exercise (RAE). The processes of scholarly peer reviewing are well described in Hefce's (2005) RAE guidance, and that also highlights the hierarchy of peer reviewing, related for example to how research will be more highly regarded if the peers acknowledging it are 'international' rather than 'national'. There is controversy over the use of the RAE to determine public funding of research, both in terms of the nature of the peer groups (i.e. there may be a built-in bias towards 'insider' research and against more truly innovative research, given the likely delay in well-established peer groups recognizing innovation from newcomers), and in terms of the proper distribution of funds (i.e. the 'selectivity' of funding) (see for example the 512 articles archived on the topic, by March 2006, at www.thes.co.uk). Notwithstanding that controversy, the process of peer review itself is broadly welcomed by academics, and is a vital example of what inclusion can mean with respect to research. The 'community of practice' into which academic researchers are inducted is a clearly identified one, and is subject to public scrutiny.

Those completing school-based research may have their research peer reviewed in this way; many will also have their research peer reviewed in other ways, too, with the process of professional and public recognition being of this broader kind. The selectivity of the RAE process (in Hefce 2005) makes it absolutely clear that much high quality research will fall outside its remit: publications of research findings in a number of journals, including a large number of peer-reviewed journals, and in books with various publishers, are of high quality and of considerable influence on policy and practice in education. For some education researchers, engagement with this form of research is part of a developmental process that might lead to RAE-type research; for others, this is itself the substance of their research engagement. It would be difficult to envisage connections being made between research and professional activity without this form of research. For example, whether research is commissioned by or used by professional bodies or government departments or agencies may be an indication of review by peers outside the 'academic peer review' community of practice, but clearly within a distinct 'professional educator' or 'education policy' community of practice. Some of the challenges of defining peer review, for subjects such as education and nursing and social work, are captured by debates on what is called 'applied practitioner research' (for which, see Furlong and Oancea 2005). However, the phrase 'applied practitioner research' as developed by Furlong and colleagues and as described in RAE guidance (Hefce 2005) adds reference to professional and other peer reviewing without very significantly reducing the reference to academic peers, and is therefore less radical in its scope than consideration of professional or policy-based peer reviewing in the absence of any academic peer review.

As well as academic peer review, and peer review by other professional or policy communities, some school-based research processes can be recognized in other ways.

Engagement in research may be said to have an impact on other aspects of work in education, and the professional recognition by peers may not be directly of the research itself, but of the person who has engaged in research. Hence, school staff who have completed research (for example, through having completed a research degree such as a doctorate) may be advantaged in the job market, simply through the recognition of the value to the profession of having completed research. The nature and extent of this kind of recognition is likely to vary from school to school, and from country to country. In some countries, for example, a doctorate or other higher degrees may be rewarded with higher pay or a smaller teaching commitment (as in Sweden), or in other benefits such as different pension rights (as in the Irish Republic). There is a role for further comparative analysis of such processes: the importance, here, is in understanding various ways in which research may be 'inclusive' in the sense of being able to be recognized as belonging to a particular community of practice.

Voicing pupils, teachers and the wider school community

School-based research can be of many kinds, including research that is intimately bound up in the processes of the school as with various forms of 'action research' (see Mitchell in Bacharach and Mundell 1995, p. 232) and school development planning (see Dalin and Rust 1983, Dalin 1993), and research that touches individual schools more lightly but is intended to have a broader national or international policy impact (see for example the Evidence for Policy and Practice Information and Co-ordinating Centre, i.e. EPPI-Centre, at eppi.ioe.ac.uk/). All, however, are at least minimally concerned with the ethics of their research, as described by the British Sociological Association, who stress that '[a]lthough sociologists, like other researchers are committed to the advancement of knowledge, that goal does not, of itself, provide an entitlement to override the rights of others', so researchers should 'have some responsibility for the use to which their research may be put' and 'should strive to protect the rights of those they study, their interests, sensitivities and privacy, while recognising the difficulty of balancing potentially conflicting interests' (British Sociological Association 1995, p. 1). Even though that statement of ethics is concluded by the slightly less committed statement that 'research relationships should be characterised, *whenever possible*, by trust' (British Sociological Association 1995, p. 1, emphasis added), the broader commitment to ensure the well-being of research participants is helpful for all school-based research. The commitment is extended by school-based researchers such as O'Hanlon to an active concern to include or 'voice' pupils, with the promotion of 'democratic or inclusive action research' (O'Hanlon 2003, p. 65). Schools as learning communities themselves imply continuing learning and therefore elements of research, and where the learning is systematically carried out, original and critical and open to public review (such as peer review), schools as learning communities are necessarily research-imbued. Pring, writing about school-based research, notes that 'it is difficult to see how good teaching can be separated from a research stance towards one's own teaching – a stance in which values (both public and private) about teaching are tested out in practice and in which both the values and the practice are the constant focus of reflection in the light of systematically obtained evidence' (Pring 2000, p. 160). This is set in a context of school-based research recognizing the 'stubborn particular' of being human, as '[c]entral to educational research ... is the attempt to make sense of the activities, policies and institutions which, through the organization of learning, help to transform the capacities of people to live a fuller and more distinctively human life' (Pring 2000, p. 17).

Despite Pring's helpful warning that 'the language of the research, reflecting the interests and requirements of those who manage the system, often gives an impoverished account of that which is to be researched into' (Pring 2000, p. 29), the need for schools to be research-imbued is both a powerful argument for the 'community of researchers' but also for those wishing to give a voice to pupils and other members of the school community. Flutter and Rudduck (2004) is a particularly useful account of the role of pupil voice and pupils as researchers. There, Myers and MacBeath note that '[t]raditionally, the pupil's role within school has been a somewhat passive one, with pupils regarded as "consumers", or even as "products", of educational provision rather than as active participants in a learning community', although in recent years it has been realized that 'conferring opportunities for active agency can have a transforming effect on pupils and, ultimately, on schools themselves' (Myers and MacBeath, in Flutter and Rudduck 2004, p. 14). Pupil involvement in research is described there as only one stage of participation, with reference to the Hart Ladder of Participation, stepping from 'pupils not consulted', to 'listening to pupils', 'pupils as active participants', 'pupils as researchers', and on to 'pupils as fully active participants and co-researchers' (Flutter and Rudduck 2004, p. 16, and see also Blaylock 2001a, b on listening to pupils in religious education). The work of Rudduck in particular (as also in Rudduck *et al.* 1996) links pupil voice to both research and school improvement, and that is a significant development in the school improvement research and development work of Dalin (Dalin and Rust 1983, Dalin 1993), just as Dalin's work built on school-based research giving voice to pupils such as the critical work of Hargreaves (1967, 1972, 1982) or Willis (1977). Hargreaves himself worked on school development planning (e.g. Hargreaves and Hopkins 1991) and specifically recommends research-based teaching (in part based on the medical model, as in Hargreaves 1996).

The voicing of pupils in inclusive research is part of a wider development, voicing all members of the school community. Teachers are typically 'voiced' in a wide range of school improvement research (such as that of Dalin, quoted above), and parents are voiced and given 'agency' in work such as that of Wolfendale (Wolfendale and Bastiani 2000, Wolfendale 2002), Vincent (2000), Munn (1993), and Barth (1990, also voicing teachers and principals/headteachers). The role of other school workers in school-based research has been the subject of less attention in the research literature, but some issues are addressed by

Lacey (2001) and Biott (1991), with the specific work of educational psychologists addressed by Newton and Tarrant whose 'motto' is that 'Children learn – so can schools' (Newton and Tarrant 1992, p. 50). Some of the difficulties of parental and non-teaching worker involvement in school developments are highlighted by Lacey, who notes the 'constant practical difficulties with making partnership work and misunderstandings about the meaning of partnership between families and professionals has, in many cases, devalued its principle' (Lacey 2001, p. 135). Inclusive school-based research is therefore tied to broader definitions of inclusive schooling, with all the challenges of that inclusivity. Various groups can be included in school-based research, and inclusion that involves activity or agency, rather than simply passive mention, is that much more inclusive.

Pupils who complete research, in the forms described here, may also be addressing the need for creativity in schooling. Creativity – itself the subject of Chapter 11 below – is described by DfEE (1999) in terms of originality, purpose, imagination and value (i.e. evaluation), in contrast to the routine, the passive and the non-evaluated. It is hardly a long way from those characteristics to those of originality and critique required of research. Links are therefore worth making between the roles of inclusive school-based research and the school curriculum and pedagogy, as influenced by policies on creativity and by the parallel set of policies related to thinking skills (for example www.teachthinking.com, www.thinkingtogether.org.uk, or www.teachingthinking.net/ and as exemplified in Baumfield 2002). Beyond issues of voice, creativity and, more generally, personal inclusion, the processes of research itself may themselves be considered more or less inclusive, and that is the subject of the next section.

Beyond false dichotomies in research

Much excellent guidance on research (such as that provided by Cohen *et al.* 2000) is presented in terms of contrasting and usually conflicting pairs: positivistic vs interpretive, quantitative vs qualitative, researcher vs object of research, objectivity vs subjectivity, mind vs body. There are situations where such contrasts are helpful; there are other times when research is limited, however, by a stress on dichotomies, especially when research is, like school-based research, built in to the central purpose and activity of the community being researched. Pring is clear on the need to go beyond false dichotomies, as '[t]here is a world of difference between the sort of enquiry appropriate for understanding physical reality and the sort of enquiry for understanding the mental life of individual persons'. Pring notes that educational research therefore often 'purports to reveal the under-standings and perceptions of the subjects of research – 'the phenomenology' of the mind' (Pring 2000, p. 31). However, he continues that '[o]ne main purpose of this book is to show that such dichotomies are mistaken ... [as] researchers have fallen into a philosophical trap ... the ancient dualism between mind and body, between the publicly accessible and the privately privileged' (Pring 2000, p. 32). The conclusion is that '[e]ducational research is both and neither' (Pring 2000, p. 32), and the idea of going beyond false dichotomies with respect to research, is therefore related to the idea of going beyond false dichotomies with respect to humanity. It is the nature of humanity, particularly dualist approaches to the nature of humanity, that can lead to a number of dichotomies, and clearly underpins the positivist/interpretive dichotomy in research. Those who, like Macmurray and Buber, go beyond dualist philosophy of humanity, also therefore provide a foundation for a methodology that avoids false dichotomies. That is the task Pring gives himself, to look beyond the battles between education research 'as a subset of the social sciences' and research of a more phenomenological kind. Instead, '[t]he qualitative investigation can clear the ground for the quantitative – and the quantitative be suggestive of differences to be explored in a more interpretive mode' (Pring 2000, p. 55).

Pring's approach is also reflected in investigations on research in religion. The so-called 'insider/outsider' problem in the study of religion (McCutcheon 1999, and see McDonald 1989 or Biott 1991 for other school-related versions of this problem) is solved not through putting oneself on one side or the other, but bridging any apparent gap. That bridging can, as Buber describes it, be an act of inclusion, as Friedman says: the 'experiencing the other side' that is referred to as 'imagining the real' (Friedman in Buber 2002a, pp. xiii–xiv). Inclusive research is therefore a matter of inclusive methodology, including a range of traditions, rather than simply siding with one tradition. This is explored further, after a series of chapters on research in religion and education (Chapters 6 to 10), in Chapter 14 on ways of developing sincerity in educational research. Come what may, this will require what McDonald refers to as the 'intimacy, empathy, and attention to the nuances of context that positivists strip away' (McDonald 1989, p. 207). A school-based researcher must 'have a sense of the immense complexities and staggering ambiguities of life on the inside and of how all outside interventions of policy, curriculum, and method are transformed by inside culture' (McDonald 1989, p. 207).

Conclusion

Education research sits between arts and social sciences, or between philosophy, psychology, sociology and history: it is not a narrowly positivistic or narrowly interpretive exercise, and it is in a peculiar position to be able to contribute to educational and social inclusion, voicing pupils, teachers and others. The distinctive commitment to dialogue, which involves acts of inclusion, can inform research. The research is part of the process, and is a form of 'listening'. The moves towards a 'listening school' (Stead 2006) are part of a more general interest in listening, reflected in the curriculum (Blaylock 2001a, b) and in the development of trust in schools (Bryk and Schneider 2002). Within religious traditions, listening is a significant theme. An interesting example is from the Sufi Muslim tradition of the Mawlawiya Dervishes (known as 'Whirling Dervishes'), whose 'music' and 'dance' is not described as such, but rather as 'listening': 'It is remarkable that the term "music" is never used, and its elements are rarely discussed ... [but] is always a question of "listening", which includes attending to dancing as well as music' (Shiloah 1976).

To close, it is worth giving voice to a 13-year-old pupil, who in response to a piece of research (available at www.pcfre.org.uk/db/, with suggestions for its use in Weston 2003) wrote in a distinctive way, voicing views well worth being heard:

I have enjoyed all my RE lessons, religion is not as boring as you may think, it can be as interesting as you make it to be. I have learnt and understood other people's religions, which have helped me understand things in life. I have learnt about the world, and how we are not all equal. Plus lots more.

Section B: Religion and education

Dogmatic certainty is the end of education (not excluding religious education).
(Mitscherlich 1993, p. 14)

Section A investigated people, communities, schooling and research, ending with the pupil who 'learnt about the world, and how we are not all equal', adding 'plus lots more'. That pupil was studying religious education, and this section therefore focuses on religion and education and their coming together in religious education. It attempts to answer two questions. Firstly, how can religious education improve further, and bridge the gap between its own self-image as a vital and vibrant subject, and the image of it portrayed by some inspectors and even some pupils, parents and teachers as something of a backwater? An answer may be for religious education as a school subject to engage more in research, both research undertaken by professional academics and research undertaken by religious education teachers and pupils. Along with the accounts of religious education and research in each chapter, there are descriptions of case studies and activities through which teachers can use research in their classrooms.

The second question addressed by this section of the book is how can research hope to understand the complex and relatively impenetrable world of school religious education? Schools are a challenge to researchers (as described in McDonald 1989), just as religion is a challenge to researchers (as described in McCutcheon 1999), so religious education presents even more problems. An answer tentatively given in Chapter 5 above, was for professional academic researchers to see pupils, their families and schools as co-researchers rather than as subjects, and to build in to their research a commitment to the improvement of people's lives, and to the improvement of religious education and schooling more generally. This is the basis for research, such as that of MacBeath 1999, Rudduck *et al.* (1996), and Flutter and Rudduck (2004), that attempts to give voice to pupils and teachers.

This section therefore uses some of the common themes in contemporary religious education and sits them alongside some of the common themes in contemporary research. It is not a comprehensive survey of research in religious education, it is a selection of some important topics; it is not an attempt to say that religious education teaching and research are one and the same thing, it is a description of complementarity.

Chapter 6

Investigating text and context

My Grandmother read to me when I was young, a piece from the Bible and taught me those things.
(13 year old, responding to the question 'Religions sometimes teach
their followers about freedom, truth, justice, love and forgiveness.
Who has taught you about these things?')

Introduction

Teachers of religious education have always been exploring texts, and the best use of sacred texts in religious education should be enlightening, imaginative, literate, provocative, and sensitive to context. However, this is inevitably not always the case, and the ways in which texts are studied in religious education differ from the ways they are studied in history or English lessons. Research on the use of sacred texts in religious education can help teachers understand what is happening and what is possible. Research on the use of sacred texts can also connect contemporary religious education to its past, as the detailed study of sacred texts is one of the few activities that teachers from centuries past might recognize in today's classrooms.

Texts themselves – in contrast to oral communication – are attempts to communicate at a distance. Space and time are not barriers to textual communication, even if the texts themselves and their significance may seem to change as they are re-read over the years, and as they are passed around the world. That is why this chapter refers to investigating context, as well as text. Amongst the research on sacred text in religious education is a small-scale study by AREIAC, the UK religious education advisors' organization (www.areiac.org.uk/). That study is a good starting point, as it simply compared the typical use of texts in history and religious education (see Figure 6.1).

It is surprising that there is evidence of such a gap between the approaches to the use of texts in these subjects, given the way the subjects both depend on old and original texts, and given that many teachers in the UK teach both subjects. It is hoped the situation will improve. The availability of texts may help, as multiple, original, sacred texts are becoming much more easily and cheaply available, notably in electronic formats. On the Internet, general sites include www.religioustolerance.org or www.sacred-texts.com/ and sites with access to key texts include www.buddhanet.net/, bible.gospelcom.net/, www.krishna.com/,

History	Religious education
Tasks tend to require pupils to:	Tasks tend to require pupils to:
• read multiple source materials	• rarely use multiple texts
• make decisions and choices about the material they are reading	• simply recycle their reading
• work with original texts	• use second hand rather than original texts
• handle challenging text material	• engage with over-processed simplified language
• process reading so that their writing output is significantly different from the material they have read.	• paraphrase reading doing little with the original; too much emphasis on low-level comprehension and recall.

Figure 6.1: Use of texts in history and religious education

www.quran.org.uk/, www.jewishvirtuallibrary.org/ and www.Sikhs.org/granth.htm. However, the availability of sacred texts does not necessarily mean they will be used most effectively in religious education classrooms. What about the 'challenge' of the material, and the ways of reading texts? Five overarching issues can be identified when dealing with sacred texts in religious education.

Firstly, the format in which sacred texts are presented, for example in snippets on dog-eared worksheets, or in the form of the full text, or somewhere in between. It is worth noting the importance of oral traditions in most religions: the *telling* of stories, not just the *reading* of stories, as in the 'telling place' project of the Bible Society (see www.biblesociety.org.uk/). A second issue is the quantity of sacred text that can be put in front of a pupil, whether in snippets or longer extracts or full texts. If English lessons comfortably handle complete novels and plays, religious education lessons should be able to handle complete sacred texts, even when only a short piece is studied in detail. Thirdly, and engaging with some long-standing debates, is the issue of the degree and format of translation, paraphrasing, and retelling, taking account of different traditions in different religious communities. There can be a tension between authenticity and accessibility, although this can be tackled directly in the lessons, as it is, for example, in countless history lessons and English lessons. The language of scripture is itself a subject of much study. In Judaism, Hebrew is generally treated as a holy language of scripture: although translation is not impossible, something is lost. The absence of vowels in written Hebrew, perhaps because vowels were considered too sacred to write as vowels represent the very act of creation in G-d's breath, complements and contrasts with the similarly ancient belief in the Hindu tradition that the 'O' in the Aum symbol (ॐ) represents the silence of the reaching

God. For Muslims, the language of the Qur'an (a form of Arabic) is perfect and untranslatable – hence many 'translations' are called 'versions', 'interpretations' or 'translations of the meaning', and so on. Within Buddhism, the languages used for sacred writings are themselves part of the divisions into schools, with Thervada Buddhism treating the Pali canon as particularly sacred. In Christianity, the languages of the Bible, and the languages that shall be used in religious services, have been a constant source of debate – heated debate in England certainly since the fourteenth century when Wycliffe and his followers (known as the Lollards), were considered revolutionary, and were banned after 1408. One of the Thirty-Nine Articles (central to the Church of England since the reign of Elizabeth I) says that 'It is a thing plainly repugnant to the word of God and the custom of the primitive Church, to have public prayer in the Church, or to minister the sacraments in a tongue not understood of the people'. As this suggests, vernacular languages were not considered appropriate by some other Christians. The Sikh Guru Granth Sahib, written (like the Christian Bible) in several languages (though predominantly a version of what would now be called Punjabi), is treated as a person, and again translation is religiously guarded.

A fourth issue consists of the assumptions brought to sacred texts, and the assumptions a believer might bring to the text, and what happens when someone comes to the text who is not a believer. Assumptions include ideas on the truth. Within religious traditions, for example, a single text may be treated as more literally true or more symbolically true. Teachers should tackle this head-on, exploring possible assumptions. Fifthly, and finally, there are issues of pedagogy, including appropriate ways of dealing with texts from the perspective of the religious education teacher and from the perspective of the member of the religious community. Pupils should feel comfortable handling sacred texts, and using all their skills and creativity to come to understand the texts. All five of these issues have been raised with respect to the Bible, by the Biblos project based in the University of Exeter (www.exeter.ac.uk).

Exploring the Bible: the Biblos project

One of the biggest religious education projects of recent years has been the Biblos project, exploring the uses of the Bible in religious education, and this is therefore a good place to start, in understanding research on sacred text. It is a superb example of the search for empirical evidence, to contribute to debates on the proper uses of the text. It also draws on that research to support the training and professional development of teachers, and, notably, bases what it says on evidence provided by pupils and teachers as well as a clear understanding of theology. The respect thereby shown to the sacred text itself, in its religious context, and to pupils as well as to teachers, is a model for research in religious education.

The project has been led by Copley, and there are several research reports on the project already published (including Copley 1998, Copley *et al.* 2001, 2004), with classroom materials already coming from the project, and Copley and Walshe (2002), from a related project, involving trialling classroom materials. For Copley (in these texts and in the Westhill Seminars), the Bible as a sacred text has a particular 'problem' in England, because it is regarded as a 'heritage text' as well as a 'sacred text'. Heritage is problematic insofar as people are more likely, for example, to visit cathedrals as tourists than as pilgrims. Biblos tackles some stereotypes of the Bible in English religious education: that the Bible has disappeared from religious education, that the Bible is only relevant to Christians, that teachers are reluctant to use biblical material, and that biblical material should be secularized.

An example of the loss of the Bible, even from nominal 'Bible stories', is the Joseph narrative as tackled with 7 to 11 year olds. Joseph becoming an oppressor is not included in the narratives used in schools, and the central role of God in the Bible is suppressed, just as the central role of Allah in the Qur'an is at times suppressed. For example, in the musical *Joseph and the Amazing Technicolour Dreamcoat*, 'any dream will do'. God appears not at all: Joseph is a 'nice guy, who succeeds against the odds'. This, says Copley, is anti-religious education. A proper consideration of biblical texts is vital, as they are relevant to three religions, Judaism, Christianity and Islam, they have a place in the history of Western civilization, and they are a proper subject for debate. The relevant cultural and historical contexts must be supplied, and for this, academic scholarship is important: the apparent 'divorce' of theology from religious education, since the 1960s, may not have helped. Comparisons may be made with Germany (Schweitzer 2006), where theology and religious education remain in a closer relationship. Work on biblical narrative might also be complemented by scholarly work on the portrayals of religious figures in various media, such as the writing by Moyise, Pearson and Telford (variously, in Beckerlegge 2001b) on portrayals of Jesus in film. One of Telford's notable, if with hindsight predictable, findings is the lack of Jewish actors playing Jesus in films.

The criteria for the Biblos project's choice of stories, or narrative themes, were that they had to be relevant, a bridge between the secular and religious, easily comprehensible, easy to remember, not exclusive, and progressive. The team, after abandoning hope (as a theme), and giving up taking 'God' seriously (as a topic), settled on 'destiny', 'encounter' and 'vulnerability' as the three themes. These themes are also themes of importance to children: what they want to grow up as, encounters with friends and enemies and teachers, and vulnerability in all those things. The Biblos project went on to study what young people know and think about the Bible, and what has shaped these attitudes and perceptions. The work is being replicated in New Zealand, to see how 'British' are the responses. There were 1,066 pupils aged 10 to 11, 13 to 14 and 16 to 17, who were asked similar questions in questionnaires and some of whom were interviewed. 70 per cent of respondents were Christian, 15.1 per cent had no religious identity, 6.2 per cent Sikh, 3.4 per cent Hindu, 2.4 per cent Muslim, 1.5 per cent 'other', 0.8 per cent Buddhist, 0.2 per cent Jewish. Most could identify passages from the Bible, but when asked about meaning,

36.3 per cent found secular ethical meanings, compared to 22.9 per cent theological, 9.1 per cent literal and 5.8 per cent irrelevant. Examples of the 'secular' meanings given to Bible passages were: David and Goliath as hope for the underdog, the birth of Jesus meaning Christmas presents, feeding the 5,000 meaning not taking things for granted and sharing things. There were numerous responses to questions on why the Bible is important, especially from respondents who themselves were members of religious groups other than Christianity. The 'heritage' importance of the Bible was certainly recognized. 'The Bible should be respected' (74.1 per cent), it 'can show people how to live' (63.1 per cent), but surprisingly 58.8 per cent disagreed or strongly disagreed with 'I look to the Bible for personal guidance'. Most positive were Christian church-attending females aged 10 to 11, with hobbies such as reading fiction/novels and watching soap operas, rather than film, music programmes on television, and computer games. What matters most to children? Family, education and religion, for those more positively inclined towards the Bible; activities and hobbies, for those less positively inclined towards the Bible.

The project's overall conclusion is that, by presenting biblical narrative in its cultural context, and by encouraging pupils to provide their own theological interpretations, the Bible can be opened for children. It is the research of teachers, to support the presentation of the appropriate context, and the research of pupils, as interpreters of the text, that can change passive lessons in comprehension into lively and scholarly religious education. There are different ways of researching and teaching the Bible, such as those of Cupitt (e.g. Cupitt 1991), Erricker (e.g. Erricker and Erricker 2000) or Hull (e.g. Hull 1998), all of whom are described by Copley as looking for meaning in the *reader*, at times more than in the *text*. The Biblos project is clearly 'partial' in this way, in looking first for meaning in the text itself, and yet the contrast between those looking at the text and those looking at the reader may be something of a false dichotomy, as the Biblos project, in common with the other approaches, looks at *engagement* between text and reader: nobody looks to the text or the reader alone. It is the intellectual culture of the classroom that supports the idea of engagement with the text of the Bible, allowing for distinct approaches, yet held together by a commitment to engage. Although the research considered church schools and non-church schools, the responses were slightly different from church schools than non-church schools, there is more work to be done on this issue. An interesting finding was that many Christian children, whether in church or non-church schools, were apparently encountering more religion in school than they did at home.

There are at least three conclusions from the Biblos research: good religious education teaching must not ignore the theological and God-centred dimensions of Bible narratives; good religious education teaching must recognize that the Bible is of particular importance to Christians, Jews and Muslims; good religious education teaching must facilitate pupil engagement with the Bible and seek to raise their valuations of it, as the religious education teacher is often the most important gatekeeper to, and cartographer of, the Bible for children. Religious education teachers can investigate how each of these can be achieved. As described in Stern 2006b, the process could involve teachers reviewing the religious education curriculum plan, to highlight examples of the use of the Bible narratives. They could then assess whether theological issues are to be raised, how important the narrative might be to Christians, Jews and Muslims, and how the lessons will help pupils to value the text. Where any of the answers are negative, the teachers could work out how to improve the plan so that, at least for some of the uses of Bible narratives, there are opportunities for theological engagement, consideration of the importance to religious believers, and pupils valuing the text. Other sacred texts can of course appropriately be studied in the same ways.

Approaching the Qur'an

The Qur'an has been widely used in the teaching of Islam, both as an artefact, in lessons about how sacred objects may be treated, and as text. However, relatively little research has been completed in the UK on its use in classrooms, although some initial surveys are being completed. From the Muslim Council of Britain, for example, Amer has considered approaches to using the Qur'an as a sacred text in the classroom (reported in the Westhill Seminars). She starts with the question, what kind of sensitivities should teachers observe when using the Qur'an in teaching religious education? On a school visit, Amer noticed one teacher, who wanted to display a copy of the Qur'an, apparently trembling, worrying about what the pupils, many of whom were Muslim, would say about her handling of the Qur'an. Such fear seems out of place: genuine respect is the appropriate attitude to this sacred text, as with all sacred texts. The Arabic text of the Qur'an is considered by Muslims to be the directly revealed Word of God, whilst a translated Qur'an is by definition part human interpretation of the meanings and is therefore no longer considered divine. However, both should be treated with respect.

Muslim pupils may memorize the Qur'an, but teachers should avoid using pupils who memorize the Qur'an as a novelty. Rather, teachers could develop a knowledge of how and when this example may appropriately be incorporated into a lesson: it should be a voluntary activity. The time and background of the arrival of the first substantial Muslim community in the UK has influenced approaches to the Qur'an, as that group had a particular religious approach, reflecting particular cultural traditions rather than universal religious traditions. Whilst remaining sensitive to the specific cultural traditions, according to Amer, becoming completely tied to a set of 'taboos' deriving from a single tradition can restrict the possibility of studying the Qur'an in classrooms. The Qur'an can be used positively in a number of ways, as a study text, as inspiration for daily life, as a catalyst for academically sound historical enquiry, as a linguistic framework, as a framework for modern ethical dilemmas, or as a way of facilitating acquisition of vocabulary for UK pupils with English as an additional language. Such uses can tie in with, but are not entirely addressed by, literacy strategies: these strategies tend to focus on literacy alone, and not on exploring the deeper meaning or the underlying messages. As with Copley's work on the Christian Bible, work on the Qur'an relates to Judaism, Christianity and Islam.

Three issues are commonly raised by religious education teachers on the use of the Qur'an:

- *What are the best ways in which school religious education can use the sacred texts of Islam?* Amer suggests the use of narrative to inspire, the use of enjoyable games such as hopscotch to learn the stages of Hajj or snakes and ladders for steps to paradise, the use of role-playing to assist in the exploration of the sense of awe and wonder in relation to the divine, and the use of poetry and creative writing (e.g. on birds, animals, insects, or water, in the Qur'an) for pupils of all ages.
- *What potential for good learning in religious education in general is there, in the development of good uses of the Qur'an in religious education?* Exploring the transfer of concepts using the vehicle of translation, enhancing opportunities for social and emotional literacy, highlighting commonalities between three Abrahamic religions whilst treating differences with integrity (as it is important to do both, especially with an increased prominence of interreligious issues), and the diversity and enrichment of religious literacy.
- *How can teachers be helped to do more and better work on Qur'anic text in religious education with the various different age groups?* This is an issue of teacher training, increasing teachers' personal familiarity with the sacred text, and having good quality inexpensive inservice training. Amer talked about some of the resources that can be used, including the patterns of texts themselves as calligraphy (for which, see the 'art' section of www.islam101.com/), patterning used in texts, materials produced by the IQRA Trust (with information at www.iqratrust.org), story books that manage to avoid portraying prophets, computer games, a CD-rom (*Living Islam*, from www.microbooks.org/), and songs (including translations of meanings of Qur'an verses). With the involvement of the Muslim community in producing more resources, there is an increasing choice of resources. Publications of the Islamic Foundation (www.islamic-foundation.org.uk) have been very helpful. Further ideas could be found from within Islam, such as from the London Central Mosque Trust & The Islamic Cultural Centre (146 Park Road, London NW8 7RG, tel 020 7724 3363), the Islam online website (www.islamonline. net), the Muslim Heritage website (www.muslimheritage.com/), and Salaam (www.salaam.co.uk), in order to give some basis to valuable celebration traditions.

Those discussing the use of the Qur'an in religious education often report a fear of making mistakes when using the Qur'an in any way. It is as though the Qur'an should, literally and metaphorically, be put 'out of reach' of the pupils. Yet it is surely better to engage with the text, even with the possibility of inadvertently making mistakes, than to avoid all engagement. Making use of a Muslim sacred text (available on paper or electronically from www.sacred-texts.com/ or www.quran.org.uk/), teachers and pupils could research examples of how the text can be used in each of the six ways described by Amer, i.e. as a study text, for example by asking pupils to study a Sura (such as Sura 2 or many others) looking at Islamic belief about Allah; as inspiration for daily life, for example by asking pupils to identify an appropriate text for a Muslim who has suffered a personal loss (again, starting with Sura 2); as a catalyst for academically sound historical enquiry, for example by asking pupils to consider accounts of events in the Qur'an, such as the account given of Jesus in Sura 4, making use of the skills of textual analysis developed in history lessons; as a linguistic framework, for example by asking pupils to compare two contrasting 'translations' (generally called 'interpretations') of a particular piece of text, in order to understand more about the process of translation; as a framework for modern ethical dilemmas, for example taking guidance on divorce (from Sura 2, 33, 55 or 56) and discussing what the implications are of this advice for life in the contemporary world; or as a way of facilitating acquisition of vocabulary for pupils with English as an additional language, for example by involving pupils with a knowledge of the Arabic used in the Qur'an to work with pupils without that knowledge, to create a 'dictionary' of key concepts.

The Bhagavad Gita and young children

A good example of research on using the Bhagavad Gita in religious education is that of Parmar (2001, and in the Westhill Seminars), who has been researching the use of translations of the Bhagavad Gita to raise questions fundamental to human experience. She worked with children aged 7, many of whom had experienced inappropriate teaching of Hinduism – for example using cartoons that made the pupils uncomfortable. Parmar's own experience of Christian education, as a pupil, was not a challenge to her Hinduism, but enriched it, so, when Parmar took up her Bhagavad Gita, she used her interpretive skills as an historian as well as her life as a Hindu. The Bhagavad Gita is set on the eve of battle, with the battle metaphorically at the heart of every person. The problem is of right choice, happiness and suffering, including the three *gunas* or qualities of light, fire and darkness. Carrington and Troyna (1988) say that children should face controversial issues, and this is important in working with the Bhagavad Gita. Although the work is clearly important, the difficulty appears to be getting teachers interested. Sometimes, new religious education teachers see the subject as being about multiculturalism alone, without having a concern for the substantial sacred texts and other religious items.

A second issue is that of oral in contrast to literary traditions. Beckerlegge (2001b) investigates how religions represent themselves in their traditions, for example in speech, texts, images or ritual enactments, and how these are affected by cultural, historical and technological contexts. The oral tradition, from which the Bhagavad Gita and other Hindu Vedic sacred texts derive, involved an immediate personal relationship between the speaker and audience. Written traditions, and later technologies such as film and the Internet, changed that relationship and therefore affected access to and relationships with the sacred. Once photography was developed, according to Beckerlegge, photographs of such religious teachers as Ramakrishna were by some regarded as *murtis*, and more recently, there have been representations of deities and sacred narratives in films and on television, notably the 1987–8 televised *Ramayana*. The qualities of the oral tradition must not be lost in all these changes. The English and Welsh national curriculum for teaching English (DFEE and QCA 1999) addresses the development of reading and writing skills, but also includes a focus upon speaking and listening. Pupils are expected to demonstrate an ability:

> To speak with confidence in a range of contexts, adapting their speech for a range of purposes and audiences ... [aged seven to 11, and to] speak fluently and appropriately in different contexts, adapting their talk for a range of purposes and audiences, including the more formal [aged 11 to 16]. (DfEE and QCA 1999)

This requirement, along with the importance of oral traditions in religion, gives considerable impetus to the use of story-telling in UK religious education, and to assess pupil skills in story-telling, and listening to stories. Assessment of pupils rarely refers to oral work, except to complain of 'too much talking'. It is possible in classrooms to tie together a sacred text with its oral origins, helping pupils develop their own oral skills as well as their understanding of religion. For example, as the Bhagavad Gita is one of the texts most used by Hindus for guidance on making difficult personal decisions, teachers might choose topics of immediate importance to the pupils in their classes, that are also addressed by the text, and create a story-telling (*telling*, not *reading*, if possible) of that text, and a lesson to follow it up. An example might be the apparent recommendation of violence in the story (generally noticed, with some glee, by more 'lively' pupils), noting the peace-loving Gandhi's response when asked about this. Questioner: 'at the end of the Gita Krishna recommends violence'; Gandhi: 'I do not think so. I am also fighting. I should not be fighting effectively if I were fighting violently' (quoted in Beckerlegge 2001a, p. 307). After working on the story-telling pupils might be asked (as recommended in Stern 2006b) what they learned about Hindu traditions or dharma from the work, what they thought Hindus would want them to learn from the relevant part of the Bhagavad Gita, and what they learned from this Hindu narrative that would help them to meet their targets in religious education or as a pupil?

Conclusion

It is worth going back to the questions set in the introduction to this chapter. When it comes to the format in which sacred texts are presented, there is a need for further research by teachers on how pupils engage with sacred texts, building on the research of the Biblos project and the others described in this chapter. How sacred text is used may also be a continuing topic for research not only by teachers but also by the other organizations interested in religious education, such as religious groups and curriculum committees such as the UK's SACREs (Standing Advisory Councils for Religious Education, for which see Ofsted 2004 and www.nasacre.org.uk).

People have asked about the quantity of sacred texts: whether they are primarily presented in short snippets (in a more fractured format), or complete texts (in a more holistic format). It is clear that this is not only an issue about presentation. The impact on pupil learning of fractured or holistic approaches has been little researched in religious education, and the subject could sensibly join with other subjects such as English and history which may have a longer tradition of considering this issue. The publishing of complete sacred texts, for use in schools, is to be welcomed (as in the *Living Religions* CD-rom series from www.microbooks.com). Of course, having complete texts available does not answer the question of how those texts have been translated, paraphrased, or re-told. The oral tradition seems most in need of further development (as described from Beckerlegge 2001b, above), and research in that area would be welcome. Pupils as well as teachers have considerable story-telling abilities, often under-exploited in schools. That oracy is so important within every religious tradition, suggests that religious education should be leading – alongside drama and languages lessons – on developing this skill.

The very act of translating, paraphrasing or retelling, indicates some of the assumptions of both teachers and pupils. How can teachers be prepared, and pupils be supported, in understanding these assumptions? Initial teacher training is important, but this must be continued throughout teachers' careers, with continuing support from advisors, examination boards, and the writers of texts for schools. Teachers and pupils need a strong sense of the various genres used in sacred texts, and use those texts across all of religious education, and not just in topics called 'sacred texts'. The framing of texts is important, that is, how an extract from a sacred text, or a complete sacred text, is introduced and explained to pupils. Such explanatory work will outline something about the text's source and its genre. 'Framing' is well developed in history textbooks such as those of the *Schools History Project* (at www.tasc.ac.uk/shp/), in which extracts from historical sources are explained in terms of how the texts were written, whether and how they are translated, what they would have been used for, and how they fit in amongst other related texts. Religious education might use some more of the skills of such historical 'framing'. School religious education of course has its own pedagogy (as also described in Chapter 9 below), and this may be different from the pedagogy of other subjects and of religious communities, when dealing with sacred texts. There is not necessarily a problem with these differences, but knowing what the differences are will help make religious education more effective. Indeed, each group understanding the pedagogy of the other groups could benefit all. Long traditions of pedagogy from every religious tradition should be 'tapped into', notwithstanding possible challenges caused by religious communities not always 'saying the right things', from the perspective of teachers, and *vice versa*. For example, memorizing texts, much used in religious contexts, is at times seen by teachers as inappropriately 'old-fashioned', yet it is a skill and practice of much value in religious education.

Sacred texts communicate with us, and are used to communicate between us. The relationship between text and reader, or between writer and reader, is much studied in literary theory. In religious education, sacred texts may have the religion extracted from them (as described by Copley with respect to the Bible), may be treated as unusable objects (as described by Amer with respect to the Qur'an), or may have their life-giving story-telling properties ignored (as described by Parmar with respect to the Bhagavad Gita). It is a measure of the importance of research that all three of these authors, along with others working in the field, can exemplify good practice with respect to sacred texts. The texts help communication across time and across distance: it is a kind of dialogue over space and time that can educate and inspire (as also in Bakhtin 1981, and Friedman 2002, pp. 353–66). A text

> carries on a continual dialogue with other works of literature. It does not merely answer, correct, silence, or extend a previous work, but informs and is continually informed by the previous work. Dialogic literature is in communication with multiple works. This is not merely a matter of influence, for the dialogue extends in both directions, and the previous work of literature is as altered by the dialogue as the present one is. (en.wikipedia.org/wiki/Dialogic)

What is called 'literacy' is therefore a complex educational topic, made complex by, and illuminated by, issues in religious education. Teaching children to read includes teaching them to discriminate qualities of text, and those qualities might include sacred qualities and profane (meaning both non-sacred, and showing contempt or disregard for sacred things or moral values), and the special significance of words (such as the names of gods or the titles given to religious leaders). 'Vocabulary development', in that context, is more like the 'concept development' described by Vygotsky: a pupil does not simply learn a concept, the concept is constantly developing (see Daniels 1996, pp. 10–14, and Veer and Valsiner 1994, ch. 9). Within religious education, key concepts (such as 'love', 'devotion', 'obedience', 'god', 'sacred') spiral up through the pupils' time in school. At least, it is hoped there is a spiralling: there is some evidence that concept development is not often maintained across the phases of schooling, and may be rather 'flat' even within phases (see Lenga and Ogden 2000). Pupils who are developing their concepts are in a sense being theologians: it is hermeneutics (the study of meaning) that most characterizes modern and much older theology.

Interacting with text, including dialogue by text, across space and time, is now also possible using computers, but the simpler technology of printing has already expanded the frontiers of dialogue in religious education just as in history, English and other languages lessons. Dialogue itself is the subject of a great deal of research in religious education, and is the subject of the following chapter.

Chapter 7

Dialogue within and between

it's like we're sort of teaching the grown ups

(8 year old)

Introduction

Dialogue has been central to religious and educational traditions for thousands of years, yet people often associate religion with authoritative monologue (such as in stereotypes of endless sermonizing), so the importance of dialogue needs stressing. One of the great defenders of educational dialogue was Socrates. Many write about Socratic methods, with Socrates having philosophized through dialogue or argument. Socrates even went to the lengths of refusing to write things down, as that would restrict his thinking and teaching. It is fascinating in today's literacy-obsessed world to think that this refusal to write was the basis of the criminal charges brought against Socrates for 'corrupting the youth of Athens'. In religion, many write – or, better still, talk – about the Buddha's dialogues or Jesus' arguments, or about the various dialogic forms in Hindu traditions, notably the Bhagavad Gita. Religious dialogues include dialogue between religions, as well as within religions. Early Christian dialogue crossed Jewish and non-Jewish boundaries, Sikh dialogue worked across Hindu and Muslim traditions (both within and beyond both, as Hindu and Muslim writers are recognized in the Guru Granth Sahib, whilst Sikhism asserts itself as a quite distinct religion), and the Sufi Muslim poet Rumi wrote of the state of heightened awareness through *dhikr* ('remembrance' or 'listening') when 'I belong to the beloved' and am 'not Christian or Jew or Muslim, not Hindu, / Buddhist, sufi, or zen' (Rumi 1995, p. 32). The Bahá'í tradition recognizes the teachings of Zoroaster, the Buddha, Jesus and Muhammad, as well as Baha'u'llah. In these and countless other ways, talking and listening within and across religions have been central to how people have lived. In the twentieth century, Buber described living itself in terms of dialogue as 'all real living is meeting', whilst also, helpfully, warning against the temptation of 'monologue disguised as dialogue' (Buber 2002a, pp. 25 and 22).

Religious education can and often does reflect the same dialogic approach, especially when the educational and religious traditions come together in a multi-religious religious education, the most widespread tradition in English and Welsh religious education since the 1960s. Ninian Smart was perhaps the most influential person in the growth of multi-religious religious education, and one of his first books was a description of a dialogue between a Christian, Jew, Muslim, Hindu, Sri Lankan Buddhist and Japanese Buddhist, 'The demand for fairness is one reason for the dialogue form', says Smart (1960, p. 13).

> The dialogue form also emphasizes anew the point that where there is discussion, there reasons are found. The possibility of argument implies that there are criteria of truth, however vague. Indeed, the man [*sic*] who refuses to argue at all is guilty of slaying truth: both the true and the false perish, and he is reduced to mere expressions of feeling. (Smart 1960, p. 14)

Interreligious dialogue, and dialogue beyond religions, is now built in to the English and Welsh national framework for religious education (QCA 2004), which says that pupils should 'reflect on ... the significance of interfaith dialogue', which should in turn help in 'promoting racial and interfaith harmony and respect for all, combating prejudice and discrimination, contributing positively to community cohesion and promoting awareness of how interfaith cooperation can support the pursuit of the common good'. That could be interpreted as rather glib, but the guidance also stresses that interreligious dialogue recognizes conflicts as well as collaboration, both within and between religions and beliefs, religious and non-religious.

Such a strong and vibrant tradition is clearly ready for detailed work on dialogue in religious education, as represented in the rest of this chapter, which describes some of the leading classroom-based research on dialogic approaches to religious education. Research on dialogue is distinctive in that the research itself may directly help improve religious education, and yet it also complements a wide range of other research in religious education such as Wright's work on religious literacy (Wright 1993, 1997, 1999) or Baumfield on thinking skills (e.g. in Baumfield 2002, 2003).

Dialogue in religious education across Europe

Jackson (2004 and in the Westhill Seminars underpinning much of this section of the book, and see Jackson 2006 for research to come) describes the tremendous amount of interest across Europe – and beyond – in addressing religious diversity in school education, and this is related to the aims of religious education as understood in England and Wales. Those aims include first-order aims of increasing knowledge and understanding, and relating new learning to one's own experience – whichever way around these go. Often, new teachers of religious education see some of the second-order aims as first-order aims, but for Jackson, these are importantly second-order aims: increasing tolerance and respect, and promoting social cohesion and good citizenship. Such aims are not just the province of religious education. Those second-order aims are particularly influential in Europe, notably with respect to social cohesion, since the various terrible events that include 11 September 2001 in USA, Afghanistan and Iraq wars, Bali, Casablanca, Jakarta, Madrid, and civil disorder in northern UK towns from 2001 – including activity by far-right organizations for several years. The need to address issues of social cohesion was further highlighted by the bombings in London in July 2005.

It is the reaction to these events that have stimulated projects such as that of the Council of Europe (made up of 45 states, with information at www.coe.int/), called *Intercultural Education and the Challenge of Religious Diversity and Dialogue*. The Council of Europe includes states with a very wide range of approaches to religious education (from none, in most of France, to confessional religious education in many countries), but the project is about intercultural education regardless of the state of religious education. Work on UK religious education will feed into more general intercultural education, then. Similarly, the UN-sponsored Oslo Coalition on Freedom of Religion or Belief set up the Teaching for Tolerance project, based at Oslo University. It is an international project, including states from the Islamic world such as Nigeria (50 per cent of whose population are Muslim, and 40 per cent Christian, according to www.wikipedia.com, quoting www.state.gov/ and www.cia.gov/). Meanwhile, the long-standing Comenius Institut in Münster, Germany, contributes widely to these and other debates, producing influential research and professional guidance (as in Schreiner 2001, 2005, Schreiner *et al.* 2002).

Within the UK, intercultural education includes work on citizenship as well as religious education. Religious education professionals in the UK, according to Jackson, need to engage with citizenship education – which includes knowledge and understanding (second-order) and appreciation (first-order) of the 'diversity of national, regional, religious and ethnic identities in UK and the need for mutual respect and understanding'. This is quoted from the English and Welsh national framework for religious education (QCA 2004), which goes on to say that religious education provides opportunities to promote 'education for racial equality and community cohesion through studying the damaging effects of xenophobia and racial stereotyping, the impact of conflict in religion and the promotion of respect, understanding and co-operation through dialogue between people of different faiths and beliefs'. The connections between religious education and multiculturalism go back over the decades, as do criticisms of the connections. For example, some specialists in antiracist education have criticized religious education for seeing cultures as closed systems, for a rather superficial treatment of cultures ('saris, samosas, and steelbands', as highlighted by Troyna 1983 and see also Troyna and Carrington 1990), and for an emphasis on the exotic more than the every-day. Minority cultures were often contrasted with the national or majority culture, as long as there was no 'threat'. This meant that there was a lack of attention to power issues in multicultural education.

Some antiracist educators in the 1990s responded to the early critique of multi-culturalism by suggesting a more sophisticated approach to cultural analysis in schools. This work was paralleled independently by Jackson and colleagues (in the Warwick Religions & Education Research Unit, www.warwick.ac.uk/wie/WRERU), through their ethnographic research on religious diversity and Jackson's development of this into an interpretive approach to religious education (Jackson 1997). Gerd Baumann's work (Baumann 1996, 1999) is a good example of the 'new multiculturalism'. Baumann completed fieldwork in London on cultural discourse, suggesting that there was a 'dominant discourse' that treats cultures as separate and homogeneous (e.g. 'the Sikh community' as a unified whole): this separation creates a superficial view of the issues. In contrast to the dominant discourse is a 'demotic discourse': the process of making new culture through interaction – as Ipgrave found in her research on children in dialogue (e.g. Ipgrave 1999, 2001). 'Culture' can in this way be seen as a possession of an ethnic or religious community, and also as a dynamic process relying on personal agency. Culture should therefore be seen as a process, including individuals making choices, and individuals drawing on their own families' and other cultural resources and sources of spirituality, as also described in recent work by Smith (2005). People must not be labelled in the way the media sometimes labels, such as 'Muslim = terrorist'. Pedagogical ideas on dialogue challenge precisely such fixed views of culture.

The 'new multiculturalism' of the 1990s included antiracist multicultural education (Leicester 1992), reflexive multiculturalism (Rattansi, in Donald and Rattansi 1992), and critical multiculturalism (May 1999). These combined antiracist and cultural concerns, rejecting closed views of cultures and antiracist fears of cultural difference as a source of division (with Modood and Werbner 1997 looking across Europe). At the same time, Jackson's interpretive approach looked at people in their contexts, covering the *representation* of religions and cultures showing their diversity (individuals, groups, traditions), *interpretation* (comparing and contrasting familiar and unfamiliar concepts), and *reflexivity* (pupils relating learning to their own views). The *Bridges to Religions* materials for 5 to 7 year olds (available from www.warwick.ac.uk/wie/WRERU) attempt to introduce children to other children in the books, as steps towards dialogue. Children reading, and those quoted in the books, are in a kind of preparatory dialogue, rather than a face-to-face dialogue. The source material is ethnographic studies of children in family and school, as also described in Chapter 14 below. Children in class compare and contrast their concepts, experiences and beliefs. Texts deal with similarity and difference, and diversity of views of children in the class is recognized. In these ways, taking account of the real experiences of children in Britain should take 'the exotic' out of religious education. The importance of context is emphasized, as are different elements of individual identity that can be expressed in different social contexts. For example, different dress codes in different contexts can be discussed, compared and contrasted (as in French and more recent UK debates over the wearing of religious dress and symbols), and cultural change over generations can be shown in order to break down stereotypes (as with an 'English' style birthday party given a 'South Asian' slant).

A simple and profound dialogue-enhancing research question (derived from Stern 2003 and described in Stern 2006b) involves asking pupils 'What more can we do to promote religious harmony?'. Similar, and similarly profound questions might be 'What more can we do to promote racial harmony?', or 'What more can we do to promote social harmony?'. Such a research task can be completed with individual pupils responding on paper to the open-ended question, followed up with groups of pupils creating plans for enacting their ideas. They might create pictures, dramas or videos to explain their views, like those respondents used in Burke and Grosvenor 2003 on *The School I'd Like*. Other dialogue work includes that of Leganger-Krogstad (e.g. in Jackson 2003 and Jackson 2004, ch. 7) in the context of Finnmark, Norway's most northerly county. This project involved pupil research on their own local knowledge, which was used for analysis and reflection. They then moved outwards from the local to the national to the global. Themes included connections, self-other, inside-outside and past-future. The work explored the practice of plurality and identity, with pupils involved in selecting topics and methods, and developing competence to handle cultural material. Leganger-Krogstad refers to this ability to handle diverse cultural material as 'metacultural competence'. She goes on to study religious practice and the environment, involving a large number of items: cultural landscape, architecture, historical signs, monuments, music, art, symbols, traditions, language and use of names, sacred texts, narratives and songs, institutions and values, clothing, food, days and hours, rites, rituals, customs, behaviour, events, discussions in the media, attitudes to the natural environment, membership and leadership. Exploring nature in northern Norway involved exploring the experience of nature in time and space, using a camera to record the midnight sun. When Leganger-Krogstad moved to Oslo, she started working on exploring the city environment, with trainee teachers exploring the city, visiting mosques and a Lutheran Christian churchyard.

A second strand of dialogic research is that of Weisse (e.g. in Jackson 2003 and Jackson 2004, ch. 7) who works in Hamburg in Germany and in South Africa. Although Hamburg schools are officially described as having confessional religious education, promoting a single religion for each pupil, dialogic approaches have been used for many years. There is both intercultural and inter-religious learning, and learning about those without religion. There are existential, ethical, social and environmental issues to be considered. It is important to allow for individual expression, not labelling students by religion, as students from different backgrounds are learning to listen to others, and to reflect and criticize, grounded in human rights theory. This approach treats conflict as *normal* and not to be avoided. Ipgrave (Ipgrave 1999, 2001, 2003, 2004 and in the Westhill Seminars) makes an important contribution to dialogue by discussing conditions for dialogue, acknowledging plurality within the school and being positive about that plurality. There are different levels of dialogue: primary (acceptance of plurality), secondary (openness to difference) and tertiary (pupil interaction). Use is made of children's religious language, and providing opportunities for structured dialogue. Children negotiate their viewpoints. The project developed from work in one school, through work across schools in a single city, to e-bridges project work making use of email dialogue across cities. *Building e-Bridges* (Ipgrave 2003) uses email in distinct dialogic stages: the dialogue of life (getting to know each other, building friendship), the dialogue of experience (finding out about each other's practices), the dialogue of action (debating moral issues, exploring issues of justice and social concern), and questions of faith (reflecting on 'big' questions and comparing different viewpoints).

Research on dialogue in schools for 4 to 11 year olds suggests that most pupils say they share parental beliefs. However, the research also showed some openness to the beliefs of peers, highlighting issues of agency, and of exploring religious language using one's own experience of religious plurality – including peer relationships. Pupils are searching for integration and coherence, and make their own current religious identity in dialogue with others, meanwhile negotiating new meanings. It is as yet unclear what opportunities pupils have in the school curriculum to be in a meaningful dialogue with other pupils. Pupils undoubtedly talk with other pupils, and discuss both personal and school-related issues. However, the degree and level of dialogue relevant to the *curriculum* has rarely been studied. Pupils working together, even in what is called 'group work', often only take part in the 'dialogue of life', and rarely take part in the other forms of dialogue. Pupils might therefore be themselves asked to describe as many examples as possible of each of the four types of dialogue, with respect to religious education, that they have taken part in over the past year. They will need quite detailed descriptions of those types of dialogue, such as those of Ipgrave (2003, p. 11 onwards, also summarized above). There is a distinction between research into what opportunities pupils have for each of these four kinds of dialogue, and having the dialogue itself. Once the initial research has been completed, pupils and their teachers might work together to plan for opportunities to promote all four types of dialogue, in the year to come.

There are three themes arising from Ipgrave's very wide-ranging research, relating to the word 'all', to time, and to teacher dialogue. One of the participants in Ipgrave's dialogue research noted that it revealed the narrowness of some children's understanding of diversity. For example, some Muslim pupils thought that all 'white' children were Christian (as also described in Smith 2005). It made Ipgrave think about religious education syllabuses, and how far they promote diversity within religions: perhaps not enough. Dealing with this issue, as the Warwick approach attempts to do, involves getting rid of the 'all' from the discussion of religions. It is rarely true to say 'all Christians ...' or 'all Hindus ...', and religious education teachers could helpfully avoid the word 'all' altogether. Secondly, as well as contemporary dialogue amongst pupils, there are opportunities for inter-generational dialogue. Schooling in general has been described as 'a continuing personal exchange between two generations' (Macmurray 1968, p. 5), and in religious education children might be involved, for example, in interviewing members of their grandparents' generation, in order to understand a tradition – not a passive 'receiving' of tradition, but as active participants in a tradition. Beyond the living generations, texts, sacred and secular, may allow for a form of dialogue across time, as described in Chapter 6 of this book above. Finally, religious education teachers themselves can be in dialogue with one another, and this will help in their own training, a critical issue for religious education – a subject with a lower proportion of specialist-trained teachers in UK secondary schools (for pupils aged 11 to 19), than almost any other subject (as described by Gates 1989, 1991, 1994, and see also Al-Buraidi 2006 for the similar situation in the Kingdom of Saudi Arabia). This should be a true dialogue between teachers, rather than the promotion of a 'body of knowledge' about religions. Some of the possible processes are described in Blaylock (2000), which reported on research with teachers having other specialisms but working in religious education.

Dialogic work with parents, though not specifically with respect to religious education, is described in work by current author (i.e. the 'inside out' work in Stern 2003), which suggested that pupils and teachers, from within a school/institution, communicate with an 'outside' group, justifying an aspect of that school. Based on that approach, a class might write to a parent or to a religious community, about why religious education is valuable. Following this, from outside a school/institution, members from a local group or community might communicate with an 'inside' group, justifying what is being done, as an outsider, for the issue covered by the school. For example, a parent or religious community might write to a school saying what they contribute to religious education. The work will only make sense if teachers and pupils really want to tell parents and others about what they are doing, and if they really want to know what they are doing.

Dialogue and children's voices

Ipgrave's work on dialogue helps to give voice to children's own lives, and these voices are themselves highlighted in this section, with quotations and paraphrases, and comments after each quotation. For example, a boy aged 10 to 11, self-identified as Rastafarian, described himself in this way:

> quite a lot of my friends only believe ... I say to them, 'Do you believe in Jesus?'. They go, 'No' ... But when they ask me, I say, 'Yes, I believe there's only one God'. And they ask me, 'What colour do you think he is?'. And most people my colour will say he's black, but I think he's all mixed colours – black, white, Asian – blue, pink. I think he's every single colour in the world. I don't just think he's one particular colour. Because, even though you have only one God, God must be like everyone's colour because to me I think he's everyone's God, because in my religion I think there's only one God and he's everyone's God, so he's got to be everyone's different colour. He can't just be black and be everyone's God.

The pupil here is recognizing both diversity and that there is only one God: his description is ambiguous, in the positive sense that it is rich with multiple meanings. It is important to note that children at this age are already talking about religion and are reconciling diversity with their beliefs. A younger child (aged 8) said:

> But you know, if more of us would be able to get along better it would boost the chance of even more people getting along better, and if the kids do it then the grown ups might try and do it too, so it's like we're sort of teaching the grown ups.

What interesting ideals are being expressed here. They illustrate the need for voicing children, if only to understand how mature they can be, when not simply trying to guess the 'right answers'. The following quotations are from a conversation between a number of pupils aged 10:

> I think there's only one [God] and he's called different things.
>
> I was going to say that!
>
> We can't actually say that because we've got so many gods.
>
> Yeah but they could be called – em ...
>
> You have to believe in all of them because all of them have got something different, like special ...
>
> Yeah, because – look, they can all – God can ...
>
> Do lots of things.
>
> Change into different – like different features. Like he can be in you.
>
> He can come into anybody.
>
> He can change into anything.

Here, children themselves are working through dialogue to develop their own theologies, and Ipgrave's e-bridges work has tried to encourage such dialogue, with the email dialogue growing out of more general dialogue work. One exercise tried in the e-bridges project is sentence starters, such as 'A Muslim is someone who ...'. This was responded to by the children in varied ways, including formal religious behaviours (goes to the mosque to pray, prays to God, reads the Qur'an, wears a topi, fasts at Ramadan), behaviour exhibiting moral characteristics (doesn't backbite and doesn't swear, is honest), and beliefs (believes in Allah and Muhammad is his prophet, believes in one God, believes in the Qur'an). All these types of response overlap with each other, and pupil explanations of their statements provide good stimulus for further dialogue. Examples of responses can also be put on cards, with these cards used for further dialogue work, and, if pre-prepared, sorted by the pupils, for example into beliefs and other characteristics, things unique to Muslims or shared by others. Another practical interpretive kind of work involves asking pupils who have worked on holy books to come to agreement, in pairs or groups, on which of the following statements come from holy books, and why: my cat likes to lie in the sun; God has done great things for us; love each other; it was Sara's birthday last Monday; do not worry about what will happen tomorrow; work honestly and give money to the poor; my favourite food is chips; don't be happy, be sad; our school is in Leicester; all human beings belong together; keep all your money and things for yourself; giraffes can be six metres tall; do not quarrel with each other but make friends; keep your body clean. Children as young as 6 can use these statements as the basis of further dialogue.

Starting points for dialogue suggested by pupils aged 8 to 9, from Ipgrave's project, were based on the moral issue of whether or not people should be allowed to hunt and kill tigers. Statements included: no you cannot because we have to save them; yes you should kill them all they killed my grandson; no they are God's lovely creatures; yes they might eat all my children; no don't kill them as tourists pay money to come to India to see them: just give them more land. This proved a good basis for discussion, with pupils saying: we're the same though because God made us and God made tigers and we're animals too really; we're the same because God made people to look after animals and he made animals to help people; tigers are more precious because there are lots of people but tigers are in danger of becoming extinct; but people can die before they should, in accidents, or they could be ill and people are in danger, too.

Children aged 10 to 11 formulated their own questions for Christian visitors, working out questions in groups, with the questions given to the visitors in advance:

In my religion, Islam, we have to respect our Holy Book, the Qur'an, because it has God's name in it – so we have to put it higher than our feet. Why don't Christians do the same with their Bible?

What do you think about Christians that don't go to church? Do you think the world would be a better place if they did?

The Bible tells us that Jesus performed many miracles. Do you think Jesus really did perform these miracles or do you think that the person who wrote the Bible just wanted us to realize that Jesus is a very special person?

Do you feel sad at Christmas because most people think about presents and food and TV instead of thinking about God and Jesus?

I am a Muslim and I believe that when people die they are judged by God. Do you believe that?

When you are praying to God do you have any ideas about what God looks like? Do you see a face, a spirit of God or a picture of God?

What makes Christians believe that Jesus was the Son of God? What evidence is there that he was?

The quality and range of the questions indicates the amount and depth of dialogue work the children had completed over the years. Interreligious issues and negotiations between different religious points of view, and getting children used to that, are well illustrated by such work. To extend such work, children can be given a number of problems and asked to solve them. For example, pupils aged 10 and upwards might be asked to design a multi-religious prayer room for a hospital serving Buddhists, Muslims, Christians, Hindus and Jews, or they might be asked to plan a menu for a party for children from Christian, Hindu and Sikh backgrounds who are about to leave their primary school (at age 11).

Another challenging question from Ipgrave's work, set for children aged 7 to 8, asked 'Why is it okay to kick a football but not okay to kick a cat?' Some children said: a football is a toy but a cat isn't; you can't put a cat in a cupboard or throw it away when you don't want it; a football belongs to you but a cat doesn't; a cat belongs to God; a cat will get hurt; a football won't say 'ouch'; a football can't be hurt: it can go flat but it can't feel it; cats are like us – we are animals; you have to look after animals; God says we must be kind to animals; cats are our brothers and sisters: it's Brother Cat but it's not Brother Ball. This work might have arisen out of prior study of ethics or of creation, or work on sacred texts. It might overlap with work in science, personal social and health education, and religious education. The dialogue is of value in itself, and it reveals children's moral thinking in a way that is valuable for all adults. Too often, it is assumed that pupils need to be taught morals, rather than that they already have sophisticated moral positions, even at a young age, to be investigated and further developed.

How then can teachers plan for more and better dialogue in religious education? There are several issues to keep in mind, according to Ipgrave and others involved in the e-bridges work. It is important to let the children respond at their own level, having built up a real rapport. In order to build up a rapport, pupils can use 'chat' at first, and not leap straight into religious education issues. It is also useful for children to find things out for themselves, in addition to the agreed questions, so they have an opportunity to become more independent learners. Children will generally have had first-hand experiences at a young age that can be the basis of a great deal of future learning, and teachers should have confidence in the tendency of children to be very open-minded, especially on email. Children who are generally shy often come out of themselves in the email dialogues, and children can often discuss on email things they would not be likely to discuss face-to-face, so that community cohesion becomes a central issue. Pupils said that as a result of the project they 'have learned that other schools have a lot of different religions'. 'The project made Christians seem like real people', 'Islamic children are as normal as they are' (from a teacher), and 'I used to think our religions were really different, but they're not'. These are all illustrations of Jackson's 'second-order aims' of the e-bridges project.

The email project included blocks of exchanges (rather than a 'trickle' of correspondence), with planning completed around subjects (religious education, and citizenship), themes and questions. A dialogue grid was used, tracing topics to be discussed, and which dialogue stages might be demonstrated, across the school year. Ipgrave's work started in one school, and has continuously developed – including her academic paper (Ipgrave 2001) and the book for teachers (Ipgrave 2003). Through this work, she sees children as presenting themselves and learning to relate in three ways, each of which corresponds to the levels of dialogue. Firstly, as a friend or 'pal', related to the 'dialogue of life'. It is often enough simply to have a name to 'feel like' a friend. How do the children try to build up friendship with their email partners? How does the concern to make friends affect the choice of the topic of dialogue? How do they want to appear to their partners – as what kind of person? How is language used to establish friendship? It is clearly important for the children that they identify as friends. Secondly, children present themselves as a member of a religious or cultural community and tradition, related to the 'dialogue of experience'. This is a 'community' element, relating to practices and traditions. What do the children tell each other or ask each other about religious or cultural background? How clearly do they explain their own practices and traditions? How do they relate to each other's practices and traditions? Some children have – and show – very little sense of membership of a religious tradition, and these same children also seem to have no explicit identity of any kind. Perhaps as a 'majority' tradition, it feels like no tradition at all. Or do the children have less of a sense of identity? However, the way the question is worded has an effect on possible responses: 'What is your religion?' may gain a different response to 'What is important to you?' The former question is common in some contexts, the latter in other contexts. This is a significant research issue, as how the question is asked does indeed affect the answer. 'Secularization' in the research literature is in some senses an indication of changes in ways of describing, as much as changes within religions and in religious belief. Smith (2005), following Davie (1994), tackles some similar issues. Thirdly, children may present themselves as thinkers, related to the 'dialogue of action' and the 'questions of faith'. What thinking skills do the children demonstrate? What kind of language is used for sharing thoughts? Pupils may want to dialogue in the form of 'puzzles', especially over issues that some regard as controversial. They might indicate this with phrases such as 'have you any comments', 'I hope to hear your comments', or 'I am surprised that ...'.

For each of these ways of presenting oneself (i.e. in terms of friendship, membership and thinking), a 'circles of importance' activity can be completed. This activity involves drawing a set of concentric circles, putting the 'self' in the middle, and the things closest to the 'self' in the inner circle, the next most important in the ring created by the next circle, and so on to the outer circles. The choice of membership and thought as themes comes from Davie (1994) and others who have written about 'believing and belonging'. The choice of friendship comes from a concern with the nature of self and friendship, as described by Macmurray (1992, see also Stern 2002). For the 'friendship' version of circles of importance, the title will be 'me and the people closest to me'. Previous research using this technique indicates that at different ages, there is often a very different balance of friends and family in the 'inner circle'. The use of this research tool is described in Smith (2005), with one quoted as saying 'I've put as closest God ... because He is everywhere ... [then] my mum, my dog, my baby sister', whilst another report indicated that 'the PS2 or Xbox was sometimes listed as a significant member of the household in network diagrams' (Smith 2005, pp. 20 and 59, with more examples at mysite.wanadoo-members.co.uk/friendsfoodfaith/fffindex.htm). For the 'membership' version, the title will be 'To what do I belong?' Previous research suggests that the venue of the research itself affects the results: within a school, school membership is likely to be more 'central' than it would be for the same people completing the exercise in their homes. Finally, for the 'thinking' version, the title will be 'What beliefs and ideas are most important to me?' Previous research suggests, as did the work on moral issues described above, that young people have very complex and sophisticated moral systems. Following each of the exercises, pupils can discuss with each other (and with their 'dialogue' friends, if involved in e-bridges work for example) why different people and memberships and ideas are so important.

Conclusion: dialogue in schools and between nations

Giving pupils a voice is important for schools (as described in Flutter and Rudduck 2004, and Ranson 2000) and important for research (as described in O'Hanlon 2003). The nature and use of that voice is vital for religious education and for life. When Smith writes about the beliefs, practices and memberships of children aged 9 to 11, one of his conclusions is a message of hope with respect to complex issues of freedom of thought, conscience and religion, and diversity, conflict and segregation:

> Perhaps the most hopeful note from this research is that we have discovered children who, in their everyday lives, are deeply engaged with these issues, aware of many of the opportunities and problems and already taking steps to work things out for themselves. (Smith 2005, p. 69, the final words of the book)

That hope links dialogue in religious education with research in religious education and with hope for the future of humanity. Including pupils in dialogue is what is allowed by religious education and increasingly required of research. The dialogue beyond schools can break through religious and national boundaries. Research by Al-Buraidi (2006) on religious education in the Kingdom of Saudi Arabia suggests that teachers and pupils of the subject have considerably more in common with their UK counterparts than might be expected. Making use of interviews with pupils and teachers as well as historical sources, Al-Buraidi suggests that the assuredly confessional, Islam-centred, religious education appears to suffer from a relatively low status (as less 'relevant' and old-fashioned), with teachers having a large number of relatively short once-a-week classes, a dearth of effective training of specialist teachers, and a lower use of teaching aids and technologies. It is, nevertheless, a vital subject of significance to pupils' personal and communal lives and to the development of society: as also in the UK. Such research, giving voice to pupils and teachers, helps include the Saudi approach to religious education in the mainstream of dialogue on the subject around the world, just as the research of Wong (2006) includes Chinese traditions. Including pupils, in the research by Al-Buraidi as well as that by Wong and by Smith, raises issues of inclusion more generally, and that is therefore the subject of the following chapter.

Chapter 8

Inclusions and religious education

People have to learn *to be adults*

> (8 year old boy with learning difficulties, saying what he had
> learned from the Zen story of the sound of one hand clapping)

Introduction: the 'church of inclusion'?

Everyone thinks inclusion is a good idea, and thinks that exclusion is a bad idea. This chapter investigates a variety of issues in inclusion for religious education, and relates those to research on inclusion, with education research identified by O'Hanlon (2003) as a method of inclusion in itself (as described in Chapter 5 above). By bringing pupils together in dialogue, as in Chapter 7, religious education can bring pupils together in all kinds of ways. It is important to base inclusive religious education on a robust description of inclusion, as any simple 'bringing together' is only the start of the story. Some have even suggested that an uncritical promotion of inclusion, without evidence for its value, is reminiscent of some methods of promoting religion: hence the reference (from O'Brien 2001) to the 'church of inclusion'. Religious education can contribute to inclusion through its content (the curriculum) and through its pedagogy (the relationships between teacher and pupils). Important research on how religious education can in itself model inclusiveness has been completed by Hull (as in Hull 1998, 2003, 2005), and by Ipgrave (on dialogue in religious education, for example in Ipgrave 2001). Both of these authors are concerned with the 'deep' issues of the nature of humanity, and both can be related to theological theories. This chapter also sets inclusion in the context of the philosophies of Macmurray and Buber. It is Buber's striking description of the act of inclusion involved in 'experiencing the other side' or 'imagining the real', described above in Chapter 2 and applied to schooling in Chapter 4 and to research in Chapter 5, that explains the importance of inclusion here. If religious education can help pupils experience the other side, it is that much more worthwhile.

Religious education curricular and pedagogic inclusiveness

There are eight contrasting pairs of descriptions of aspects of the religious education curriculum, and eight pairs of descriptions of religious education pedagogy (first used in Stern 2006b), that can be used to describe and analyse inclusion in the subject. The curriculum and its pedagogy are closely related, yet their separate consideration reflects the need to consider both the content and the intentions of those dealing with the content. Just as Figure 3.1, at the end of Chapter 3, is a model at the centre of all the Section A themes of personal life in learning community, the following sets of contrasting pairs of descriptions of religious education form the centre-piece of all the work on religious education of Section B. They therefore incorporate work from a wide range of sources, and present an agenda for further research.

Firstly, then, the pairs relating to curricular inclusiveness. For some purposes, pupils, teachers and researchers could place each item of the pair at either end of a Salmon Line (as described above in Chapter 1), in order to see where the subject might be on that line, now, where the respondents might wish it to be in the future, and how it might be moved from the first to the second point on the line.

- *Countable vs valuable learning in religious education.* Countable learning can be described as presenting 'facts', and only facts. Pupils are given plenty of facts, or 'knowing that', rather than 'knowing how'. Valuable learning can be described as every fact coming with a thought. Perhaps, 'What does this tell us about . . .?' or 'What do you think the members of this group would like us to learn from this fact?' or 'What can you do with this fact?' or 'If facts had a monetary value, what is the value of this fact, and why?' These might be called 'thinking skills' exercises, as described at www.teachingthinking.net and by Baumfield (2002).
- *Purposeless vs linked learning in religious education.* Learning is purposeless if no connection is made between facts, they are left unlinked or lonely. Linked learning, in contrast, might involve pupils having to find another fact that is similar to, or contrasts with, that fact. For example, play 'odd one out', with groups of three facts (as in Baumfield 2002).
- *Meaningless vs meaningful learning in religious education.* Learning is meaningless if no systematic connection is made between facts, they are left unpatterned and not, for example, linked to central concepts. Learning can be more meaningful through constructing concept maps within topics, to link facts and concepts systematically (as in Erricker and Erricker 2000, ch. 8, and Novak 1998). For a thinking skills activity related to this, teachers might try 'maps from memory' as a useful strategy: this involves a group of pupils attempting to draw a map or diagram, with each member of the group, consecutively, spending 20 seconds looking at the source map (as in Baumfield 2002).
- *Loose vs mapped learning in religious education.* Loose learning means no connection is made between systems, cultures, religions and world views. Mapped learning can be helped if pupils, in describing any system, are also asked to say what contrasts with that system. This is particularly important in religious education, as religious education is beset by descriptions of religious systems that make them all sound the same (such as 'be nice to

people'). The mapping, in this case, is less about links and patterns (as in the previous paragraph), and more about borderlines and contrasts. There is a danger in exaggerating contrasts, and yet an account of any system that provides no boundaries is more dangerous, as it is liable to give the impression that there is no alternative.

- *Every classroom is its own world vs connected learning in religious education.* Classrooms can be isolated worlds, with no connection made between different kinds of world views, for example, cultures, religions, philosophies, political systems. Pupils can learn to isolate subject classrooms from each other, as described (as working against inclusion) by Daniels (2001). He uses Bernstein's concept of classification, to describe the degree of insulation of categories, and the weaker the classification (that is, the lesser the degree of insulation), the greater the likely inclusiveness. Daniels extends this to a model of good practice, such that 'collaborative patterns of staff working ... [is a] key indicator ... of what we define as good practice' (Daniels 2001, p. 139). Religious education should not teach about religions in isolation from other systems: it must connect with citizenship education, for example, and other curriculum areas. There are numerous examples of religious education activities that stretch across curriculum boundaries, with one (from Stern 2006a) for example involving describing the activities and consequences of a putative 'religion police', and many science and religious education activities in Sankey *et al.* 1988, and the Science and Religion in Schools Project (www.srsp.net).

- *Pupils are 'learning school' vs schools as learning communities through religious education.* The former might be described as pupils merely learning about how to be successful in school, not life as a whole. No connection is made between world views and 'real life' or living communities beyond the school. In this sense, the 'community of practice' to which pupils are being inducted is that of school itself (as in Wenger 1998 and Lave and Wenger 1991 described in Chapter 4 above). Poor attempts at widening the 'communities of practice' might include attempts at 'relevance' that are simply added to schooling, rather than integrated into the curriculum. Perhaps this is what is attempted in the 'thought for the day' slots, so ambiguously popular on BBC Radio 4 (www.bbc.co.uk/radio4/religion and elsewhere in the BBC network), and so insulted by the English school inspectors Ofsted, who note that 'many teachers fail to cope satisfactorily with the "Thought for the Day" that typically passes for the spiritual element in tutor periods' (Ofsted 2000b, p. 45, but see also the use of the 'thought for the day' below, Chapter 13). In contrast, if pupils are in a learning community, a community of and for learning, religious education is about life, and life stretches beyond school (as also in Chapter 13 below). Religious education teachers and pupils should frequently ask, 'How would life in these communities be different if people believed (or did) this?'.

- *Learning is for teachers, and pupils are merely the audience vs learning is for everyone, pupils and teachers alike.* The former is exemplified by pedagogies based on teachers as performers, whilst pupils merely listen. No connection is made between world views and pupils, and pupils do not justify their views. 'It's boring' may at times simply mean 'it has no connection to my current life or to my expected future life'. In contrast, teachers conducting learning, with all in the classroom performing, and all (teacher and pupils) listening, retains the teacher's essential professional role, whilst broadening the sense of active involvement. If religious education teachers and pupils frequently ask, 'How would your life be different if you believed (or did) this?', there would be the basis for discussion of the significance of any element of study in religious education.

- *Island or siege learning vs learning in a community of communities in religious education.* Island learning suggests that no connection is made between world views, pupils and pupils' communities, with 'siege learning' implying an active battle between the school community and external communities. Where the school involves learning in a community of communities, the multiple communities of practice to which pupils belong will all be recognized in school. In religious education, for example, pupils could have homework that captures the views and ways of life of people outside school. Straightforward examples (from Stern 2006a, and used in Chapter 13 below) include counting up and analysing the breaking of the Five Precepts or the Ten Commandments in a soap opera, or accompanying a member of the family to a shop and agreeing what would be the most appropriate gift (from the available goods) for Jesus as a baby. A more complex issue, also addressed below, is the curricular inclusion of pupils' own religious or non-religious beliefs and ways of life, and those of communities to which pupils might belong.

These eight overlapping ways of analysing curriculum inclusiveness in religious education can be applied to other subjects. The significance of religious education, here, is that religious education has systematically engaged in debates on these issues, with the UK pattern of multi-religious religious education attempting to reflect the diversity of the communities it serves, along with the methods of developing Agreed Syllabuses, being distinctive examples of engaging with complex and overlapping communities of practice in the curriculum (as described below). That involvement is, in turn, an aspect of pedagogy, and in analysing religious education's pedagogic inclusiveness, it is possible to bring together themes from throughout this book, in a second set of contrasting pairs of descriptions that might be operationalized by researchers using a Salmon Line. There are themes here that apply to all subjects; again, what is distinctive about religious education is a history of engagement with many of the themes. For example, religious education in the UK is rarely seen as training for a specific religious community or for the academic community of theologians, whilst physics might be so described (as in Lave and Wenger 1991, pp. 99–100, quoted above in Chapter 4). Non-confessional religious education, in contrast, is not even close to developing that relationship to the 'professional' religious community of practice, whether defined in terms of religious belief (as in 'Why do I have to do religious education? I don't want to be a vicar or a nun', Broadbent and Brown 2002, pp. 16–17), or in terms of professional theology or religious studies. The questions to be asked of non-confessional religious education pedagogy will therefore reflect the subject's rejection of an external, religious, community of practice. Here are eight contrasting pairs of descriptions of pedagogy:

- *Obedience school vs a school of human development in religious education.* In the former, pupils work for teachers: they do, and only do, as they are told. A government report into behaviour in school, initiated as a response to public concern about 'disobedience', concluded that there should be a move away from school rules that simply describe what should not be done, and a move towards behaviour policies that describe what should, positively, be done, with pupils and parents as well as staff engaged in developing such a policy. This report, the Elton Report (DES 1989), helped change the culture of schooling in the UK with respect to behaviour and discipline in general. Within religious education in the UK, the importance of developing a positive agreement on what should be taught is embedded in the current system of agreeing the syllabus. The UK's Agreed Syllabus approach is described by Hull (1998, p. 1, on how 'religious education is rooted in local communities'), Grimmitt (2000, ch. 1), Blaylock (1993), and various government reports (such as HMI 1989, Ofsted 1997). Schweitzer (2006) compares the UK and German approaches to local and state-level agreement on the religious education curriculum. Lowndes (1999), Stern (2001e) and Zamorski (2000) all address the implementation of Agreed Syllabuses.

- *Martyr school vs every person matters in religious education.* Teachers and other school staff are martyrs if they deny themselves, working for pupils at the expense of their own health or humanity, acting as though only the children matter. If every person matters, then all school staff and pupils can be treated well. '[T]he school must care for and provide for a full and free adult life for the members of its staff' and '[t]he tendency to sacrifice the adults to the children is as disastrous as it is widespread' (Macmurray 1968, p. 37).

- *Institutional loyalty vs a sense of community in religious education.* If teachers and pupils are all, primarily, working 'for the good of the school', then they will be working for an aim external to themselves. The 'common purpose' of the school as an institution may emerge from the activities of the members, including from the activities of religious education that bring together people from diverse backgrounds to understand each other, but the school is only a community if that common purpose is secondary to the sense of community. 'The fact is that the creation of common purposes presupposes a unity of persons already achieved; *not* through purpose' (Macmurray 1968).

- *Exam factory vs learning community in religious education.* The position of teachers who see examinations as their main aim has been discussed above (in Chapter 4), where the abolition of examinations was suggested by Macmurray – but only if it stands in the way of learning. Good exam results are a bonus in religious education, as in every other subject, not a purpose. There is no denying the significance of examinations for pupils' and teachers' futures: simply focusing on them and ignoring the intrinsic worth of religious education will ultimately mislead pupils, and will potentially open the way to the 'learned monsters, skilled psychopaths, educated Eichmanns' warned against by the concentration camp survivor in an open letter to a teacher (much quoted, including in Erricker and Erricker 2000, p. 81).

- *Social engineering vs living learning in religious education.* Even if religious education does indeed make for the moral development of pupils and a more tolerant and equitable society, to everyone's benefit, seeing religious education in terms of such social engineering can distract, once again, from the intrinsic value of the subject for human development. Extrinsic social benefits, like examination results, are a bonus. As Jackson vividly describes the situation:

  > It is impossible to establish a necessary connection between the instrumental goal of using religious education to promote social cohesion and the adoption or propagation of relativism or theological pluralism. However, a religious education that sets out only to promote tolerance or social cohesion is inadequate. Elsewhere I have argued that a key aim for RE is to develop an understanding of the grammar – the language and wider symbolic patterns – of religions and the interpretive skills necessary to gain that understanding ... Religious education develops self-awareness, since individuals develop through reflecting upon encounters with new ideas and experiences. Religious education is thus a conversational process in which students, whatever their backgrounds, continuously interpret and reinterpret their own views in the light of what they study. (Jackson 2004, p. 169)

- *Learning for the academy vs learning to be human in religious education.* The apprenticeship model of subjects, tentatively indicated as their proper purpose by Lave and Wenger, might suggest that 'the academy', or the academic study of theology or religious studies, should be served by the subject. If not the 'academy', perhaps the religious communities considered by the subject would be their purpose, with religious education teachers more or less successful according to attendance at church or mosque, recruitment to religious communities, or numbers becoming 'vicars or nuns'. Learning to be human, in contrast, requires a religious education, but not necessarily an academy. That is a proper pedagogic aim of religious education, and, in equivalent ways, of each school subject.

- *Hedonistic learning vs learning for flourishing in religious education.* Happiness seems such an obvious objective for religious and every other kind of education. It depends, of course, on what is meant by happiness. For Macmurray, '[t]he ancient and widespread belief that the supreme good of human life is happiness – for all its persuasiveness – is false' (Macmurray 1993, p. 2). His contrast is with freedom, which 'has a higher value', 'and this is what we recognize when we honour those who have been ready to sacrifice happiness, and even life itself, for freedom's sake' (Macmurray 1993, p. 2). More recent accounts of happiness in education have been provided by Noddings, who promotes happiness but does not deny the struggles in life, simply stressing that 'students who are generally happy with their studies are better able to bring meaning to difficult periods and get through them with some satisfaction' (Noddings 2003, p. 2). Hedonistic learning, learning for the sake of entertainment and current, temporary, happiness, is not a proper aim for religious education. A more complete, human, aim is that recommended by Macmurray and Buber, and by this book. It is a form of human flourishing also recommended by Aristotle, whose *eudaimonia* (often translated simply as 'happiness') is defined by him as applying to a person 'who is active in accordance with complete virtue, and who is adequately furnished with external goods, and that not for some unspecified period but throughout a complete life' (Aristotle 1976, p. 84). A better translation of *eudaimonia* is therefore flourishing, and learning for such flourishing in religious education is entirely worthwhile. As Reeve says of Aristotle's writing on education,

> [I]t is only by being brought up and educated in a city-state that human beings can acquire virtue ... The very thing that distinguishes a city-state from all other sorts of communities, indeed, is that it alone educates its citizens in virtue (1280a34– b15). Nature provides the potential for city-state life, then, while education helps to realize that potential, giving men the traits needed to perfect their natures as citizens and achieve happiness. Education is a part of politics for this reason. (Reeve in Rorty 1998, p. 51, and see also Howie 1968)

- *Equality of the shallows vs respect notwithstanding inequalities in religious education.* Religions and people within religious education are not equal in every way. If all people and all views and all learning are regarded as entirely equal, then there can only be an equality of the shallows: an equality that recognizes no wisdoms or truths or values. Religious education, of all subjects, must deal robustly with truths and falsehoods, and a radical equalizing, a kind of stereotype of post-modernist relativism, is anti- educational. Teachers and pupils must be striving for truths and greater humanity, in a community that is respectful, and one that recognizes the need for epistemic trust: believing that some will have greater knowledge or understanding than others (as also described in Chapter 4 above).

Religious education pedagogies can be more inclusive, the more they reflect the second of each of these contrasting pairs. Further consideration of the pedagogy of religious education is completed in the following chapter. However, the inclusiveness of the teaching is also to be reflected in the range of pupil needs addressed by religious education, and case studies of work attempting to meet a wide range of needs are described here.

Religious education and special educational needs: three case studies

How can religious education meet a wide range of needs? Pupils with special educational needs (SEN, determined by the possibility of being registered and statemented, as described in Wearmouth 2001, 2000), and those with other special needs (such as the gifted and talented, or those in English contexts with English as an additional language), have always completed religious education. Religious education has notable advantages in meeting a wide range of needs, as it can exploit the richness of religious and other traditions and the ways in which all those traditions have, in turn, had to meet the needs of the whole range of adherents. Yet there is some evidence that religious education does not have a distinguished record in meeting such needs. The English chief inspector commented in 2000 that 'achievement in religious education is also often weak in schools for pupils with EBD [emotional and behavioural difficulties]' (Ofsted 2000b, p. 56). Fortunately, in recent years there has been a significant growth in research and professional development concerned with religious education meeting the range of needs. Brown has written widely on the 'regular' teaching of religious education to pupils with special needs (as in Brown 1996), and has also researched and written on important issues for religious education such as dealing with bereavement (Brown 1999). Krisman (e.g. Krisman 2001) and Hull (e.g. Hull 2004) have written on a range of religious education and special needs issues. The National Society (www.natsoc.org.uk) has supported excellent development work in religious education and special needs, for example O'Brien (2002) for pupils on the autistic spectrum and those with severe and complex learning difficulties, and Orchard (2001) for challenging pupils aged 11 to 14. The British and Foreign School Society (BFSS, www.bfss.org.uk) supported work on additional support needs in mainstream schools for religious education (Beadle 2006). The biggest area of growth has been that supported by the Farmington Institute, who had a large number of Farmington Institute Special Needs Millennium Awards (FISNMA) award-holders, along with a number of other Farmington reports on religious education and special needs (from www.farmington.ac.uk).

It is helpful to describe case studies of research involving pupils with special educational needs. These case studies were carried out by Marie Stern, at that time head of a London special school, and Julian Stern. The first of the case studies involved taking a group of pupils aged 9 to 11 from the special school to a Hindu *mandir* (the Shri Swaminarayan Mandir and Hindu Mission, London, www.swaminarayan.org/), and, after the trip, asking the pupils three questions: 'What did I learn about Hinduism?', 'What do Hindus want us to learn from a *mandir*?', and 'What did I learn from Hinduism to help with meeting my targets?' Prior to the visit, the pupils had worked on some Hindu beliefs and stories (from Rose 1995), making use of some *murtis*, images on cloth, and a *puja* tray. However, most of the work was planned for after the visit. All the pupils had what are described as severe learning difficulties, and were working below the levels of attainment described in the English and Welsh national curriculum (DFEE and QCA 1999), but the purpose of this case study is not to highlight the needs of the pupils, but to describe how religious education can help meet the needs of pupils including those having considerable difficulties with learning.

The first exercise, aiming to explore the first question, was an 'adjectives' exercise. This involved attaching adjectives to pictures of the *mandir*, a school and a hospital, and saying why they had chosen them. The adjectives were 'angry', 'frightened', 'cold', 'peaceful', 'relaxed', 'busy', 'safe', 'happy', 'sad', 'beautiful' and 'interesting'. Figure 8.1 shows how the pupils justified putting particular adjectives by particular pictures.

Adjectives	Mandir	School	Hospital
Angry	I was afraid they would be angry if we teased them about their precious things.	Cussing.	Upset and crying.
		Nasty people.	Angry when the baby died. [This pupil's new-born sibling died on the day of the visit. The same pupil is the second of the contributors to hospitals being 'cold'.]
Frightened	Before we got there, I thought they might be mean. [Why?] Because they had so many rules.	Cussing.	Going to die.
		Bullying.	Loads of needles.
		Kicking.	Heart attack.
	I was scared because I'm a Christian and I thought that when I was there I wouldn't know if I'm a Christian or a Hindu.	Punching.	Meningitis.
Cold	It was warm.	School can be cold, warm or hot.	Hospitals can warm you up from the cold.
			My mum was cold when the baby died.
Peaceful	When we went 'Aum'.	When your friends are there.	If you get good news.
	No shouting.	When there was praying.	
	When we walked and saw stuff.		
	When you are playing.		
Relaxed	When the music made my headache go.	When we did yoga.	When you rest and calm down.
	When we took our shoes off.		
	Nice music.		
	The people were excellent to us.		

Busy	There were lots of people looking around.	Teachers do lots of work.	It is very busy, with lots of patients and doctors.
	Some people were working and giving us advice.		Helping babies to come out.
Safe	It's peaceful there because there is no talking and no silliness.	You can see the teacher so she will look after you.	If you're really sick, they can protect you.
		Teachers protect you.	Nurses help you.
	There was no bad people.	Teachers are good to you.	
	There's no fighting.	You do nice things.	
	It's all nice and peaceful.		
	It's relaxing.		
Happy	It's peaceful because there is no talking and no silliness.	You are happy when you learn.	You are happy when someone's alive.
	The statues made you happy.	It's better than staying at home.	
	I liked the flowers, and books in the shop.	You can play with your friends.	
Sad		You might hurt yourself.	If someone's dying or hurt or has a heart attack.
		If you hurt yourself.	
Beautiful	The building was beautiful.	It has all the things we need.	–
	The statues were beautiful.		
Interesting	You can go and listen and see what they do.	You do lots of work.	–
	It makes you go to sleep when you are looking at the ceiling. [The ceiling at this *mandir* is very ornately carved.]		
	The elephant god [i.e. *Ganesha*] was interesting.		

Figure 8.1: pupil responses on adjectives

Then the pupils were asked more about what they learned about Hinduism from the visit, and what they thought Hindus wanted them to learn from the *mandir*.

Pupil (a): They believe in gods and I saw beautiful statues of Sita and Rama like a Princess and a Prince. They put money in a bowl.

Pupil (b): I learned about where Hindus pray and that they like to do yoga. I liked the ornaments and you had to put your hands on the light.

Pupil (c): I saw the temple.

Pupil (d): I learned how to do the hand movements [copied, perfectly], and how to do *Aum*. They put red spots on their head.

Pupil (e): I learned about the music and how they use the *Aum* sound. [Why do they do this?] To help them pray.

Pupil (f): Before I went there I didn't know they had so many pictures and you could see so many things.

Pupil (g): I learned that they do yoga there to help them pray to the gods.

Pupil (h): Now I know why they put a red mark on their head and I know that they ring the bell when they want to pray.

Pupil (i): The Hindus made the temple with carving then the man blessed the gods. The monks wear orange and lay on the floor.

The teachers involved in this case study tried to evaluate these responses in terms of the levels described in the national framework for religious education (QCA 2004), and said that the responses were working at least at levels 1 or 2, considerably higher than the level of work the pupils achieved in the rest of their school work. This suggested that the engaging, experiential learning, based on traditional Hindu teaching, enabled the meeting of many of the pupils' needs. The pupils themselves were asked about how the visit might have helped them meet their own targets, formally set in their IEPs (individual education plans). This is what some said:

Pupil (j): The music helped me to be quiet. [A pupil with an IEP including avoiding inappropriate shouting.]

Pupil (k): It was good – it made me good. [A pupil with an IEP including attempting to take responsibility for his own actions.]Pupil (l): I learned some new words. [A pupil with an IEP including learning new words.]

Pupil (m): Not to be rude. [A pupil with an IEP including avoiding rudeness.]

Pupil (n): It was quiet; it helped me to be quiet. [A pupil with an IEP including calming.]

There are various conclusions that could be drawn from this work, not only for teaching pupils with special educational needs, but for pupils with a wide range of needs, including those deemed 'gifted and talented'. One is that, when teaching religious education, trying to meet a wide range of pupil needs, it is valuable to focus on the key concepts. Religious education can easily become a set of descriptions of religious 'phenomena' such as clothing or celebrations, with the descriptions made more simple or complex for pupils with different needs. Yet it is the concepts – concepts in the case study such as 'calm', 'respect', the *Aum*, 'safe' – that carry more of the essence of the religious traditions to be studied. Unlike some literacy strategies, religious education does not simply add a 'word' to a vocabulary list and then move on. Rather, it introduces concepts like change, peace, kindness or happiness early in a pupil's education, and then helps 'deepen' that concept year after year. Progression in religious education, then, is a matter of deepening concepts, not simply increasing vocabulary.

Another conclusion is that religions themselves have a long history of attempting to meet a very wide range of learning needs of members, and religious education can follow suit. Think about the 'multi-sensory' methods of establishing and promoting religions – making use of text, art, music, smell, dance and so much more. Simply using religious music, as described in detail in Stern 2004 (and more briefly in Chapter 11 below), can allow pupils access to authentic elements of religious and other traditions, and can do so in a way that allows a profound response from all pupils. Thirdly, pupils' own needs, including special educational needs, may provide insight into religions. For example, although aspects of autism can be understood as barriers to learning, the need for and comfort in ritual is often better understood by those on the autistic spectrum than by others. One might as easily consider the insights provided by a pupil's speech difficulties into the life of Moses (who appeared to consider himself unworthy to be a prophet, due to his stutter), or pupils' literacy difficulties with the 'unlettered' Prophet Muhammad (Qur'an Sura 7.157–8). Similarly, those with behavioural difficulties are more likely to understand, say, the Buddhist story of Angulimala, the fierce robber who learned how to change (as described by Padmasri and Adiccabandhu 1997, Chödzin and Kohn 1997, www.angulimala.org.uk or by searching for 'Angulimala' at www.buddhanet.net/). That story was therefore used for a second case study by the same team (Julian and Marie Stern), again with pupils having special educational needs.

The work follows the advice of Chödzin and Kohn, who say that Buddhist stories 'reflect many profound truths of the Buddha's teaching, but no matter how profound, the truth is always simple and can usually be grasped by young children at least as easily as adults' (Chödzin and Kohn 1997, p. 5). It seemed from their comments that the pupils' special educational needs helped give them insights into this religious story. Here are some of their comments, with the teachers' comments added in square brackets:

> Pupil (o): When that man [the Buddha] came along it made Angulimala chuck away his swords. [So, what do Buddhists want us to learn from this story?] Buddhists want to be peaceful.
>
> Pupil (p): The Buddha thinks that everyone deserves to be treated with respect so when he met Angulimala, the Buddha thought he should be treated with respect. So he took him to his home to meet his friends. Then, the King came and saw Angulimala and the King saw he wasn't bad, so Angulimala stayed with them. [So, what do Buddhists want us to learn from this story?] Being kind to people.

Pupil (q): That [i.e. Angulimala] looks like me! It [the story] was like me. It is true cos I used to be extremely naughty but I'm good now. [So, what do Buddhists want us to learn from this story?] Be good. Being bad didn't make Angulimala happy. It learned me a lesson.

Pupil (r) (a pupil on the autistic spectrum): Angulimala was stealing fingers and nobody was his friends. The Buddha wants Angulimala to be good. He teaches everyone to be good and not kill each other.

Pupil (s): The Buddhist people don't like bullies. Bullies upset people because they feel upset inside.

Pupil (t): I don't like the story. Because ... [no reason given]

Pupil (u): The Buddha didn't like people who bullied. If bullies stop, people will like them. The Buddha likes people when they stop bullying.

Pupil targets imply change, and change can be difficult. The story of Angulimala is often told in order to show that change, real change, is indeed possible, despite the fact that people might try to prevent change, and keep people 'bad'. Here are some of the pupil comments, again with the teachers' comments and extracts from IEPs in square brackets:

Pupil (p) [a pupil whose IEP stresses his need not to give up easily when he finds work difficult]: [Can this story help me meet my IEP?] Yes. Buddhist books are like friendship books. The story shows how the Buddha never walked away from the finger man. The story teaches you that you can change. It can help me try harder.

Pupil (o) [a pupil whose IEP stresses the need to encourage him to be less argumentative, and to attempt more work on his own and not to give up so easily]: [The story] can help me with my behaviour, because you were good while you were listening to the story – you're interested, so you're not naughty. It teaches you to be good and kind to people.

Pupil (q) [a pupil whose IEP stresses the need to encourage him to work cooperatively with his peers]: When you get your work wrong, you should count up to ten and start again instead of getting angry. If you're naughty, a story like this makes you good then you're happy all day.

One could generalize about the role of story in Buddhism, and how that is particularly suited to meeting pupils' targets. Story in Buddhism is often seen as 'situational' – as being told for a specific reason in particular circumstances. Bandits might be told of Angulimala, the bereaved of Kisagotami, and so on. When a man travelling through the jungle reaches a river he cannot cross, he may build himself a raft out of the materials to hand. Using this to cross the river, he must decide whether to carry the raft with him, or leave it there. (What would you do? Why?) Many Buddhists would say that he should leave the raft behind, as it would only be a burden. This also, they would say, is what you should do with stories. (Indeed, the most common interpretation of the story is that the river is all of existence, and the raft is the teachings of the Buddha. The other side of the river is

Nirvana.) Stories, and other 'teachings', are neither 'true' nor 'false', but are 'rafts' with which to cross rivers, to be discarded when they have served their purpose.

When considering religious education and dealing with truths, it may be worth considering some issues related to autistic spectrum disorders (for which see also Delf *et al.* 1999). There is the need within religious education to understand that people have different world views, and that the teacher may at times encourage pupils to 'suspend judgement' on these different, conflicting views in a way that might be particularly difficult for pupils on the autistic spectrum. The teacher, too, will be presenting different, mutually contradictory views without describing them simply as right or wrong. Similarly, the ability to empathize with people from different religious traditions, and from no religious tradition, to understand how and why they maintain their beliefs and behaviours, may be a real challenge for pupils on the autistic spectrum. However, these challenges also highlight the important strategic role for religious education in school with pupils on that spectrum.

The third case study is from the same team in the same school, further building on the ideas that Buddhist narratives contain truths 'that can usually be grasped by young children', and that the situational approach of Buddhist texts can mean that pupil difficulties may themselves provide insights into complex religious issues. There are many versions of the narrative used, all derived from the Japanese Zen Buddhist koan devised in the eighteenth century by Hakuin, asking the question 'What is the sound of one hand clapping?' (for example in Olson 2005, pp. 310 and 356–7, Erricker 2001, and www.io.com/~snewton/zen/onehand.html). The 'story' narrative used describes an impatient 13 year old who wishes to be set an 'adult' task, and is set the task of working out what the sound is of one hand clapping. He comes back week after week, listening hard each week and trying to describe what he thinks the sound is, eventually giving up and saying 'nothing' as the answer. Following a telling of the story, one teacher said:

> The pupils' reaction to this method and story was wonderful. I do suggest they all shut their eyes and focus on your voice which would be very quiet. The children do learn and do take the comments made within the story on board (some more than others).

Pupils in the school listened carefully to the story, itself a real achievement for many of them, and said how much they liked it: 'It's a good, nice story, because you wanted to find out what happened'. They were asked what they thought Buddhists wanted us (and the boy in the story) to learn?

Pupil (v): Because the boy was scared, to always go back and keep trying.

Pupil (w): They wanted the boy to learn to be quiet.

Pupil (x): Buddhists want us to learn – how to read and count and *listen*.

Pupil (y): They wanted the boy to grow up but take his time.

Pupil (z): People have to *learn* to be adults.

Pupil (aa): At the end of the story, the boy learned to be quiet. That is important, so you can hear the fire alarm.

Pupil (bb): To listen.

Pupil (cc): It's like [pupil name] trying to ignore [another pupil name].

Pupil (dd): Not to listen to things you hear outside – listen to things inside your head, like ideas.

What did the pupils learn from this story? Did the story help them with meeting their targets? One said that 'It would help me to ignore things', another that 'It's like, when everyone teases me, I read'. One could again note the 'situational' nature of story in Buddhism, as described above. Fidgeting impatient people may be set the 'one hand clapping' koan, others would be set other koans.

The three case studies described here, all involving pupils aged 7 to 11 with moderate to severe learning difficulties of various kinds, are valuable for religious education teachers in illustrating the ability of serious, authentic, religious narratives and practices to be understood by pupils with a very wide range of educational needs. It also demonstrates how such narratives and practices can help pupils meet their own educational targets.

Religious education, inclusion and exclusion, and new religious movements

When considering inclusion, it is not just those pupils with special educational needs who need to be included. Broader groups – indeed, according to the English school inspection service, all pupils and wider communities – need to be included, as described by the English inspection service as being:

> girls and boys; minority ethnic and faith groups, Travellers, asylum seekers and refugees; pupils who need support to learn English as an additional language (EAL); pupils with special educational needs; gifted and talented pupils; children 'looked after' by the local authority; other children, such as sick children; young carers; those children from families under stress; pregnant school girls and teenage mothers; and any pupils who are at risk of disaffection and exclusion. (Ofsted 2000a)

This therefore becomes a general issue of the ethos of school and the nature of subjects, relationships with parents, the overcoming of racism and sexism and various forms of bullying. The history of English and Welsh religious education has in recent decades been dominated by the incorporation of various religious and of non-religious traditions, and the rejection of 'confessionalism' or the promotion of religious belief. This is a distinctive tradition, even within Europe, and there is a need for research to investigate the impact of this policy, in terms of inclusion, especially as there is some tentative evidence that religious education may be a lesson where – ironically – pupils who are religious may feel most ostracized or excluded (as in White 2001). Jackson has worked on inclusion and exclusion in religious education across Europe, most recently working on religious education as a way of overcoming intolerance in plural societies, for example in Jackson 2004; Joy Schmack and Brendan Schmack (for example in White 2000 and 2001, Lovelace

2001) have worked on how pupils of religion can be included; Ipgrave has investigated pupils' own religious backgrounds and how they can be used in religious education for children aged 4 to 11 (in Ipgrave 2004); and Dodd (e.g. Dodd *et al.* 2002) has looked at issues of Islam and intercultural education. Good examples of inclusive practice across religious and non-religious traditions is embedded in the work of every SACRE (Standing Advisory Council for Religious Education) in the country (as described in Hull 1998 and Rudge 2001, and see also Chapter 6 above). The active approach exemplified in Lovelace 2001, in which pupils and adults talked about their beliefs and ways of life, can also be used in research, as described in Chapter 7 above (the 'inside out' work derived from Stern 2003).

All this research investigates how the religious education policies of inclusion are implemented, and how at times religious education may unintentionally exclude some pupils. However, there are some ways in which religious education policies may intentionally, rather than unintentionally, exclude. In the UK, for example, parents or carers of pupils may withdraw them from religious education (or from parts of religious education) church schools may reject applications from pupils on religious grounds, and the subject as a whole may exclude some traditions from syllabuses. Religious education teachers can research the inclusiveness of their subject, with their own pupils, by systematically asking the question 'When do you feel more included?' This question should be asked after pupils have been presented with an appropriate definition of inclusion, such as that from the English inspection service:

> An educationally inclusive school is one in which the teaching and learning achievements, attitudes and well-being of every young person matter. ... This does not mean treating all pupils in the same way. Rather it involves taking account of pupils' varied life experiences and needs. (Ofsted 2000a)

Then pupils can be asked to describe when they feel more included, in religious education lessons. The question should be asked of individual pupils, as an open question, initially, to allow for answers of different kinds. Pupils should then work in groups of two, three or four, to agree on a list of situations in which they feel more included in religious education. When this question has been asked, pupils have given a wide variety of types of answer. Some have written about the topics of lessons (topics that seem more 'relevant' or simply more enjoyable), and others have written about the style of teaching and learning (discussions or project work or group work). One surprising response was that of a pupil who felt most included when allowed to work on her own. Perhaps allowing for individual interests to be met, rather than always working collaboratively, can itself help include pupils.

It seems particularly strange that some religious traditions might themselves feel excluded from the religious education curriculum. Of course, no syllabus could cover absolutely every tradition, yet some traditions are not only unlikely to be included in syllabuses, but may be actively rejected as inappropriate. Examples include paganism and other traditions referred to as 'new age' religions (as described at www.paganfed.org and www.newageinfo.com), and other new religious movements (NRMs), such as Christian Science, Scientology and Jehovah's Witnesses (www.dianetics.org/ and www.scientology.org/ and www. watchtower.org/ with information on many groups at www.religioustolerance.org). Holt has researched and published on the Church of Jesus Christ of Latter-day Saints (CJCLDS), and on Jehovah's Witnesses (JW) (i.e. Holt 2002, 2004, and the Westhill Seminars), and is completing doctoral research on NRMs, especially Christian NRMs.

What is an NRM? Barker (1982, 1984, 1989) writes of the members of NRMs being first-generation converts, atypical of society, with a founder or leader who wields charismatic authority. Chryssides (1991, 1994, 1999, 2000, 2003) writes of NRMs being recent, outside the mainstream, and attracting converts from the indigenous culture. Holt himself writes of an NRM as having been founded within the past 200 years, and placing itself or being placed, by the majority of its 'parent faith', outside of the mainstream – either because of tradition or doctrine. The idea of a 'parent faith' is determined by the group itself. For example, the Nation of Islam identifies with Islam and the CJCLDS considers itself Christian, whether or not the 'parents' acknowledge their 'offspring'. Bahá'í no longer identifies with any 'parent', so although it is new, it should not, according to Holt, be considered an NRM. Under this definition, Christian NRMs include the CJCLDS, the New Church, the Exclusive Brethren, the Christadelphians, Christian Science, Jehovah's Witnesses, Seventh Day Adventists, the Worldwide Church of God, the Unification Church, the Jesus Movement, some Rastafarians, and many more groups. They are Christian in the sense that they consider themselves Christian, although other approaches might try to define Christian in terms of membership of the World Council of Churches (although that would exclude Roman Catholicism), groups founded before the nineteenth century (although that would exclude a number of recent groups), or groups that accept the Trinity (although that would exclude Unitarians). Curriculum representation on SACREs can, ironically, be damaged by the groups' self-identification as Christian. There are roughly 150,000 Buddhists in the UK, and 174,000 CJCLDS, but as the latter will call themselves Christian, the group is not as well represented on SACREs as are Buddhists. Pupils' own views are important. *Speaking for Ourselves* (Lovelace 2001) includes a Jehovah's Witness and a Rastafarian, which is helpful. Bolton (1999) writes about the importance of recognizing children from pagan backgrounds ('defined in terms of Wicca, Druidry, Shamanism and Odinism').

Religious education could continue without NRMs, but it would miss a lot of diversity, a lot of discussion points, and the backgrounds of a lot of pupils. For Holt, the best approach would be phenomenological, that is, the clear systematic study of individual NRM traditions, so that the curriculum is richer, and pupils from NRMs feel free and confident enough to share their beliefs as appropriate in lessons. Exam boards might also recognize the possibility of a number of NRMs being used in answers to examination questions on ethics. In the study of religions, there will always be issues of proportionality: it would be impossible to give substantial time to all religious traditions, even within the most generous timetable. More important than a simple statistical proportionality is an appreciation of the reasons for the inclusion or exclusion of a particular tradition. If for example there are pupils in the school following a tradition, this seems to be a good reason for inclusion. In contrast, if a tradition is included only if it is 'safe' and 'respectable', this seems to be a weaker justification for inclusion.

Conclusion

When it comes to inclusion, religious education has the immense advantage of access to thousands of years of multi-sensory, affective teaching that uses various forms of language, symbols, music, art and dance. On the other hand, religious education also encompasses traditions of rejection and exclusion – not only in religious traditions, but in its own history as a subject. The former advantages can be used to outweigh the latter disadvantages, to help schools as well as religious education become more inclusive. One strategy that would help pupils and teachers alike, in religious education, would be for teachers to feel able to say 'I don't know', if that is accompanied by 'so I/we will try to find out'. This might lead on to what is called 'reciprocal teaching' (taken from literacy work, as in Oczkus 2003), making the classroom environment acceptable for asking questions. Reciprocal teaching involves a dialogue between teachers and students for the purpose of jointly constructing meaning from text, with five strategies for structuring the dialogue: predicting, clarifying, visualizing, question generating and summarizing.

It is helpful to include in the chapter a description of an activity that has a long religious history, and a shorter history as a research tool that can help with inclusion in a number of ways: Moksha Chitram (adapted from Mackley 2002). The Moksha Chitram game originated in Hindu communities in India, helping players think about how to achieve the ultimate goal of *moksha*: release from the cycle of births and rebirths. The game was adapted by British Christians in India in the nineteenth century, based around the 'seven deadly sins' and corresponding virtues, but continuing to use the original Indian symbolism of snakes and ladders. Commercial, secularized, versions of the game became popular under the title 'snakes and ladders'. The activity involves pupils reflecting on any 'goal' including, for religious education, the purpose of life itself. Then, each pupil or group of pupils can be provided with an empty 100-square grid, with the squares numbered from 1 to 100, and a way of drawing snakes and ladders. Pupils should consider what they want to achieve in life, and represent that in a drawing or piece of writing in square 100. Then, they will think about some of the things that might hinder them from achieving their goal, the 'snakes', with the length of the snake representing the degree of hindrance. Each pair might produce four or five snakes, each labelled according to what they represent. Then, they will think about some of the things that might help them to achieve their goal, the 'ladders', with the length of the ladder representing the degree of help. Each pair might produce four or five ladders, again labelled according to what they represent. The completed games can be used as display items, for further discussion, and can also be played and reviewed for their 'realism'.

Having made use of research in religious education to investigate, illuminate and inspire further inclusion of pupils, it is important to retain a sense of teachers, too, being included. The lives of teachers are complex and challenging. Everington and colleagues are currently studying the life histories of religious education teachers (Sikes and Everington 2001), and I'Anson (2004) is studying the transition from religious studies student to religious education teacher. The research indicates that the need for the inclusion of teachers is as significant as that for pupils, and there is sufficient indication of teacher stress for it to be worth pointing out such a need. Many would recognize the comment from Macmurray, quoted above, that '[t]he tendency to sacrifice the adults to the children [in school] is as disastrous as it is widespread' (Macmurray 1968, p. 37). The following chapter looks in more detail at pedagogy, therefore: the role that religious education teachers fulfil, and how that can be enhanced.

Chapter 9

Teaching and learning: about and from

Teacher: Come on you still have all those questions to finish. You can finish colouring in that candle after you have done them.

Pupil: But miss, you said to make it look nice!

(Trainee teacher, responding to the question 'What is typically said in religious education?')

Introduction

The religious education curriculum brings together teachers (whose work is pedagogy) and pupils (whose work is learning). 'The curriculum' describes *what* may be taught and learned, whilst 'pedagogy' describes *how* it might be taught and learned. The *what* and the *how* are of course intimately linked. This chapter investigates some of those links, starting with the role of religion in religious education (part of the *what*), continuing with the nature of pedagogy in general (part of the *how*), and bringing both together in models of religious education pedagogy. Research has been completed on all of these areas, especially on the nature of the religious education curriculum, and research can stimulate further development of the subject and of the teachers of the subject. However, Grimmitt has noted that, of the various approaches to religious education pedagogy represented in his book,

> [i]t is quite remarkable that to date there have been no extended, independent evaluations of any of the pedagogies of RE represented in this book, other than as pilot studies undertaken during the life of the projects themselves. This is a serious deficiency because it means that there is no empirical *evidence* of the reasonableness or otherwise of the claims that each project both implicitly and explicitly makes about the viability of the pedagogical procedures or strategies that it adopts in accordance with its central pedagogical principles in order to meet its aims. (Grimmitt 2000, p. 22)

Some of the research on religious education pedagogy will therefore need to draw on research on pedagogy in other subjects, and that is one of the purposes of this chapter.

Research on religious education

It is hardly controversial to quote Wintersgill, who says that 'what RE offers uniquely is *the study of religion*' (Wintersgill 1995), or to quote Teece, who says:

> I judge good RE to be happening when students are enabled to develop their own beliefs, values and critical faculties by learning about and from the interaction between the study of living religions and our common, shared human experience of the world. (Teece 2004)

This approach, related to that of the Westhill Project (published for example in Read *et al.* 1988), is often described as the three-circle model of religious education, addressing traditional belief systems (beliefs and spirituality), shared human experience (issues and ultimate questions) and individual patterns of belief (beliefs and values). Yet it is still not clear what 'traditional belief system' or 'religion' mean in the model. For Teece, a member of the Westhill Project team, one of the problems is that religions are often understood naturalistically, non-religiously, sociologically, phenomenologically, anthropologically or historically: religions are not always understood 'religiously'. Teece's concern is to have a religious understanding of religion that is more spiritual than phenomenology, broader than theology, and that better aids pupil learning from religion. According to Teece (in these texts and in the Westhill Seminars), relating his views to those of Hick (1991), religions share a view of human nature as essentially unsatisfactory or incomplete, along with the possibility of human transformation. They share these views, but interpret them in many different ways. The unsatisfactoriness or incompleteness of human nature and the possibility of transformation, according to the world religions, is described by Teece as including:

- Buddhism: *tanha*, *dukkha* and understanding the four noble truths, following the eightfold path and keeping the five precepts in a path of meditation and skilful living, developing *metta* and *karuna* to the state of *nibbana*.
- Christianity: *falleness* and *sin*, and redemption found within the person of Jesus Christ and the development of the 'fruits of the spirit', leading to eternal life.
- Hinduism: *avidya* and *maya*, attachment (spiritual blindness), and following one's *dharma*, non-attachment leading to *moksha*.
- Islam: *ghafala* as 'heedlessness' and *fitra* as a good state, and obedience to the will of Allah in terms of the *Shari'ah* and *tariqa* and the development of the Islamic personality leading to paradise.
- Judaism: *yezer ha-ra* and *yezer ha-tov*, good and bad inclination, because of free will, and atonement by bringing *kedusha* into the world through the development of right relationships with fellow humans and with God.
- Sikhism: *haumai* and *manmukh*, and following a path of *nam simran* and *sewa* and developing *gurmukh* leading to the state of *mukti*.

This can lead to us viewing the phenomena of religions in a transformed way. As Smith says, it is not 'religion' but 'religiousness' that should be understood through religious education:

> Religion is … inherently human, and integrally so … if abstracted from … the men and women whose humanity it informs it wilts, even if it is abstracted for the purposes of intellectual scrutiny … It is not a thing but a quality: of personal life (both individual and social).

> … [Smith is here considering an example of a Hindu man:] If we would comprehend … we must look not at their religion but at the universe so far as possible through their eyes. It is what the Hindu is able to see, by being a Hindu that is significant. Until we can see it too, we have not come to grips with the religious quality of his life. And we can be sure that when he looks around him he does not see 'Hinduism'. Like the rest of us, he sees his wife's death, his child's minor and major aspirations, his money lender's mercilessness, the calm of a starlight evening, his own mortality. He sees things through coloured glasses, if one will, of a 'Hindu' brand. (Smith 1978, p. 138)

As Fowler (1981) says, students of religion should not be asking 'What do you believe?', but instead should be asking 'How do you see the world?' Teece's own approach is well expressed in *A Third Perspective* (Baumfield *et al.* 1994). There, the work on the human condition, for 11 to 14 year olds, fits with the way people are, focused around guilt and reconciliation, why people are not perfect, what is the problem, what should people be like, facing up to the truth about ourselves, and an ideal human being in an ideal world. In such ways, Teece says, teachers need to help pupils gain a greater understanding of what religion is all about, as so many people fail to understand this issue.

What makes something 'religious' is worth investigating by all religious education teachers. All teachers can have their own views of religiousness, but it is understanding the views of pupils as well as colleagues that can help clarify and, it is hoped, improve the subject. The question should be asked in a way that is appropriate for those of any religion and of no religion. All can be asked both of these questions: 'If you say someone is "religious", what do you mean?' and 'If you say someone is "not religious", what do you mean?' Pupils could produce their own answers, and then work in pairs and fours, to come to an agreement about what they think 'religiousness' means. It is important that there is not a simple 'right answer' to the question: the question can be answered in various useful and meaningful ways. Once the pupils have generated some answers to the questions, they can be asked the following questions: 'What has been done in religious education lessons that helps us to understand being "religious"?', and 'What has been done in religious education lessons that helps us to understand being "not religious"?' These four questions are helpful in analysing pupil views on religiousness, and pupil views on how religious education lessons tackle religiousness. They are therefore central to understanding how the subject works in a school.

Research on pedagogy

The previous section looked at religion, ending with work on the subject of religious education itself. Here, the issue of pedagogy – the *how* of teaching – is tackled more directly. Understanding pedagogy is centred on understanding learning theory, and there are two traditions of learning theory worth describing here: behaviourism and constructivism. These initial descriptions can be followed up in standard textbooks such as Wood (1988), or Daniels and Edwards (2004).

Behaviourists tend to look at how people respond to 'stimuli' (so they may be called 'stimulus-response' theorists), which in practice generally means 'rewards and punishments'. If the theory underlying teaching is based on giving pupils incentives to do the 'right' thing, and sanctions to prevent them from doing the 'wrong' thing, then the teaching is working on behaviourist principles. The rewards may be praise or marks or stars or credits or exam results or sweets or bicycles; the sanctions may be criticism or detentions or missed breaktimes or fines. Of course, every teacher will use rewards and punishments. It becomes more 'behaviourist' if the teacher believes this is the *only* way in which to get pupils to act in a certain way. Distinguished behaviourists include Pavlov, Skinner and Eysenck, with Pavlov famous for demonstrating that dogs can be trained to salivate on the ringing of a bell if the bell has been rung every time the dog is fed. Their theories are not so 'fashionable' amongst contemporary psychologists, or amongst religious education researchers, but within schools the practical application of behaviourist theories can dominate teachers' lives. As well as star charts and merits, a concern with physical conditions (for example, having carpeted rooms in order to reduce noise) might – if it dominates teaching – be based on these same theories. It is an unfair stereotype of behaviourism to say that teaching is like training dogs, but it is a memorable analogy (and is entertainingly applied to 'training husbands', Sutherland 2006). Equally unfair, and equally memorable, is the description by Rumi, the thirteenth-century Sufi Muslim poet who wrote in *Two Types of Intelligence* of 'acquired' intelligence that flows into a schoolchild from books and teachers, weighing them down as 'retaining all that knowledge is a heavy load' (Rumi 1995, p. 178, www.sufism.org/books/barks and www.sufism.org/books/jewels/rheart.html). What behaviourist approaches tend to have in common is the idea of adding extrinsic rewards or punishments, to what is happening in the learning itself, and having more rewards than punishments (see, for example, Canter and Canter 1992).

For religious education, behaviourism might mean getting pupils to learn religious education by rewarding the completion of work, marking and returning work quickly (so that the feedback 'stimulus' is associated with the original work), rewarding good-quality work, being careful to avoid associating religious education work with punishment – especially unfair punishment. A behaviourist approach could also lead to setting up religious education classrooms with good conditions for studying (tables, lighting, displays, resources) to help stimulate positive feelings about the subject. Many see behaviourism as tied in to debates on 'standards of achievement', as a concern with standards leads people to introduce incentives and punishments related to the achievement of such standards.

Constructivists tend to look at each pupil's current understanding or 'worldview' (whatever subject is being studied), and see teaching and learning as building on, or reconstructing, that worldview. (It is easy to see how controversial this might be, in terms of religious worldviews, if pupils or their families think that the role of religious education is to 'reconstruct' pupils' worldviews.) Pupils are seen as active rather than passive learners: they are not 'empty vessels' into which teachers pour knowledge or 'behaving machines' that teachers can re-programme with appropriate stimuli. Vygotsky used the term 'scaffolding' to describe constructivist approaches. Helping children understand what it is that they know and can do, and giving them the tools with which to develop or change their understanding, is typical of those supporting this theory. Classical, or more individualist, constructivists include Piaget, who sees the process of learning primarily as an individual pupil and teacher working together: pupils are sometimes like 'lone scientists'. Social constructivists include Vygotsky and Bruner, who see children as learning 'in conversation' with peers and teachers, and may look at systems (classes, families, schools, communities) rather than just at individuals. The process of learning involves groups of pupils working collaboratively with a teacher to build up their understanding. (Vygotsky and Bruner, then, can be 'blamed' for group work.) It is an unfair stereotype of constructivists to say that teaching is all about waiting around while pupils discover everything for themselves, but it is a memorable analogy. Equally unfair and equally memorable is Rumi's description of the learning that comes from within, from the heart or soul, and that flows outwards and 'gushes continually from the house of the heart' (Rumi 1995, p. 178, www.sufism.org/books/barks and www.sufism.org/books/jewels/rheart.html). What constructivist approaches tend to have in common is the idea of looking at the intrinsic features of learning, to support learning 'from the inside', either individually (often using 'cognitive' strategies) or collectively (using social strategies).

For religious education, constructivism means getting pupils to learn religious education by encouraging pupils and teachers to talk about the topics and tasks, encouraging purposeful and interesting and creative activities, that provide intrinsic motivation. Pupils can work long hours on tasks that really interest them, making incredible discoveries, whilst extrinsic rewards and punishments may have little effect and will never make routine and repetitive work interesting. Indeed, constructivists will often say that extrinsic rewards and punishments will distract, not encourage, pupils: if you are working on a project because you will get a merit mark or avoid a detention, you will not be wanting to learn the subject, and will be unlikely to develop a life-long interest in the subject, but will merely be learning how to get a reward. Teachers expressing an interest in religious education, and demonstrating how important it is as a subject, should help, too. The more that religious education can build relationships and conversations within and particularly beyond the school, the more the social constructivists will say this is how people learn best. Many see constructivism as more loosely tied in to debates on 'standards of achievement', and yet in the last ten years, debate on how to raise standards in UK schools has been dominated by various versions of 'assessment for learning' (well described in Assessment Reform Group 1999, Black and Wiliam 1998a, 1998b, Weeden *et al.* 2002, and at arg.educ.cam.ac.uk/), which is clearly based on constructivist theories of learning.

Most of the traditions of religious education pedagogy (as described in Grimmitt 2000) are broadly in the constructivist tradition, although it is only Grimmitt himself (within that book) who writes extensively about constructivism. A constructivist approach also matches UK government descriptions of the importance of religious education, as national guidance focuses on intrinsic values of the subject. The national framework document asserts:

> Religious education encourages pupils to learn from different religions, beliefs, values and traditions while exploring their own beliefs and questions of meaning. It challenges pupils to reflect on, consider, analyse, interpret and evaluate issues of truth, belief, faith and ethics and to communicate their responses.

> Religious education encourages pupils to develop their sense of identity and belonging. It enables them to flourish individually within their communities and as citizens in a pluralistic society and global community. (QCA 2004)

Nevertheless, as has already been said, teachers' lives in schools are often dominated by behaviourist, not constructivist, approaches. In that context, some research on how pupils and teachers themselves see their learning is worth carrying out, in order to understand which traditions are most influential in the classroom. This might follow Daniels' (2001) work, itself an investigation of the social constructivist approaches to schooling of Vygotsky. The key concepts are 'classification' (also referred to above, in Chapter 8) and 'framing', taken by Daniels from the sociologist Bernstein. Stronger and weaker classification and framing refer to the divisions between subjects ('classification') and the degree to which pedagogy is teacher-centred rather than pupil-centred ('framing'). Stronger classification and framing are more likely in schools using more behaviourist approaches, and match Rumi's view of 'acquired' learning. Weaker classification and framing are more likely in schools using more constructivist approaches, and match Rumi's view of learning 'from the inside'. The differences are illustrated by Daniels from art lessons in two of the schools. In the school with stronger classification and framing,

> the teacher read a story called 'Where the Wild Things Live' [*sic*]. She then told the children that they were going to 'make pictures of the wild things'. The teacher had prepared a number of different pieces of sugar paper and proceeded to assign children to these pieces of paper. Each piece of sugar paper had an outline of a 'Wild Thing' on it and most of them had sections/areas of the paper marked off. Each section contained a code number and thus could be translated by a key at the bottom of the piece of paper. The children followed the key which dictated the material to be used to 'fill in' the sections/areas marked on the paper. The 'Wild Things' were thus constructed. The

department head said of art lessons, 'We are interested in the results of art, of good productions rather than "experiencing" the materials'. (Daniels 2001, pp. 162–3)

In the school with weaker classification and framing,

> the children were given different grades of paper, powder paint and a piece of foam rubber or sponge. The teacher then told the children to wet the paper and flick paint at it with the sponge. The children were encouraged to use different kinds of paper with different degrees of dampness. They were told to experiment with ways of applying the powder paint. (Daniels 2001, p. 163)

In this way, Daniels contrasts classrooms where 'you paint what you see' and those where 'you paint what the teacher sees' (Daniels 2001, p. 170). He suggests a research task (adapted and described in more detail in Stern 2006b) to investigate classification and framing. Pupils and teachers can be asked for religious education and for one or more other subjects 'What is typically said in religious education?', and in each other subject. In analysing responses, analysts should bear in mind the indications of 'classification' and 'framing'. Indications of stronger or weaker classification will be seen in how different the descriptions are of different subjects, or how 'bounded' those subjects seem. Indications of stronger or weaker framing will be whether pupils are 'painting what the teacher sees' or 'painting what they see'. According to Daniels, weaker classification and framing are likely to be more inclusive, that is, more suited to classrooms where pupils have a wide range of educational needs. Discussion of the outcomes of this exercise – completed by teachers, as well as by pupils – suggests that there is a concern with the difference between the 'self-image' of religious education, and how the subject works in classrooms. Pupils often see religious education in terms of 'right and wrong factual answers', and/or a confessionalist promotion of religious belief, with the former illustrated by a trainee teacher's description of what is typically said:

> Teacher: Come on you still have all those questions to finish. You can finish colouring in that candle after you have done them.
> Pupil: But miss, you said to make it look nice!

Daniels' broader conclusions are that teaching is and should be creative, and although Vygotsky might be interpreted as saying pupils 'internalize' the surrounding culture, it is more appropriate to think of him as saying that pupils 'participate' in the surrounding culture more actively. An example of the latter is given in how people learn to dance. In that way, people (including teachers and pupils) do not 'create' society, they 'reproduce and transform' it (Daniels 2001, p. 43).

The varieties of religious education pedagogy

Blaylock (2004, and in the Westhill Seminars) describes six schools of thought in religious education, with phenomenology providing a platform, a 'given', for religious education, even if it is not the whole pedagogical toolkit for religious education. What is interesting is that, for Blaylock, phenomenology and the other pedagogies described here can be cumulative, and can work in any order. A 'humaniser' start can be complemented by a 'post-modern' piece of work, and, crucially, *vice versa*. It is worth noting that Blaylock is not describing all the possible pedagogies of religious education, and that confessional religious education is not included in his modelling, despite its popularity across many countries, and its continued existence (sometimes almost as an 'underground movement', as in Thompson 2004a, 2004b) in the UK. Figure 9.1 is Blaylock's diagram covering six schools of thought (adapted from Blaylock 2004, with each also represented in Grimmitt 2000).

The following approaches could be described as competitors or as complementary, with complementarity illustrated in this narrative below, also adapted from Blaylock 2004.

Six ways around Easter: a pedagogical fantasy

At the start of term, the new religious education teacher Miss X noticed in her syllabus that she was to teach the 11 year olds about the Festival and stories of Easter, the beliefs associated with the celebration, and the impact of these beliefs in the Christian community. She had just been trained by some phenomenologists (as in Smart 1969), and so planned two lessons on the phenomenon of Easter. Using artefacts – a variety of crosses, some icons, some 'He is Risen' badges, hot-crossed buns, and a video of the Easter celebrations in an Orthodox and an Evangelical setting – she taught them about the Festival, its terminology and its diversity.

After two lessons, Miss X read Michael Grimmitt's book on religious education and human development (Grimmitt 1987), and realized she had been neglecting pupils' learning from religion. She planned some fresh activities: pupils were asked some provocative questions. What if you were in charge of the Easter celebrations for the two churches nearest school: what music would you choose for Good Friday and Easter day? What does the idea of 'life out of death' or 'resurrection' or 'life after death' mean to you? Can you explain an occasion when hope seemed hopeless, but you held on anyway? More good work emerged as pupils related the festival to their own experiences.

After these two lessons, she went on a course with Trevor Cooling, and learned the methods of 'concept cracking' (as in Cooling 1994b). Inspired by the new pedagogy of the conceptual analysis of truth claims, she planned two lessons of biblical study in which the claims of the resurrection were presented to the class. They responded to the challenge – some who thought it would be impossible discussed their view with others who thought it a miracle. Some Christian children in the class stayed at the end to say how affirming they had found the exploration of their own faith.

	Focus	Impact	Questions raised
Phenomenology E.g. Smart 1969	Learning in religious education is focused upon assembling, broadening and deepening understanding that takes each religion's phenomena on its own terms. Examining the 7 Smartian dimensions of religion brings balance to the study.	From the 1970s until now, this set of approaches has defined a baseline for English and Welsh religious education: children should learn lots of information about the religions. Its best practice takes comprehensive account of whole religions.	Is it supportable to argue that 'dry factuality' goes with phenomenology? Can a phenomenological pedagogy which takes theologies and philosophies on their own terms be envisaged? Practised?
Religious education as human development E.g. Grimmitt 1987	Pedagogy is guided by the need for religious education to enable human development. The links between psychology and other social science disciplines, and philosophy and questions of meaning, establish a creative tension. The place of religion as a distinctive human discourse, in flux and flexible, is defended even in relatively secular cultures like those of the UK.	The term 'learning from religion' originates in this articulation of religious education's purposes, and has been highly influential as an 'attainment target'. The focus on finding and making meaning through religious education has become axiomatic for many religious education teachers.	Is this set of approaches tied to an existentialist philosophy (the idea of meaning making)? How can the tensions between religionists and educationists be balanced? If religious education is a part of the curricular 'meaning making' then should religionists control what is taught at all? Or is it enough to 'treasure the questions'?

	Focus	Impact	Questions raised
Spiritual development E.g. Hay with Nye 1998, Hammond *et al.* 1990	Concepts of spiritual dimensions of life lie behind the intention to enable learners to access their own spirituality. The psychological defence of the spiritual dimension is linked to the examination of spiritualities from various different religions.	Hammond *et al.* 1990: widely influential on some teachers, but the momentum is slower now. The emphasis on spirituality and psychology leads to opposition from phenomenology, and little government interest.	Are these approaches to religious education dualist? Individualist? Is there a danger for religious education in being 'more spiritual but less religious'? Does the spiritual focus here draw religious education too far from religions and their communities as found in the UK?
Religious literacy – conceptual approaches E.g. Cooling 1994a, 1994b, Wright 1993	Since religion is about truth, the critical evaluation of claims and schemes for establishing the truth about religious propositions are the key skills for young people in their religious education. These skills are especially necessary in a philosophical climate of relativism and post-modernity.	Through teacher training and academic writing, these approaches, allied to 'critical realist' philosophical discourse about religion in a post-modern society, are popular with many teachers. It is a bit less clear that there are resources to support classroom work in this style.	By focusing on the conceptual, and the 'truth-claiming' elements of religion, what is marginalized? Does a conceptual approach carry the danger of making too little space for cultural and social aspects of religion? Do these approaches set phenomenology and community cohesion too lightly aside?

Interpretive pedagogy E.g. Jackson 1997	In religious terms, the focus is on internal diversity as well as religious plurality, and on a serious engagement with the layering of religion, culture and philosophy. In terms of learners, the key skill is interpretation.	By linking resources, methodological publications and research, the 'Warwick school' has made a substantial impact on teaching and learning. Versions of interpretive pedagogy are practised, increasingly widely, from 5 to 16.	Is it possible for teachers to grasp this set of methods with sufficient clarity to be effective? Do the subtleties of reflexivity suit the learning needs of all 5 to 16s? What is the place of 'neutrality' in the stances of the teacher and the learner now?
Deconstruction and the 'world view' E.g. Erricker and Erricker 2000	If the task of education is constructing the 'self', then pedagogies for religious (and spiritual and moral) education should facilitate this task with regard to the 'philosophical' or 'spiritual' self. To enable this, some 'inappropriate' prior practice must be swept away.	The national framework (QCA 2004) and the lobbying interests of the British Humanist Association (www.humanism.org.uk) have created a climate in which 'worldviews' are part of the religious education of the future. As yet, few curricular resources supports this, but the impact is likely to grow.	What effect would deconstruction in religious education have for children whose family culture is evangelical Christian, traditional Islamic or humanist? What effects would follow if the deconstructionist tools were turned upon consumerism or soft agnosticism? Is this their commonest use?

Figure 9.1: Blaylack's six schools of thought

During half term, she checked her notes from college, and remembered all about the deconstruction of religion for post-modern young people (as in Erricker and Erricker 2000). The next two lessons were used to dissect how the Easter festival is sometimes used to keep people in their place – a heavenly reward for a life of drudgery. One child asked 'So, Miss, is religion just a way of keeping people in their place?' She knew she was getting somewhere when a group of boys announced they didn't believe in Easter, and wouldn't be bothering to wait till Sunday before eating the chocolate.

There was another course on interpretive approaches to religious education (as in Jackson 1997), and Miss X was edified. She decided to plan a couple more lessons, the first on the diversity of Easter as Christian children describe it (she used accounts from 13-year-old Catholics, Methodists and Quakers, from Bristol, Birmingham and Nigeria). Then she asked pupils to write interpreter's notes on the *Hallelujah Chorus*, making sense of its origins, use today and impact within and beyond the Christian community.

As term wore on, Miss X was visited by the local adviser, who was signed up to a spiritual and experiential approach to religious education (as in Hammond *et al.* 1990). She realized what was missing in the term's lessons and used a guided fantasy based upon the appearance of Jesus to two disciples travelling to Emmaus. Pupils finished the term creating works of art inspired by the work on a choice of themes: 'Back from the Dead' or 'My Hope for the Future'.

These descriptions of six perspectives can be complemented by further investigation of each of them in Grimmitt (2000). In any one school, there may be elements of all six perspectives, or one perspective might dominate. Perhaps by swapping evidence from a number of schools, religious education teachers may discover the extent to which the various approaches to religious education pedagogy dominate religious education. Asking pupils for their views (as suggested throughout this book, and supported by Rudduck *et al.* 1996 and Flutter and Rudduck 2004) will be important, too, as will understanding the cultures and perspectives of university theology and religious studies departments which generate religious education teachers (as researched by I'Anson 2004). It may be that the culture and pedagogy of each school, rather than the training and beliefs of the religious education department, will dominate, especially if many of those teaching religious education have not trained in the subject (as described by Gates 1989, 1991, 1994, referred to in Chapter 7 above). Clearly, a school dominated by a more behaviourist approach to learning is unlikely to find it easy dealing with constructivist approaches to religious education or any other subject. Yet the variation between departments within UK secondary schools for pupils aged 11 to 19 is wide ('the range of variation by department *within* schools is probably three to four times greater than the average variation *between* schools', Reynolds in Stoll and Myers 1998, p. 167), suggesting that there may be room for departments as 'islands of constructivism'. I'Anson's research on trainee teachers negotiating a route between post-structuralist religious studies (at Stirling University), and what he describes as 'modernist' school religious education, gives further hope for intelligent negotiation between the world views of university and school studies of religion, rather than giving up and saying 'there is nothing we can do'.

Conclusion

This chapter has touched on a small part of research on the religious education curriculum – itself probably the most-researched aspect of religious education – and on some broader issues in pedagogy that could be applied to religious education. Despite the relative scarcity of good research on pedagogy specific to religious education, it is clear that some work is going on in this area, and that teachers wishing to develop themselves will want to be researching their own pedagogy, using some of the techniques described here. By researching religious education pedagogy, teachers can thereby come to understand the impact and value of their work. They may also come to feel a part of the whole process: not merely 'speaking textbooks', but members of the community of learners, learning and developing together with colleagues and pupils. This links back to the previous chapter, on inclusion (in this case, the inclusion of teachers, not just pupils), and it links forward to the next chapter, as that deals with the values embedded not only in schools but in wider communities and societies. Religious education is and always will be a controversial subject, not because its status is in doubt (even if it is), but because it deals with real religions, religions that have been at or near the heart of most of the world's controversies and conflicts.

Chapter 10

Religious education and citizenships

RE lessons give you the peace of mind in a world, where peace and mind no longer go together.

(17 year old)

Introduction

There is no question that religions are related to human rights, values and the nature of citizenship. The question addressed by this chapter is the extent to which religious education as a school subject is related to these issues. For example, what impact can religious education about values have upon pupils' moral and social development, and can religiously-originated approaches to values education and moral formation be offered to all pupils in a plural school? What, indeed, does religious education offer to dis-traditioned, non-religious or secular young people, in terms of human rights, values and citizenship? What can those same young people learn from religion? The emergence in England and Wales of a statutory citizenship curriculum (e.g. DfEE and QCA 1999) and a national framework for religious education (QCA 2004) has helped religious education in this country to re-evaluate itself and its purposes, including especially its role in broader values and citizenship education. Chater (2000), for example, connects citizenship education to liberation theology *via* Freire (1993), while Gearon (2004) writes of teaching citizenship through religious education, and Baumfield (2003) writes of 'democratic religious education' in communities of enquiry. Others, such as Rudge (2001), look instead at the impact of religious education on its pupils. It is worth starting by bringing all these debates together, with an emphasis on how research in religious education can illuminate and help develop not only the subject but also, potentially, pupils' lives, values and roles in social and political structures.

Values and citizenship

Are values education and citizenship education subjects in their own right, or approaches to schooling as a whole? Both have been taught as separate subjects, yet both are also well embedded in personal social and health education and religious education lessons. Teachers of many subjects in secondary schools (for pupils aged 11 to 19) say 'I trained as a teacher of this subject, not of personal and social education or values', rather than 'I trained as a teacher of pupils'. This raises the question of whether any school subjects – including religious education – are ends in themselves or are means to educate *children*. Macmurray, the philosopher of community, said that teaching is dangerous if it only thinks about subjects, as '[y]ou have one person very anxious to make Tommy a good mathematician and another to make him a good historian and another all out to develop his knowledge of science or to teach him to speak French or read Latin', yet 'who is now concerned to make him a good human being and to teach him to live?' (Macmurray 1968, p. 114).

> Somehow the all important thing has got squeezed out in the process of professionalizing education. ... The golden aim of education – to teach the children how to live, has vanished over the horizon – crowded out by a multiplicity of little aims. ... They are learning that life is a bundle of more or less unpleasant tasks which are a weariness to the flesh, to be performed because they have to be performed, and that to escape from them is a blessed relief. (Macmurray 1968, p. 114)

This is a partial view, of course, and there are many subject specialists, including religious education specialists, who see their subjects as most important. The statutory curriculum documents (such as DfEE and QCA 1999) tend to address issues of 'child development' and 'subject development' together, rather than as in competition, although present UK policy related to the Children Act 2004 (DfES 2004a, b) has moved towards child development as the dominant influence on schools (as also addressed in Chapter 14 below).

On citizenship, a further question might be, how would you know a good citizen if you saw one, and of *what* would you be a citizen? These are related questions: to judge a 'good citizen', it is necessary to understand what a person may be a citizen of: the world, a country, or what? The official English and Welsh citizenship curriculum refuses to say 'of what' a citizen is, for the purpose of citizenship education, but there are three common traditions: an 'exclusive' citizenship, an 'inclusive' citizenship, and a citizenship that extends horizons. 'Exclusive' citizenship expresses distinction or special privilege. St Paul says that he is a 'citizen of no mean city' ('I am a man which am a Jew of Tarsus, a city in Cilicia, a citizen of no mean city', KJB Acts 21:39), as a way of getting out of trouble: the Romans would not dare treat a citizen of such a city in the same way as they might treat an 'ordinary' person. Citizenship of particular places is still used as a mark of distinction, nowadays referring to the nation state. The last 75 years have seen more migration and refuge-seeking than any other period in the history of the world, and claims of citizenship, attempts to block citizenship, withdrawal of citizenship, and so on, have characterized political struggles throughout the period. Many of these issues derive from religious conflicts. Just within Europe, Jewish migration, population movements in the former Yugoslavia, political developments in Northern Ireland, and recent responses to terrorism, all have religion and citizenship as important themes. So St Paul was not the last person to rely on a claim of citizenship to save his life. Indeed, it is important to note that in schools throughout the world, today, there are many pupils studying religion and citizenship who are seeking asylum and do not yet have, but would like to have, 'exclusive citizenship'. There are many others objecting to people being given such citizenship. It is citizenship of the nation state, the sort of citizenship that is related to entitlement to a passport, that is the most common kind in debates on the issue.

However, another quite contrasting approach to citizenship is to see it as an inclusive and universal characteristic, something that unites all human beings. Aristotle might have been thinking of this when he said that people were 'born for citizenship' ('. . . man is born for citizenship', Aristotle 1925, p. 12, also translated as 'man is by nature a social being' and 'man is by nature adapted to a social existence'), although he probably wanted to exclude slaves and women from his 'universalism'. Bacon used the term in a clearly inclusive way, saying that

> If a man be gracious and courteous to strangers, it shows he is a citizen of the world, and that his heart is no island, cut off from other lands, but a continent, that joins to them. (Bacon 2002, p. 363)

This idea of a 'citizen of the world' is one that might well appeal to teachers, and the English and Welsh national curriculum (DfEE and QCA 1999) does indeed refer to the 'local, national and international' dimensions of citizenship, and QCA guidance has mentioned 'global citizenship', so there are good grounds for doing work in this area. Macmurray talks explicitly about the role of education and citizenship. He says that 'to be educated today means to have learned to be human – not Scottish, not British, not even West-European – but human' (Macmurray 1968, p. 145), and, on citizenship itself, that there is a

> tendency to conceive education as a training for citizenship. Such training has its place in a good system of education. But it is a subordinate place. To use citizenship as a co-ordinating conception for education as a whole is merely one way of identifying the personal with its organic aspect. (Macmurray 1968, p. 12)

Whatever its definition, citizenship is still to be defined more clearly, and there is a third tradition that goes beyond exclusive and inclusive definitions. Curriculum documents and the influential work of Crick (as described in Lockyer *et al.* 2004), are themselves heavily influenced by the nineteenth-century reformist philosopher and economist John Stuart Mill, who saw citizenship education as pushing outwards, or extending horizons. (This has, within the education system, often been described in terms of 'spiritual development', as a recognition of the 'other', or of something unselfish.) Mill himself, when talking of citizenship education, referred to

> the peculiar training of a citizen, the practical part of the political education of a free people, taking them out of the narrow circle of personal and family selfishness, and accustoming them to the comprehension of joint interests, the management of joint concerns – habituating them to act from public or semi-public motives, and guide their

conduct by aims which unite instead of isolating them from one another. Without these habits and powers, a free constitution can neither be worked nor preserved; as is exemplified by the too-often transitory nature of political freedom in countries where it does not rest upon a sufficient basis of local liberties. (Mill 1974, p. 181)

In linking citizenship education to the idea of an extension beyond the self-and-family, Mill also links it to various personal and social issues, and to links between schooling and parents, families and local communities. It is therefore not surprising that religious education links to citizenship and also to personal social and health education. After all, what is a 'person'? Is a person really, essentially, a social being as Aristotle said, or even more? For Macmurray, '[o]ur human Being *is* our relations to other human beings' (Macmurray 1995a, p. 72, as quoted above in Chapter 2), and that approach pulls together various curriculum areas: teachers are teaching young people, and according to Macmurray have a duty to help them become more 'real' or more 'human'.

Research into the impact of religious education and citizenship education

Research by religious education specialists such as Rudge (1998, 2001, and in the Westhill Seminars), studying the impact of religious education and citizenship education, an impact promised by syllabuses and policy statements, suggests that account must be taken of the following five issues. Firstly, education programmes covering religious, moral and social issues *may or may not* have an effect on pupils' development. Their impact is worth questioning and cannot be taken for granted. Secondly, the religious education curriculum *may or may not* offer something of value to pupils of non-religious backgrounds. Descriptions of such pupils (terms such as 'dis-traditioned' or 'secular') will themselves need clarifying in order to answer the question. Thirdly, there are positives *and* negatives to be found in interreligious dialogue and encounter in the plural school (and all schools are plural). Dialogue is not a neutral process, and its positive impact should not be taken for granted. Fourthly, it *should be* possible for the non-religious to learn from the religious, and the religious to learn from the non-religious about values. Learning from religion is something broader than acquiring *knowledge*. Religious education may have a 'bias' towards the 'religious' as the norm, and in that way might differ from other curriculum subjects: this may be, and may be seen as, a hindrance for the subject. Fifthly, and finally, 'impact' is hard to define, track and record, and individual programmes do not happen in isolation, as all education is likely to have its own impact.

All of these issues come down, here, to two questions: what does religious education aim to do for pupils and society (and how is this known), and what effect does it have (and how is this known)? On the first question, of the aims of religious education, some answers are immediately accessible in government policy statements, inspection frameworks, syllabuses, school policies, classroom resources, published articles, and on professional association websites (accessible through www.REOnline.org.uk). The English and Welsh national framework (QCA 2004) says religious education 'actively promotes the values of truth, justice, respect for all and care of the environment'. It also 'places specific emphasis on pupils valuing themselves and others, the role of family and the community in religious belief and activity, the celebration of diversity in society through understanding similarities and differences, [and] sustainable development of the earth' (QCA 2004). Furthermore, religious education 'also recognises the changing nature of society, including changes in religious practice and expression, and the influence of religion in the local, national and global community'. The whole school curriculum 'should aim to provide opportunities for all pupils to learn and achieve', whilst religious education 'should be a stimulating, interesting and enjoyable subject' (all from QCA 2004). The document goes on to discuss pupils' self worth:

> The national framework aims to promote religious understanding, discernment and respect and challenge prejudice and stereotyping. ... A central concern of religious education is the promotion of each pupil's self-worth. A sense of self-worth helps pupils to reflect on their uniqueness as human beings, share their feelings and emotions with others and appreciate the importance of forming and maintaining positive relationships. (QCA 2004)

The 'learning about' and 'learning from' aspects of religious education, described in the national framework, owes a debt to the work of Grimmitt (1987, 2000), in describing learning *about* and learning *from* religion, and there is an assessment system including a 'levels' scale, with, for example, level 4 (expected of average 11 year olds) described as follows:

Attainment target 1
Pupils use a developing religious vocabulary to describe and show understanding of sources, practices, beliefs, ideas, feelings and experiences. They make links between them, and describe some similarities and differences both within and between religions. They describe the impact of religion on people's lives. They suggest meanings for a range of forms of religious expression.

Attainment target 2
Pupils raise, and suggest answers to, questions of identity, belonging, meaning, purpose, truth, values and commitments. They apply their ideas to their own and other people's lives. They describe what inspires and influences themselves and others. (QCA 2004)

These have many implications for secular pupils. Citizenship also has a transformatory aspect, transforming both pupils and society, although religion may in some ways be sidelined into narrow issues of personal identity and some community issues. In summary, the policy base for religious education does indeed expect religious education to have a specific impact on pupils' personal development.

A second research question would be to ask what effects or impact might religious education have, and how is this known? Whatever syllabuses say about the hoped-for impact of religious education, its actual impact needs separate study. Where there is a gap between the stated aims and the reality of religious education, this can lead to considerable frustration, especially if religious education gives the impression that it is easier to show respect for ancient religions, than it is to show respect for the current lives (including some of the religious lives) of today's pupils. In terms of academic performance, there is some evidence – albeit unclear evidence – in the inspection data. A recent English inspection report on religious education (Ofsted 2002), said that pupils' achievements 'remain disappointingly low', but attitudes remain at least 'satisfactory' in over nine in ten schools and 'very positive' in over seven in ten schools. The 'Making Religious Education Work' project (Bell 1999, Rudge 1998, and Zamorski 2000, also summarized in Rudge 2001) focused on three chronologically sequenced, overlapping, themes of the relevance of religious education to social justice, human rights and interreligious dialogue, in the UK; the tensions between local and national provision for religious education in the context of the standards agenda in the UK; and the emergence of citizenship education in the UK that itself questioned some of religious education's aims and outcomes. The research looked in enormous detail at the need for training, and more broadly the need for effective strategies to support schools and pupils. However, the related project on effective pedagogies for religious education (Agombar *et al.* from www.uea.ac.uk/care/nasc/ NASC_home.htm), the Norfolk Area Schools Consortium (NASC) study, gave a less promising view of UK religious education, citing religious education, along with business studies, economics, and personal, social and health education, as contributing to disaffection amongst school pupils. In summary, then, despite some evidence of relatively low standards, some evidence of a positive contribution to social justice, human rights and interreligious dialogue, and some approaches to pedagogy that might generate disaffection, there is mixed evidence on the impact of religious education. There is therefore plenty more for religious education researchers still to do in this field.

Pupils do value the opportunity to have a voice, and are indeed 'voiced' in the national framework document (QCA 2004). Pupil quotations on the value of religious education, taken from the PCfRE religious education festival database (available at www.pcfre. org.uk/db/), themselves can be researched, or the questions used for further research (as suggested in Weston 2003). The following work (derived from Stern 2006b) goes to the heart of the issue of the value of religious education, and helps give a voice to pupils. It asks pupils to consider the relative value of different subjects of the curriculum, assuming the whole curriculum is valued at 1,000 units, and asks pupils, further, to consider the basis of their decisions. For example, to what extent is the value intrinsic to the subject (the value of the subject in itself, for example in helping pupils develop their own ideas), and to what extent is the value extrinsic to the subject (the value of the subject for other purposes, for example in helping qualify pupils for a job)? More sophisticated analysis can be achieved if other characteristics are included on the response sheet, such as the age and gender of the respondent, and other social or religious characteristics. It could be used, for example, to analyse whether religiously active pupils set a higher value on religious education, as long as responses were suitably anonymous to avoid ethical research problems of requiring responses on issues that pupils may wish to keep private. A more sophisticated use of the exercise might involve more 'modelling', where one variable is changed in order to see the impact on other variables. For example, if religious education were abolished, which other subjects might increase their 'value' in order to compensate for this loss, and how would they change? Or, if religious education were to become the study of a single religion, what 'value' would it lose or gain? More informal 'modelling' of such a kind has been completed by Gearon (2004) modelling the curriculum in such a way as to emphasize the complementarity of religious education and citizenship, and Crick (2004) contesting that position in a review of the book (see also Lockyer *et al.* 2004).

Religion within citizenship and human rights education

One of the leading researchers on the interconnections between religious education, religion and citizenship education is Gearon (e.g. 2002a, 2002b, 2003a, 2003b, 2004, 2005, and in the Westhill Seminars). His work can be described in terms of religion's place in the world, its relationship to the United Nations and citizenship or human rights education, and the connections between religious education and citizenship or human rights education. He starts from the idea that religion's role in public and political life has been underplayed. Talk of 'secularization' has often meant that religion, in Western contexts since the eighteenth-century Enlightenment, has been pushed into the 'private' sphere. However, this appears to be changing as there is increasing evidence of the importance of religion in post-Cold War public and political life, often but not exclusively centring on issues of human rights, including freedom of religion or belief. The post-Cold War context is particularly important, with Bowker and Smart working on this since the 1960s, attacking the secularization thesis (well described in Smart's final book, Smart 1999). For example, in 1998 the US legislature passed the International Religious Freedom Act: a requirement for the US government to have a report on religious freedom every year (available on the Internet, in the US Department of State's website at www.state.gov/). Religious freedom is therefore seen as a barometer of wider freedoms, although this should not be regarded as uncontroversial.

The United Nations system incorporated and defined freedom of religion or belief since the 1948 UN Universal Declaration of Human Rights (see www.unhchr.ch/udhr/), but the early history of the UN tended, according to Gearon, to downplay religious and ideological diversity. The notion of 'universal' human rights itself may downplay diversity, as the universality of the declared rights itself seems to deny the specificity of religious context: the Declaration can in that sense be described as a 'humanist' text. However, it may be the religious contexts that provide, for many people, the reasons for having such rights. Freedom of religion and belief, incorporating non-religious beliefs, was eventually incorporated in the 1981 UN Declaration on the Elimination of All Forms of Intolerance and Discrimination Based on Religion or Belief (www.ohchr.org/english/law/religion.htm). This has meant that, after a long neglect or low level treatment of religion, the UN system from the late 1970s and with the 1981 Declaration began to recognize the international significance of religion for a stable world order. There is a UN Special Rapporteur on Religion and Belief, with that role having considerable relevance to education, including UNESCO, work (see www.unesco.org/). The 1992 UN Declaration on the Rights of Persons Belonging to National or Ethnic, Religious and Linguistic Minorities (www.ohchr.org/english/law/minorities.htm), is further evidence of a move to considering these issues as important, despite or perhaps related to the conflicts precisely over those issues in the 1990s.

It is worth considering, as a separate issue, the role of religion in civic education, citizenship, human rights education, as that has, according to Gearon, been significantly underplayed in the UK. The Crick Report (Crick 1998, and see also Lockyer *et al.* 2004) is evidence of this, although the English and Welsh national curriculum orders on citizenship (as described in DfEE and QCA 1999) slightly redresses that imbalance. Reflecting broader global trends, there is increasing recognition of the importance of religion in citizenship and human rights education, although the recognition of the importance of teaching about religion remains arguably less strong in civic or citizenship education than in religious education. Paul Marshall of Freedom House in the US (Marshall 2000, and on the web at www.freedomhouse.org/religion/), publishes on religious freedom in the world, with a slightly more objective approach to that of the US Department of State. He gives the US a top rating (i.e. 1), with the UK getting a lower grade (i.e. 2) (due to the establishment of the Church of England), Burma, Turkmenistan, China and Saudi Arabia getting lower grades (down to 7). There are major issues relating to apparently conflicting rights, such as religious rights perhaps being in conflict with other human rights. Gender is an important theme in this, as is the balance between freedom of expression and freedom of religion. The latter has recently been brought out in the conflicts in the UK over the play *Behzti* set in a Sikh gurdwara, and over the televizing of *Jerry Springer: The Opera* (both able to be investigated from, for example, www.guardianunlimited.co.uk/ with an archive of religion news at www.guardianunlimited.co.uk/religion).

This brings the research back to the issue of religious education and citizenship or human rights education. Religious education is a subject that often, understandably, stresses the positive in religions. That positive approach, however, is one that can lead to avoiding some of the more difficult issues, and so the political has often been underplayed in religious education, and contentious historical contexts have, according to Gearon, been sidestepped. For example, a Christian tradition of complicity in colonialism and imperialism is one such 'avoided' issue, with a stress instead on liberating and anti-establishment figures such as Oscar Romero. A similarly negative topic such as genocide is also useful as a case study for considering religion in its global context (as in Gearon 2005). From a religious and cultural perspective, genocide is important, as there are often religious and cultural bases to genocide (described for example in Power 2003, and see also Smith 2003). In 1948, the Universal Declaration of Human Rights was signed on 10 December, the day after the declaration on genocide. In other words, it was the context of genocide that set the scene for 'universal' human rights. Gearon 2005 follows this up, as does (in an applied approach) Gearon 2004. There is, according to Gearon, 'an increased emphasis on fostering tolerance and freedom of religion or belief through school education', and 'an increased emphasis on religion and culture in international politics'.

Case studies of citizenship work in religious education

Citizenship is integral to schooling, then, although it is not all that schools do. The question remains, whether schools are actually teaching citizenship, in any of the forms described here. One case study of such work brought together religious education, human rights, values and citizenships in a kind of model of the United Nations (and see also various Model United Nations projects such as that at www.un.org/cyberschoolbus/modelun/, and the description at en.wikipedia.org/wiki/Model_United_Nations). Pupils can take a position as if from within a nation state, and expand their horizons by listening to positions from other nation states, perhaps also gaining an understanding of how small the world is and that their humanity is as well described in universal as national terms. The pupils, in this case study aged 14 to 19, have countries or continents allocated to them, and each pupil (or group) is then to become a representative of that country. The task is to write a script for a United Nations speech on the significance of religion in their country, using information from one newspaper from that country, using that day's papers (from www.onlinenewspapers.com/). The reports could be word-processed, and the combination of all reports might be made into a big 'world newspaper' for the day, with added reportage on the debate to follow. Pupils continue the exercise by having a UN debate (also making use of www.undcp.org/unlinks.html or www.unsystem.org/), on the motion 'religion is the most important influence on the world today'. Pupils would take part in the debate, representing their countries and only able to speak 'in role', with a choice of for or against the motion, depending on their initial research on how important religion is in 'their' country.

A second case study reports some tentative research by the current author on responses school pupils gave to the PCfRE religious education festival database (www.pcfre.org.uk/db/, with further suggestions of use in Weston 2003, Fageant and Blaylock 1998, and Blaylock 2001a, 2001b). That questionnaire elicited 18,000 responses from across the UK, currently archived at Brunel University. Almost 10 per cent (1637 in all) were transcribed onto a database (which has not been published), with that database further edited and cleaned up and published on the Internet (at www.pcfre.org.uk/db). The research reported here quotes either from the original responses or (in most cases) from the first database. It is an unusually revealing account of young people's views. One of the questions in the questionnaire is in this form: *Religions sometimes teach their followers about freedom, truth, justice, love and forgiveness. Who has taught you about these things? What have you learned?* One 17 year old responded by saying

> Everybody who has come into contact with me has taught me about freedom, truth, justice, love and forgiveness in many different contexts. I have learned that everybody needs these factors in order to be in perfect harmony with themselves.

Incidentally, this same person referred to religious education in an interesting way:

> RE lessons give you the peace of mind in a world where peace and mind no longer go together.

These two responses start to address the two issues raised by the research: from whom do young people learn about freedom, truth, justice, love and forgiveness, and what is the role of schooling in this process?

An initial rough quantitative analysis was completed on a stratified random sample of 100 responses, 50 from pupils aged 7 to 11 in primary schools, 50 from pupils aged 11 to 19 in secondary schools. As pupils gave free text resonses, the totals for influences, identified by pupils, add up to more than 100 per cent. One 9 year old, for example, described four influences by saying *I lurned by my Mum and family and teachers i had lurned of the Bible about freedom, truth, justice, love and forgiveness.* It appears that pupils aged 7 to 11 in primary schools feel they learned about these things mostly from their family (24 responses, from the 50 pupils), then from school (19 responses, for example *School has taught me thing about RE The teachers have taught me everything I know which is a lot* and the slightly more critical *I have been learned by teachers that are good teachers*), and to a lesser extent from religious groups, sacred texts, people, or divine beings (9 responses), and very little from friends, other people, or other books (only 1 response for each of those categories, although one lucidly said *People have taught me about the truth – it helps if you do tell the truth*), and none from television. Pupils aged 11 to 19 in secondary schools prioritized family even more (39 responses, although the responses were often qualified, as in *My parents have taught me lots but I have also learnt alot on the walk of life* or *My family have taught me these things but I can't say exactly what I have learned because its lots of little things*), and rather downplayed the influence of school (11 responses). These secondary pupils also said religious groups, sacred texts, people, or divine beings had some influence (7 responses, for example *God has taught me about love, justice and freedom and god has taught me this*), and there was a little more influence of television (2 responses) and other books (4 responses). The big difference between primary and secondary school respondents, however, is in the older pupils' perception of learning from friends (4 responses) and even more, learning from 'experience' (11 responses, such as *I have learnt these things though my journey of life* or *I've learnt by myself, no one can teach you stuff like you have to learn by experiences, by yourself*). On the other hand, a number felt they had learned little, in the words of one respondent *Nothing Smeg all*, or as another said, rather sadly, *I don't think any one has told me anything like this*.

This tentative initial analysis suggests four kinds of answers to the two initial questions of who taught and what might be the role of schools. The first is that family is seen by pupils as most influential, across the ages. Although this might be unsurprising for younger pupils, the continuing influence may be more interesting. Certainly, the significance of family has implications for schools in involving parents in schooling (as in Stern 2003), and in setting appropriate homework that captures what happens in homes rather than simply imposing the school on the home (with this debate continued in Chapter 13 below, and in Stern 2006a). It also clearly complements Macmurray's view that the 'school community stands between family and the wider community and looks back to the first and forward to the second' (Macmurray 1968, p. 35).

A second answer to the initial questions relates to how pupils describe the importance of school in teaching them about freedom, truth, justice, love and forgiveness. The perceived influence of school is lower for older than younger pupils, yet is still of some significance. It might have been expected that school would have been seen as more important for older pupils, and especially more important relative to family, and yet this was not the case. With respect to topics and issues regarded as more closely associated with school subjects, the responses might have followed this pattern. Perhaps the responses therefore indicate how freedom, truth, justice, love and forgiveness are not associated with school subjects. The questionnaire was completed prior to the introduction to citizenship as a compulsory school subject in England and Wales, so there is a question as to whether pupils would respond in the same way after that curriculum change from 2002, and yet this should not be regarded as the most significant change, as citizenship was still a part of the statutory curriculum from 1988 as a 'cross-curricular theme'. Rather, the declining influence of school indicates how important it is for schools to make their teaching relevant to such issues. It is an argument for raising the status of such important issues, and the subjects supporting them such as religious education, citizenship and personal and social education. In these ways, Macmurray's claim is supported that '[w]e may act as though we were teaching arithmetic or history ... [i]n fact we are teaching *people*' (Macmurray 1968, p. 5).

A third item worth considering is friendship. It is not surprising that friends or peers (as pupils did not appear to regard teachers as Macmurrian 'friends') are perceived to have more influence on older than younger pupils, but it is a little surprising that they appear less important than other influences, with only 4 out of 50 secondary pupils identifying friends as teaching them about these issues. It might be that, as the question asks 'who taught you' rather than 'who influenced you', it is entirely possible that this would lead to an exaggeration of the influence of those identified as 'teachers', and an underestimate of the influence of friends not identified in that way. The fourth aspect of the responses to be considered is the relatively high number of older pupils who talked about learning from themselves or 'experience', as in the quoted example of the pupil who said *I have learnt these things though my journey of life* or *I've learnt by myself, no one can teach you stuff like you have to learn by experiences, by yourself.* Pupils who perceive their own learning about freedom in this way need to be engaged in schools in a way that exploits such experiential learning. Having engaging and experiential learning may seem like an obvious approach to schooling, but it is by no means universal. There is a 'Campaign for Real Education', for example, which suggests that the curriculum 'should be subject-centred' rather than 'child-centred and relevant' (Campaign for Real Education 2001). Similarly, Armstrong gives an account of US fundamentalists campaigning against 'open-ended questions that require students to draw their own conclusions' (Armstrong 2000, p. 315). As well as such explicit opponents of pupil-centred learning, schooling that is dominated by external targets – such as exam results – can all too easily become less experiential and more didactic, simply through being distracted from the real purpose of education. As Macmurray said, perhaps with even greater relevance for today's schooling than for 1931 when originally published, there is a danger that '[t]he golden aim of education – to teach the children how to live, has vanished over the horizon – crowded out by a multiplicity of little aims' (Macmurray 1968, p. 114).

Overall, the pupil responses give a good idea of what might be important to consider, when planning to prepare pupils for learning about freedom. Very little mention was made by pupils of learning from television or other media, or people encountered through those media, whilst family and school encounters loom large. There is a job to be done by schools, and from this analysis, it looks like it could be done.

Conclusion

Religious education is of necessity controversial, and yet religious education teachers in the UK and elsewhere are often defensive about the subject. It might be appropriate to think of how religious education can be more confident, and tackle the difficult issues. When someone complains to a religious education teacher, 'but religions have caused most of the world's wars and terrorism', the answer need not be 'no, that is not real religion'. The answer could be 'yes, and that is why it is worth studying, and why it is worth getting people together from different religious and non-religious traditions to discuss and argue about these very issues'. There are various aspects of religious education, human rights, values and citizenship that can be illuminated by research, with the research drawing on a wide variety of disciplines. From research on world politics and the impact of religious education described in this chapter, it is clear that religious education needs all the researchers it can get in the classroom. Despite the enormous range of skills of full-time professional researchers working on religious education – many of whom are represented in this book – it is only if religious education teachers and pupils are themselves involved in research, that the full potential of research to support the subject can be exploited. Particular approaches to research, involving teachers and pupils as researchers, and putting research at the centre of religious education, is therefore described in Chapter 14 below.

Section C: Learning, research and practice: schools and religions with attitude

Or perhaps he does not know!

Rig-Veda (X, cxxix) in Zaehner 1992, p. 14

This third section reviews the theorizing of the first section of the book, in the light of religious education as described in the second section. In a book subtitled 'imagining the real', a systematic attempt is made to describe creativity in schools and religions, informed by religious education. In a book linking schools and religions, the work of schools transcending themselves, connecting schools, communities and the rest of the world, is described and analysed. By analysing the structures and boundaries of schools, hierarchical and divided as they can be, the relationship between schools and broader political structures is clarified, in the light of the citizenship education addressed in Chapter 10 above. The book concludes, however, with a call for research of particular kinds, ethnographic and sincere, as ways towards truth. Schools can develop themselves as learning communities, drawing on and engaging with a variety of religious and political ways of living. A school need not be, in Buber's terms, an 'animated clod without soul', and can be understood through research. With respect to creativity, the relationship to the rest of the world, hierarchies, and research, the common theme is attitude: schools and religions have 'attitude' and proper attitudes take them a long way towards a better future. The book is, in the end, 'a philosophical and methodological analysis that aims to support a humane, social-justice orientation for educational organizations, ... and the research conducted in and about them' (Milley 2002, p. 47). This approach is based on the mutuality of schooling, in which '[t]he true teacher is not the one who pours information into the student's head as through a funnel – the old-fashioned "disciplined" approach – or the one who regards all potentialities as already existing within the student and needing only to be pumped up – the newer "progressive" approach'. Instead, '[i]t is the one who fosters genuine mutual contact and mutual trust, who experiences the other side of the relationship, and who helps his pupils realize, through the selection of the effective world, what it can mean to be a man [*sic*] ... [as a]ll education worthy of the name is education of character' (Friedman in Buber 2002a, p. xviii). Friedman concludes that the 'education of character takes place through the encounter with the image of man that the teacher brings before the pupil in the material he presents and in the way he stands behind this material' (Friedman in Buber 2002a, p. xviii).

This is a version of schooling that is not dogmatic, and yet does not 'surrender before the orgy of tolerance' (Eco 2004, p. 428).

> Our institutions, to the extent that they address issues of learning explicitly, are largely based on the assumption that learning is an individual process, that it has a beginning and an end, that it is best separated from the rest of our activities, and that it is the result of teaching. ... To assess learning we use tests with which students struggle in one-on-one combat, where knowledge must be demonstrated out of context, and where collaborating is considered cheating. As a result, much of our institutionalised teaching and training is perceived by would-be learners as irrelevant, and most of us come out of this treatment feeling that learning is boring and arduous, and that we are not really cut out for it.
>
> So, what if we adopted a different perspective, one that placed learning in the context of our lived experience of participation in the world? What if we assumed that learning is as much a part of our human nature as eating or sleeping, that it is both life-sustaining and inevitable, and that – given a chance – we are quite good at it? And what if, in addition, we assumed that learning is, in its essence, a fundamentally social phenomenon, reflecting our own deeply social nature as human beings capable of knowing? (Wenger 1998, p. 3)

The 'what if?' is answered here. Here, the philosophy is informed by the school-based research, to make for action philosophy.

Chapter 11

Creativity and creation: beyond the cuckoo clock

These are days when no one should rely unduly on his "competence". Strength lies in improvisation.
All the decisive blows are struck left-handed.

(Benjamin 1997, p. 49)

Introduction: a dialogue of creation

To be engaged in dialogue requires imagination, imagining the real, as described in Chapters 2 and 8. Dialogue is central to schooling, and its imaginative requirement rightly signals a relationship with what is called 'creativity'. The history of the use of the term 'creativity' is complex, and the current chapter attempts to theorize creativity in education, drawing on the broader literature on creativity and creation whilst focusing on further developing those elements of educational theory described in Section A, in the light of accounts of research on religious education in Section B. The contexts in which this is set will be contemporary policy on creativity in education, notably the current UK government policy dominated by the document developed by Robinson (DfEE 1999), and a range of religious and philosophical responses to creation, creativity and human nature. It is the variety of voices in dialogue that can be heard in religious education, that can also characterize creative education more generally. Ways of imagining and creating in community are described, using music in religious education, and this in turn can enable a kind of imagined world, a world of globalized learning far from Ritzer's 'McDonaldized' learning (see Ritzer 2004, Wilkinson 2006).

The presence and absence of creativity

'First things first', Boden starts: '[h]uman creativity is something of a mystery, not to say a paradox ... [as o]ne new idea may be creative, while another is merely new' (Boden 2004, p. 1). Boden goes on to puzzle over what the difference is between the creative and the merely new, how creativity is possible, and indeed how something truly new can be created. It is an ancient question, and religious creation narratives are full of mystery. Buber insists that creation as a 'magic trick' was developed 'falsely by later theology in the language of bad philosophy', whilst the original biblical account starts 'wholly in mystery' (Buber 2002a, p. 224). In the Hindu tradition, the Rig-Veda (X, cxxix) account of creation ends

> Whence this emanation hath arisen,
> Whether God created it, or whether he did not, –
> Only he who is its overseer in highest heaven knows.
> He only knows, or perhaps he does not know! (Zaehner 1992, p. 14)

If creativity and creation are mysteries, the absence of creativity in creation is just as much of a mystery. This is exemplified in debates over evolution by natural selection. Darwin described the possibility of a mindless, purposeless, process that apparently led to the development of complex organic structures (Darwin 1971), and realized the power of such argument in religious debates when he wrote in 1880 that '[i]t seems to me (rightly or wrongly) that direct arguments against Christianity and Theism hardly have any effect on the public; and that freedom of thought will best be promoted by that gradual enlightening of human understanding which follows the progress of science ... [so] I have therefore always avoided writing about religion and have confined myself to science' (quoted in Gould 1977, pp. 26–7).

Balancing the 'truly creative' and 'serendipitous chance' also informs debates on the possible differences between human creativity and computer creativity, as noted by Craft (Craft *et al.* 2001, p. 57). True creativity must surely involve some kind of intention or purpose, as in Buber's vivid account of how '[c]reation happens to us, burns itself into us, recasts us in burning – we tremble and are faint, we submit', continuing that '[w]e take part in creation, meet the Creator, reach out to Him, helpers and companions' (Buber 1958, p. 108). That is a rather dangerous kind of creativity, and danger is rarely absent from accounts of creativity, even in sober accounts of creativity in education. '[S]ome of the characteristics of creative teaching and learning are also acknowledged as being potentially dangerous ... [so] it is less easy to convince politicians and policy-makers that creative teaching and learning, which might also involve questioning current perspectives and practices, is beneficial to society, in spite of an economic discourse that, to some considerable extent, demands it' (Craft *et al.* 2001, p. 9, and see also chapter 1 of the same book by Joubert). It is the association of creativity with danger that inspired Graham Greene's infamous account in the film *The Third Man*:

> In Italy for thirty years under the Borgias they had warfare, terror, murder, bloodshed – but they produced Michelangelo, Leonardo da Vinci, and the Renaissance. In Switzerland they had brotherly love, 500 years of democracy and peace, and what did that produce? The cuckoo clock. (Greene 1949)

Notwithstanding the incorrect attribution of the invention of the cuckoo clock to Switzerland (in fact it was invented in Schönwald im Schwarzwald, Germany, en.wikipedia.org/wiki/Cuckoo_clock), the point is worth making that creativity can be generated by conflict at least as much as by its absence. The development of risk-averseness in education policy, an apparently benign development, can in its application work against creativity, in a way that might be recognized by Craft and even Greene. For example, the education, health and social care policy in the UK currently brought together by the policy known as Every Child Matters (DfES 2004a), requires public services help children 'stay safe', and that there should be public intervention not only 'where families are facing difficulties' but also where 'children might experience risk' (DfES 2004b, p. 27, and see also Stern and James 2006). In such a risk-averse culture, it seems less likely that creativity will be able to be promoted as effectively. For Buber, this is a religious as well as educational issue, given his belief that all take part in creation, and that therefore '[c]reation is not a hurdle on the road to God, it is the road itself' (Buber 2002a, p. 60). Human life is created not by feelings or by institutions, but by 'the central presence of the *Thou*, or rather ... by the central *Thou* that has been received in the present' (Buber 1958, p. 66). People take part in creation, then, in dialogue, in between, in the *Thou*. Such creativity is not an 'anything goes' creativity, but a disciplined one. There is a long history in Chinese education of using calligraphy, including copying out classic texts, to understand and make connection with people from the past (as described in Wong 2006). Copying and also memorizing texts are embedded in other religious and educational traditions, and may at times be used as mindless time-fillers (as described in Murphy 1999, p. 202). However, the disciplined, creative and spiritual potential of copying should be recognized, as it is by the cultural theorist Benjamin. He says that the difference between copying a text and reading it, is like the difference between walking along a road and flying over it by aeroplane. Whereas from the air, someone sees how the road travels through the landscape, but '[o]nly he who walks the road on foot learns of the power it commands, and of how, from the very scenery that for the flier is only the unfurled plain, it calls forth distances, belvederes, clearings, prospects at each of its turns like a commander deploying soldiers at a front' (Benjamin 1997, p. 50). It is therefore the copied text that 'commands the soul of him who is occupied with it', which is why, he says, copying books is so important to China – as 'an incomparable guarantee of literary culture', so that copying is 'a key to China's enigmas' (Benjamin 1997, p. 50).

Benjamin's views on writing are complemented by his views on reading. Indeed, his is one of the best descriptions of the creativity of reading by children, as children, he says, are amongst the most creative of readers:

> *Child reading* – You are given a book from the school library. In the lower classes they are simply handed out. Only now and again do you dare to express a wish. Often, in envy, you see coveted books pass into other hands. At last desire was granted. For a week you were wholly given up to the soft drift of the text, that surrounded you as secretly, densely and unceasingly as snowflakes. You entered it with limitless trust. The peacefulness of the book that enticed you further and further! Its contents did not much matter. For you were reading at the time when you still made up stories in bed. The child seeks his way along the half-hidden paths. Reading, he covers his ears; the book is on a table that is far too high, and one hand is always on the page. To him the

hero's adventures can still be read in the swirling letters like figures and messages in drifting snowflakes. His breath is part of the air of the events narrated, and all the participants breathe with his life. He mingles with the characters far more closely than grown-ups do. He is unspeakably touched by the deeds, the words that are exchanged, and, when he gets up, is blanched over and over by the snow of his reading. (Benjamin 1997, pp. 71–2)

A burning, risky creativity that is embedded in everyday activities, even those as apparently 'ordinary' as copying or reading, is needed in schooling, and its absence would be a sign of anti-educational schooling.

Agency, originality and value

Developing and implementing a policy on creativity may seem like a risky business itself, but Robinson and colleagues were commissioned to investigate educational creativity, and their work led to the UK's current influential policy on creativity (DfEE 1999). That policy identifies four characteristics of creativity, 'thinking or behaving *imaginatively* ... [in an activity that] is *purposeful*: that is, it is directed to achieving an objective ... [, and] these processes must generate something *original* ... [and] the outcome must be of *value* in relation to the objective' (DfEE 1999, p. 29). Other charactistics identified by the authors in Craft *et al.* 2001 (some of whom were also co-authors of DfEE 1999), are 'control, ownership, relevance and innovation (Woods); imaginative activity to produce outcomes both of originality and of value (Joubert); possibility thinking and problem-posing (Craft); seeing, thinking, inventing and questioning (Lucas); mindful learning (Safran); knowledge from society, self-confidence from social situations and time to play (Boden); risk-taking (Joubert)' (Craft *et al.* 2001, p. 2). These two lists of creative characteristics seem to be able to be captured by three concepts: *agency, originality* and *value*.

Agency implies creativity as making, that is, a generative or spontaneous in contrast to a passive or externally-directed process. The degree of agency is indicated by the nature and degree of a person's responsibility and purposes. It does not rule out collective responsibility. For many years, people have tended to think of artists, musicians and designers as individual creative spirits, and products as easily attributable to such single geniuses. This belies the co-operative creativity of past times and other cultures, such as the emergence and development of folk songs, vernacular architecture, or decorative sculptures on medieval cathedrals (as described in Stern 2006a, pp. 79–90). It also belies the co-operative nature of much of what is thought of as 'solo' creativity, with debates over the contributions of uncredited painters in ceramic workshops of 'names' like Clarice Cliff, or the influence of producers and session musicians on 'stars' like Lennon and McCartney. The co-operative creativity demonstrated here is not a problem (unless you are the person being accused of being less of a genius), but an opportunity, a potential strength, and it can play a big role in the way in which art, music and design and technology are taught, and how homework can be set. Looking for co-operation can mean creating a sense of collaborative and communal endeavour, critical for a school's own inclusiveness. For example, a car will have been developed by a team including specialists in manufacturing, in electrical systems, in design aesthetics, in aerodynamics, in economics, in marketing, and many more processes; a house will have been developed by a team including specialists in surveying, in materials, in architecture, in marketing, and many more processes. The teacher should choose one type of object, and work with the pupils in class to analyse the different people involved in developing that object. For homework, the pupils should be put into groups and given each of these roles, with the task being to come up with a co-operatively-produced design for a product. In these ways, pupils can come to understand that creativity may 'belong . . . in "communities" rather than residing entirely in the individual' (Craft *et al.* 2001, p. 11), and creative acts may 'necessarily involve being "in relationship" with someone or something, or both – one cannot be creative with respect to nothing' (Craft *et al.* 2001, p. 55).

The second of the three concepts, *originality*, implies a novel in contrast to a copied, imitated or routine process, related to context: that is, the relationship of the process to other processes known to the person. It is hard to see originality as an absolute quality, at least as it applies to human endeavour. Being 'absolutely original' has little meaning, as all products or processes will have something in common with what has gone before. Rather, there is a continuum, so that something can be more or less original. As Boden notes, 'new' may be 'new with respect to the whole of human history' or 'new with respect to the person's previous ways of thinking' (Craft *et al.* 2001, p. 95). The determination of originality will be part of the process of understanding the person, the immediate context, the communities to which the person belongs, and broader social and historical contexts, and will be entirely dependent on the choice of the scope of context. Within schools, originality can be understood socially, by pupils and staff sharing and discussing the creative work completed. It is through others commenting on the originality of a piece of work that a person can immediately understand how distinctive the work is; simple social affirmation, such as displaying work on classroom walls, can affirm the degree of originality within the school context.

If agency is difficult to determine, especially for an individual involved in a collective activity, and originality depends on what context is decided upon, *value*, the third key concept, is even more problematic. For Boden, '[b]ecause creativity *by definition* involves not only novelty but value, and because values are highly variable, it follows that many arguments about creativity are rooted in disagreements about value' (Boden 2004, p. 10). Value is embedded within the concept of agency, in the sense that a person's responsibility is itself implied by the person being in a position to make evaluative judgements. It is also embedded in originality, in the sense that the scope of originality can also determine the degree of value: a work of art by a six year old may be said to be 'beautiful' for that child, whose originality is likely to be small scale (i.e. original for that child, rather than for a broader social group or historical period), but may be said to be less 'beautiful' when set in a broader group. 'Beauty has never been absolute and immutable but has taken on different aspects depending on the historical period and the country: and this does not hold only for physical Beauty (of men, of women, of the landscape) but also for the Beauty of God, or the saints, or ideas' (Eco 2004, p. 14). As Joubert says, 'there may be differences between the evaluation of the creator and others' (Craft *et al.* 2001, p. 21). She continues that '[t]here may also be cultural differences regarding creativity and its evaluative judgement ... It is thus important to also make use of peer review and self-evaluation by pupils, as this may produce a variety of value judgements, contributing to an evaluation profile' (Craft *et al.* 2001, p. 21).

Those teaching religion will be particularly sensitive to the variety of value judgements that must be encompassed by the study of religion, as well as the religious issues of agency and originality. Eco worryingly concludes his study of beauty, for example, by saying that people can 'no longer ... identify the aesthetic ideal diffused by the mass media of the twentieth century and beyond ... [so] will have to surrender before the orgy of tolerance, the total syncretism and the absolute and unstoppable polytheism of Beauty' (Eco 2004, p. 428). How can these insights, and these concerns, be used in education? In the following section, the implications of creativity for schooling in general are complemented by a case study of creativity in religious education.

Creativity in schools and religious education

Creativity involves agency, originality and value, and is not restricted to individuals but implies dialogic communal endeavour, as 'creativity arises out of a spirit of friendship characterized by dialogue rather than debate ... [and] arises from the generative or more specifically the implicate order' (Craft *et al.* 2001, p. 142). It is at the heart of schooling and indeed the heart of humanity. Creativity has a history of being implicated in human nature, and this history runs through political and psychoanalytical traditions. For Marx and Engels, people 'begin to distinguish themselves from animals as soon as they begin to *produce* their means of subsistence, a step which is conditioned by their physical organisation ... [so a]s individuals express their life, so they are ... [and w]hat they are, therefore, coincides with their production, both with *what* they produce and with *how* they produce' (Marx and Engels 1970, p. 42). For the psychoanalyst Hillman, '[w]e need to talk of the work instinct, not the work ethic, and instead of putting work with the superego we need to imagine it as an id activity, like a fermentation, something going on instinctively, autonomously, like beer works, like bread works' (Hillman 1990, p. 171, and see also Bleakley 2004). These complement Buber's religious view that creation is the 'road to God' (from Buber 2002a, p. 60, quoted above), and that creativity is central to humanity and therefore central to the education of children. In a presentation to a conference on 'the development of the creative powers in the child', he notes that '[e]veryone is elementally endowed with the basic powers of the arts, with that of drawing, for instance, or of music; these powers have to be developed, and the education of the whole person is to be built up on them as on the natural activity of the self' (Buber 2002a, p. 100). This 'basic power' is described as 'an autonomous instinct, which cannot be derived from others, whose appropriate name seems to me to be the "originator instinct"' (Buber 2002a, p. 100).

Within schooling, then, creativity must be recognized and positively supported, as '[w]hat the child desires is its own share in this becoming of things: it wants to be the subject of this event of production' (Buber 2002a, p. 100), so '[r]eal education is made possible ... by the realization that youthful spontaneity must not be suppressed but must be allowed to give what it can' (Buber 2002a, p. 104). Macmurray, more closely involved in the everyday activities of schools (as a school governor for many years), described in more detail the role of creativity in the curriculum.

> I would seek to use the normal and necessary subjects and disciplines of any curriculum as a medium for the development of spontaneity of feeling and imagination; within an atmosphere of positive community and co-operation. History, for example, can be taught as an exercise in intellectual technique which extends the range of knowledge and understanding. But is can also be used as an instrument of imaginative self-transcendence and of emotional expression. It can be dramatised and re-enacted; not merely in the mind. In this way it becomes a medium of cultural development. (Macmurray 1968, p. 44)

Creativity in this way involves making meaning as well as making artefacts. This is a communal process in which teachers as well as pupils are creating and creative. The term 'constructivism', applied to a set of learning theories, also captures the generative nature of teaching and learning: 'the work of a genuine teacher can never be stereotyped or routine; the teacher's work always carries a profoundly creative character' (Daniels 2001, p. 29, quoting Davydov). An absence of creative teaching and learning is dangerous for schools, especially for schools as learning communities. For Fielding, schools have little to say about community, and '[s]chool effectiveness and school improvement are moribund categories of a frightened, unimaginative society that values control over creativity, a society whose priorities and dispositions lie in the stultifying language of audit and the tyranny of targets' (Fielding 1999, p. 75–6, and see Fielding 2000, 2001).

A more positive view is given by McCarthy. For him, the policy framework in the UK supporting creativity has a similar role to the even longer-established policy commitment in the UK to spiritual development in schools. Indeed, one of the key policy documents on spiritual development explicitly links the two traditions, noting that amongst the 'many aspects of spiritual development' are 'Creativity – Expressing innermost thoughts and feelings through, for example, art, music, literature and crafts; exercising the imagination, inspiration, intuition and insight' (SCAA 1995, p. 3–4). McCarthy links them in other ways, too, as '[t]he literature of each is full of paradox and ambiguity, of gaining and losing the self, of uncertainty and complexity and mystery' (McCarthy in Craft *et al.* 2001,

p. 129). Each involves search and journeying, each has 'moments of illumination'. 'And beyond the inspirational "moment in the rose garden", each has traditions of disciplined apprenticeship, lifetimes of dedication to the patient and steady working out of the "craft"' (McCarthy in Craft *et al.* 2001, p. 129). Creativity and spiritual development each also 'has its altered states of consciousness, its crossing of the threshold from the daily experience, a liminal quality' (McCarthy in Craft *et al.* 2001, p. 129). It is in the school subject of religious education that McCarthy finds most hope for both creativity and spiritual development. In religious education, there are many possibilities for creativity, notably when there is

> an emphasis [placed] ... on *the variety of languages which give expression to this experience.* There is the creative linguistic expression of song, poem or story; the artistic expression through music or drawing; the physical expression of dance and drama. It is an approach which embraces the *interconnectedness of our knowledge,* crossing the artificiality of subjects. (McCarthy in Craft *et al.* 2001, p. 139)

Music in religious education

Taking up McCarthy's reference to music, this case study of the use of music in religious education (adapted in part from Stern 2004) describes some of the creative processes used by religious education teachers of pupils of all ages, working with pupils of a very wide range of abilities. It is a description of religious education as a vital subject in the inclusion of pupils and staff alike, as it brings together ways of life and communities, the personal and the social. The work investigates ways of 'marking time', understanding and celebrating times and events in schools. Music, embedded in religious and other ways of life, here adds a communicative dimension that strengthens inclusive religious education and intercultural communication, including communication of the most ineffable kind – as Aldous Huxley noted, 'after silence that which comes nearest to expressing the inexpressible is music' (Huxley 1931, p. 19). Religious education with music can be used as a form of community-making, engaging the imagination to such an extent that pupils, teachers and all members of school communities can, in Buber's words, 'imagine the real'. Musical creativlty in religious education can therefore support the creation of people-in-communities, using imagination to re-make the world.

Seeing schools as particular kinds of learning communities can help determine the nature of teaching and learning, providing as it does a focus on meaningful dialogue and treating people as complete or 'whole' human beings rather than as means to some external ends. Or, as Blue Murder (for example) sing, from a Christian perspective, *No One Stands Alone* (Blue Murder 2002). Teachers of religious education and other subjects have sometimes said that they envy those teaching music (as in Stern 1998), as music teachers have opportunities to work through a medium that can appeal so directly to pupils' sensibilities. Yet religious education should be doing this, too, and music of religions and other worldviews can therefore be at the heart of the religious education curriculum. There is a comparison by Jackson of learning music and phenomenological approaches to learning religion (Jackson 1997, pp. 20–1). In religious education, pupils are expected to 'learn about' religions and other worldviews, and also 'learn from' religion and other worldviews (QCA 2004). Similarly, in music, pupils are expected not only to 'learn about' music, but also 'explore their thoughts and feelings through responding physically, intellectually and emotionally to a variety of music from different times and cultures' (DfEE and QCA 1999). This dual nature of both subjects is itself an indication of how important dialogue – as defined by Buber and others – is to these subjects. Dialogue requires an engagement of the full person with another person, rather than the passive or functional 'speaking and listening' (or their musical equivalents) that pass for communication in so many contexts. Sennett explains respect in a world of inequality through the analogy of music.

> When I first began to play chamber music, my teacher ordered me to respect the other players without ... explaining what she meant. But musicians learn to do so, usually by using their ears rather than words. (Sennett 2003, pp. 50)

> I don't suggest accepting or accommodating inequality; rather, I argue that in social life as in art, mutuality requires expressive work. It must be enacted, performed. (Sennett 2003, p. 59)

The engagement, through the use of music in religious education, is with communities, not simply individuals, and music marking special times – festivals, ceremonies, and so on – are by their nature communal expressions, expressions of communal memory and belief. Jim Copper, a member of the well-known family of folk singers, describes the significance of singing well:

> When we looked down from those old hills, we saw nothing but farmland, the white cliffs and the sea. Now it's houses, houses, houses on the land that we used to plough. I don't like it. In fact, there's only one thing that's come through from my young days unchanged, and that's our old songs. My brother John, who used to be a shepherd, and his son Ron, and me and my son Bob, we still have a good old sing together when we get the chance. (Jim Copper in 1951, in Engle and Hall 2001)

Hence, the use of music in religious education can support both learning about, learning from, and indeed *making* communities. That is, religious education, using music, can be comprehensively inclusive, can make the very community that school should and can be. The role of music in schooling, explored since Aristotle (as in Aristotle 1962, pp. 301–3 and 305–16) is well described by Deal in terms of the creation of culture (in Bacharach and Mundell 1995). Macmurray referred to music as 'an instrument for the exploration of all possible worlds' (quoted in Warren 1989), with the ability to 'explore' being a central theme in access and inclusion. He also approvingly quotes Browning 'The rest may reason, and welcome: 'tis we musicians know' (in Macmurray 1991a, p. 42).

Similarly, the *Oxford Dictionary of World Religions* describes music in religion particularly lucidly, as having 'powers to alter and match moods, to sustain and evoke emotion, to induce trance or ecstasy states, to express worship, and to entertain', whilst being 'supremely a corporate activity: it not only binds together performers and audience, it is an activity in which many people can be engaged at once' (Bowker 1997, p. 667). Indeed, '[i]n India, sound itself (sabda, Om, ॐ) is the sacred source of all appearance: music therefore has the capacity to articulate the order and ordering of the cosmos' (Bowker 1997, pp. 667–8).

Further, music can have a distinctive role in multi-religious and multicultural contexts. On 'what difference does plurality make', one suggestion of Rüppell and Schreiner relates to music. They say that '[m]ost people find music as an easier way of entering into religious traditions other than their own ... [and m]usic, whatever the tradition may be, draws people into an experience of community and togetherness'. Whereas the words of religions may divide, '[p]eople feel drawn to one another in powerful ways through music' (Rüppell and Schreiner 2003, p. 165). It is worth investigating the musical contributions to each of the religious traditions studied in school, as well as the contribution of people's 'musical intelligence' (as in Gardner 1993, p. 9 and *passim*) to their overall learning. These contributions are hugely varied within as well as between religions, and music may be used to explore a huge range of religious concepts or theories or rituals or themes. On the topic of death, for example, the Sikh *Guru Granth Sahib* links music and life, in a hymn that includes these lines by Kabeer contemplating death:

> In the past, I have taken many forms, but I shall not take form again. The strings and wires of the musical instrument are worn out, and I am in the power of the Lord's Name. Now, I no longer dance to the tune [of Maya]. My mind no longer beats the drum. (Guru Granth Sahib, pp. 482–3)

Perhaps this could also be compared to Wordsworth's 'still, sad music of humanity' (from *Tintern Abbey*). As well as concepts and rituals, music may be used to express emotions, relevant to religious education, and it may be used to make beliefs public – as in the large body of 'protest' songs.

Story-telling, central to religious education and to all religious traditions, is often best done with or through music. Some musical traditions are particularly prone to story-telling, and these can be exploited in religious education, whether or not they have explicitly religious origins. A piece of music like Bach's *St Matthew Passion* tells a story as powerfully as any in the history of Christianity. A narrative like that of Psalm 137 (people unable to sing in a 'strange land', as presented by Attia 1994, or as sung by Sweet Honey in the Rock 1988) tells a memorable and striking tale important to Jewish, Christian and other diaspora and 'minority' traditions. As Nesbitt says, based on her extensive research with young people and adults, '[m]usic is recurrently mentioned by young people of different faith backgrounds in connection with heightened awareness and wellbeing' (Nesbitt 2004, p. 131), and '[y]oung people's – and their elders' – accounts of the benefits of singing together are a reminder that spirituality is not only individual but requires involvement in a community with a shared spiritual focus' (Nesbitt 2004, p. 132).

Music can be used in religious education to develop a whole range of skills (as identified in SCAA 1994a, b) such as investigation, interpretation, reflection, empathy, evaluation, analysis, synthesis, application and expression. Starting with the skill of *investigation*, the teacher might find music to suit particular situations, or perhaps investigate distinct traditions of religious music, or attitudes to music of believers and non-believers. For example, a teacher might choose a religion and an event or time such as dawn, afternoon, evening, spring, summer, autumn, winter, birth celebration, coming of age, marriage or funeral. Play one track of music, and get pupils to provide other tracks from any suitable tradition to complement or extend this track. A piece of 'winter' music such as *Souling Song* or *Wassailing* (The Watersons *et al.* 1996) could be complemented by pupils choosing other winter or Christmas music to match the season. Similarly, one of the 'afternoon ragas' (Ghosh *et al.* 1987) might be played each afternoon, with a discussion of the appropriateness of that music and other pieces to suit the time of day. It is worth noting how effective it can be to repeat a piece of music for particular occasions in the school day and year – both school events and religious, seasonal and other calendered occasions and festivals. To repeat music, from particular traditions, at certain times of the day, term and year, is itself a critical form of education for all pupils, that can be participated in and understood by pupils with an enormously wide range of needs. Just as Benjamin and Wong, referred to above, stress the value of copying texts, repeating music encourages a deeper engagement in the tradition. There are many older people who have been through the UK education system, whose only memory of religion is a memory of hymns, and it is often those hymns that are then chosen for adult ceremonies such as weddings and funerals. There are good educational critiques of the use of hymns in compulsory collective school worship (such as Hull 1975, Cush 1994), but the power of the music itself is nonetheless remarkable.

When considering *interpretation*, pupils can explore how music may add to or perhaps change the meaning of religious texts, looking at different settings of the same text. Pupils might listen to two pieces of music on a theme, and justify attaching one of a list of words such as contemplative, stimulating, anxious, threatening, happy, sad, exciting, resigned, angry, frightened, cold, peaceful, relaxed, busy, safe, beautiful and interesting (related to the account given in Chapter 8 above, applying adjectives to places). *Reflection* has always been a popular activity in both religious and musical traditions, and, to a lesser extent, in schools. Music could be used for reflective exercises in class, either as 'background' or as positive aids to concentration, and much popular music addresses issues of relationships and of ultimate questions. A piece of meditative music (e.g. the *Buddhist Peace Chants*, Jin Long Uen 1996) could be played, with pupils asked to think of nothing (or to think of 'nothingness'), or to look at a candle flame, and to describe, after the event, some of the things they were thinking about. It would probably be better to give this exercise a quite specific context. For example, at Wesak, pupils could think about the Buddha's birth, enlightenment, and/or death, accompanied by the music, and then talk about their thoughts. Similarly, a piece of 'celebratory' music, such as *In Praise of Guru Nanak* (Bhattacharya 1999), could be played on that person's birthday (for Guru Nanak, in November), with the pupils thinking about what the music tells us about the musicians' views of the person.

In order to help pupils develop *empathy*, the teacher might simply explore music from different cultures. Taking this further, pupils could choose music for an event for someone with different beliefs, for example choosing music for the celebration of a birth of a member of a different religion or culture. This would help pupils understand empathy-in-action, and could lead to the kind of dialogue important to Buber as exhibiting I–Thou relationships. Pupils might choose a piece of music appropriate to another person in the class, when that person is troubled in some way – for example through loss or illness. Or, using a piece of music including words, pupils might write another 'verse' or some other extension of the words, suited to the religion and style. Continuing this work, pupils might paint a picture to represent all the ideas in a piece of music, including 'feelings' as well as 'events', with the picture to be appropriate to the religious tradition from which the music comes. And, following up any of the previous activities, pupils could write a thank-you letter to the musicians/composer, saying what they liked about their music, and what they learned about their religion from the music.

There are so many examples of 'positional' music – i.e. music that attempts to promote a particular viewpoint (religious or other) – that examples of such music should be easy to find, to be used as the basis for *evaluation* exercises. The music would include, for example, much 'protest' music, just about all rap music, music for evangelizing, music attacking (and, carefully-framed, perhaps promoting) different forms of racism and sexism, and so on. Pupils could write, compose or choose a 'reply' to a piece of music, or a piece of music to represent the 'opposite' feelings. For example, *Mangalan* (Shankar 1997) is about peace, so pupils might in contrast choose a suitable piece of music to reflect how they would say they were angry. In order to develop skills in religious *analysis*, pupils could use religious music to investigate differences between the features of religions. For example, looking at hymns in the Orthodox and non-conformist traditions might be used to explore distinctions and common themes. On the theme of 'times', pupils could compare and contrast two or three pieces of music related to the same occasion or time of life but from different religious traditions, such as the Sufi *Old Man's Song* (Tekbilek 1994), the Russian Orthodox *Cast Me Not Away In My Time Of Old Age* (Soglasie Male Voice Choir 1995), and from the Jewish tradition *Di Elter* (The Klezmatics and Chava Alberstein 1998). This work would mean listing as many as possible similarities and differences, and then saying what this tells us about each of the traditions.

The skill of *synthesis* – linking features of religion in a coherent pattern, and connecting different aspects of life into a meaningful whole – is often a difficult aspect of religious education to deal with, yet work here might be central to creating community, as community is by its nature something of a synthesis. Pupils might select, or even better compose and perform, music from different religious and other traditions to commemorate or celebrate a particular event, such as marking the opening of a new or combined school, or as a remembrance service for a teacher or pupil who has died. They might tell a story of significance to various religions, such as the battle between good and evil. In such ways, they will attempt to synthesize ideas, without compromising individual beliefs. Working 'outwards' from a piece of music, pupils could use one track such as *Under Your White Stars* (Patinkin 1998), which deals with a child's attitude to religion when in traumatic conditions. They could put together a performance for a communal school event that includes readings, role-play and questions from that tradition, marking a special event.

Very much at the heart of any use of music in religious education is *application*: making the association between religions and individual, national and international life. People need only think of the application of music for special occasions, such as the use of Beethoven's ninth symphony at international sporting events and at the foundation of the United Nations, or the use of the hymn *Nkosi Sikelel' iAfrica* as one of the new South African national anthems (as in Soweto String Quartet 1994). For a forthcoming international event such as the Olympics, the World Cup, a United Nations meeting or other international summit meeting, pupils could choose the music to suit the occasion. It is worth choosing a range of music, from different traditions, to represent the different people involved in the meeting. Pupils might write the introductions to each piece, or tell the story of each piece, justifying its use. Similarly, music is clearly one of the richest sources of religious *expression*, involving explaining concepts, rituals and practices, and identifying matters of deep conviction and concern, responding to religious issues through a variety of media. Music such as that in *A Vision of Heaven* (Atlanta Symphony Orchestra and Chorus 1994) could be used to look at Western European classical expressions of heaven. Hell is not so often described in music, although a favourite classical 'vision of hell' is Mozart's death scene for *Don Giovanni*. The long tradition of Sufi Muslims using music and dance to practise dhikr, or 'remembrance', particularly in the well-known Whirling Dervish practices (as in Hamza 2000) goes back to the mystic Rumi. Rumi lived in the thirteenth century CE and wrote *Where Everything Is Music*: 'Don't worry about saving these songs! / And if one of our instruments breaks, / it doesn't matter. // We have fallen into the place / where everything is music' (Rumi 1995, p. 34). The music – especially if accompanied by pictures or video of the practitioners – can help pupils understand what Rumi described as a 'longing' for Allah. To contrast with this, pupils might try an exercise on the expression of chaos or confusion, perhaps using the idea of musical 'dissonance', and tracks such as Tavener's *Representation of Chaos* (Tavener 2000), or the last movement of Chopin's second sonata on confusion/storm.

Conclusion

Using music related to 'times' from a number of religions can develop religious education skills (as described above), and can help promote spiritual and cultural development. The activities described here were originally developed for and with teachers of mainstream classes in both primary (aged 7 to 11) and secondary (aged 11 to 19) phases, and teachers working in special schools catering for pupils with a very wide range of needs. Clearly it is impossible to provide comprehensive guidance for work with pupils of all ages and needs (other ideas can be found in Grice 1997), yet one of the joys of working with music in religious education is that affective and intellectual responses to a single piece of music can defy the most rigorous determination of 'ability'. All can have agency, all can be original, and – although it is often ignored in schools – all can value and evaluate music from different religious traditions. Religious education is therefore a vital subject in the inclusion of pupils and staff alike, bringing together ways of life and communities, the personal and the social. It is not that music is culturally 'neutral'. As Morris says,

> Music plays an enormous role in the construction of communities, [as] to listen together binds audiences into an imagined community, whether nation, subculture, congregation. We listen with others and the way the music addresses us determines us as a collectivity with a certain character and a certain potential moral career. (Quoted in THES 1997)

Rather, music has for millennia been effective not only in such potentially 'exclusive' communities, but in more inclusive communities and in intercultural communication (and now Internet communication, as in Abbott 2002, p. 27), and can be used as a form of community-making of the most comprehensive kind. Music can engage the imagination to such an extent that pupils, teachers and all members of school communities can even, in Buber's words, imagine the real. Rather than Eco's 'orgy of tolerance, ... total syncretism and [an] absolute and unstoppable polytheism' (Eco 2004, p. 428), it is hoped that this case study demonstrates a sober multi-religious and multicultural approach to the search for truth in religious education. Music engages in such a way that creativity happens, often unpredictably and in ways that cannot be captured by lists of facts and competences. In a world increasingly affected by globalization and even McDonaldization, and riven by conflicts, creative education is still possible. Pupils can make more than cuckoo clocks. As Benjamin said (in the chapter heading),

> These are days when no one should rely unduly on his "competence". Strength lies in improvisation. All the decisive blows are struck left-handed. (Benjamin 1997, p. 49)

Creativity is not just for pupils, of course: school communities should be creative at all levels. The issues of the hierarchical nature of schooling, and how that is illuminated by religion and religious education, is therefore the subject of the following chapter.

Chapter 12

Blinded by the vision: schools, religions, policies and politics

Some ... would love the government to have a clear policy ..., whatever its content, so that they could pay homage to it. Others, of whom I am one, would prefer the government consciously decide not to have policies on a whole range of life, including lifelong learning.

(Lee 2005)

Introduction: vision and policy

With an approach to schooling and religion taken from Macmurray and Buber, the personal, communal relationships involved in teaching and learning are necessarily at the forefront of the analyses. Multi-religious religious education requires connection to broader national and international issues. This too would be expected of Macmurray and Buber, themselves involved in the turbulent international politics of the twentieth century, although some might claim the emphasis on smaller-scale relationships could be a distraction. In this chapter, the scale and nature of politics is tackled, as it is important both to clarify the position of the personal philosophies in a political arena, and to reassert the significance, for schools and religions, of broader political activity. The work starts from an analysis of 'vision' and 'policy' in educational and political contexts, including how they are related to religious issues. A modelling is therefore attempted of the hierarchical relationships found in schools: relationships compared with the hierarchies of various religious traditions.

Whereas 'vision' has a rather mysterious character, 'policy' is rather taken for granted and assumed to be necessary. Neither is well understood. Vision is currently expected of many educational leaders, and policy may be expected to be visionary. In this context, 'vision' derives from religious traditions of having and following 'visions', as in its definition as 'something seen in a dream, trance, or ecstasy; esp: a supernatural appearance that conveys a revelation' or 'direct mystical awareness of the supernatural usu. in visible form' (Merriam-Webster in Britannica 1994–8), or '[s]omething which is apparently seen otherwise than by ordinary sight; *esp.* an appearance of a prophetic or mystical character, or having the nature of a revelation, supernaturally presented to the mind either in sleep or in an abnormal state' (Simpson/OED 2005). Even in a more limited form, vision still retains a religious edge, as in a person of 'unusual discernment or foresight' (Merriam-Webster in Britannica 1994–8) or 'mystical or supernatural insight or foresight' related to 'statesmanlike foresight' (Simpson/OED 2005). The English inspection service, Ofsted, sets out the requirements for vision in its inspection framework. Under 'how well is the school led and managed?', the framework asks of the governing body whether it 'helps shape the vision and direction of the school', and asks of the headteacher, senior team and other staff with responsibilities, whether their 'leadership shows clear vision' (Ofsted 2003, p. 41). This is a recent development. As an American principal is quoted as saying

> If I had said twenty years ago that I had a vision, I would have been put in an institution. Now I can't get a job without one! (Quoted from Fullan in Hoyle and Wallace 2005, pp. 10–11)

The religious background to the term 'vision' is recognized in a genuine if somewhat ironic advert for a headteacher asking 'Can you walk on water?' (Hoyle and Wallace 2005, p. 11). Rather more seriously, in analysing the impact of policy on schooling, use will be made of religious models in explaining how policy can influence authority and power within education.

Policy, meanwhile, is variously defined as 'a high-level overall plan embracing the general goals and acceptable procedures especially of a governmental body' (Merriam-Webster in Britannica 1994–8) or '[a]n organized and established system or form of government or administration (of a state or city)' and '[a] course of action adopted and pursued by a government, party, ruler, statesman, etc.; any course of action adopted as advantageous or expedient' (Simpson/OED 2005). Under those definitions, it is possible to have or not to have policy, and for policy to have or not to have any impact. The questions can range across whether there is a plan, whether that plan incorporates general goals and procedures (as a plan can be made up of a description of an unconnected set of practices), and who determines the policy. The reputation of policy has in recent years been reduced by the need to produce policies in order to satisfy audit and inspection regimes, to such an extent that many in schools believe that a 'policy' is no more than a piece of paper held by administrators with significance only for outsiders and with no impact on the school itself. Where this is true, the policy is no longer a real policy because it is not part of a plan with a description of procedures, and so there is little difference between having such a 'pseudo-policy' and having no policy. This chapter therefore explores the existence of policy, the nature and impact of policy on educational approaches to authority and power, and how policy impact can be researched.

On the issue of authority and power, there is a wide range of approaches to educational policy, from centralized, through localized, to universally dispersed models: these parallel the range of approaches to religion. All points on that range are likely to have a distinctive impact on educational institutions. The effect of policy will be studied, here, through a consideration of leadership and followership. This hierarchical dimension of schooling helps in the understanding of schools as inclusive learning communities. For example, policy of one kind may mean that leaders are expected to have 'vision', and if that is restricted then they can be described as 'blinkered'. Such policy may also mean that followers are expected to follow the vision of others, and can therefore be described as 'blinded' by the vision. Another kind of policy may 'enlighten' rather than 'blind', and may enable more inclusive schooling. A modelling of policy of the latter kind, and the implementation of such policy, is attempted here. That will be informed by what Sennett (2003) refers to as 'respect in a world of inequality', such that educational leaders and followers can all see and be seen.

Policy or not?

Whether or not there is a policy can be investigated in the first instance by looking for planning, and in the second instance by looking for principles. It should be admitted that things may happen without planning, an issue with a significant history in both science and religion. Finding non-planned causes is best exemplified by Darwin on natural selection (Darwin 1971, as mentioned in Chapter 11 above) and the controversy surrounding that theory. He developed a mathematical model of change over time that could explain evolution without any purposeful planning. Rather than attempting to prove directly that there was no plan, he attempted to demonstrate that planning was not *necessary*. The theory was religiously and politically controversial at the time, and since. Those who do not understand why the theory was so controversial, may wish to put forward the view in an educational or government organization, that planning is unnecessary and that things happen whether or not they are planned. Insulted and undermined planners and policy-makers may be found repeating the defence of the deity offered by Darwin's critics: how could all this happen other than as a result of the purposes and plans and interventions of a superior being? The 'dangerousness' of Darwin's approach, highlighted by Dennett (1995), is by analogy dangerous for policy-makers. Scientists critical of some aspects of Darwinian theory such as Gould, still agree on the central 'dangerous' idea. As Gould says, '[s]hall we appreciate any less the beauty of nature because its harmony is unplanned?' (Gould 1977, p. 27). It is Gould's concern to avoid the 'skyhooks' Darwinism (Dennett 1995, pp. 262–4) that has led him to be interpreted at times as 'proving Darwin wrong', yet Gould is clearly a Darwinian (Gould 1977, *passim* and pp. 39–45) and one who understands the power of the idea, throughout *The Origin of Species*, that planning and purpose are simply unnecessary (also the argument of Ruse 1986, p. 2). Indeed it is Darwin's first task in *The Origin of Species* to contrast the intentional choice by pigeon-fanciers of better pigeons (i.e. 'selection by man [*sic*]', Darwin 1971, pp. 38–41) to the selection by nature (i.e. 'natural selection'), in the sense that the latter has no need of a mind directing the process.

The difference between 'mere' planning and 'proper' policy might be taken to be differences between how principles are used in the processes. Where a coherent set of general goals and principles are used, this might be regarded as evidence of a policy, as long as the goals and principles are themselves connected to the processes or activities described elsewhere in the policy. A helpful example of how goals and principles can be added to a plan, to make it more like a policy document, is the change to the English and Welsh statutory curriculum documents between 1988 (DES 1988) and 1999 (DfEE and QCA 1999). Both documents include broad principles of schooling, and are 'policies' in that sense. However, with respect to individual curriculum areas – the subjects of the curriculum – the first of the documents and the accompanying guidance did not describe the aims or broad purposes of each of the subjects. This was remedied in the second document, as each subject was then introduced by a description of its importance, as in this account of 'the importance of mathematics' which notes that maths 'equips pupils with a uniquely powerful set of tools to understand and change the world', that it 'is important in everyday life, many forms of employment, science and technology, medicine, the economy, the environment and development, and in public decision-making', that it 'transcends cultural boundaries' as a 'creative discipline' which 'can stimulate moments of pleasure and wonder when a pupil solves a problem for the first time, discovers a more elegant solution to that problem, or suddenly sees hidden connections' (DfEE and QCA 1999).

A distinction can therefore be made between, or a continuum described from, policy as more principled and connected 'holistic' planning, and non-policy as planning that is merely a collection of unconnected, even if principled, activities and processes. There is no problem in people working to plans of the latter kind: it is simply that people are not thereby following policy. As Lee (2005) describes it, this is a hard distinction to make, but there is a common, if not conclusive, example given from the legal system: '[i]t is often said that unelected judges should decide hard cases according to principles, leaving policy decisions to elected representatives'. Lee's doubts about the clarity of that example (as 'I have never found the distinction that easy', Lee 2005) suggest a continuum from policy to non-policy, rather than a simple contrast.

Who makes policy?

The next way of analysing policy is to investigate who has the authority to make policy. Policy-making powers may be given to individuals, or to schools, or local, national or international government bodies. With increasing and increasingly diverse globalization (Bottery 2004 *passim* and ch. 3, Bottery 2000, ch. 1, Wilkinson 2006), it might be expected that policy-making would be shifted to national and international bodies. Although the experience in schools is of an increasing expectation to generate policies at a local level, these policies are often modelled on guidance and examples developed nationally or beyond. For example, a school policy on inclusion may have been written by staff in a UK school in 1996, but that would have taken account of national policy (the UK's SEN Code of Practice, DfE, Welsh Office 1994) written in an international policy context (the UN's Salamanca Statement, UNESCO 1994), and supported by a range of very similar policy guides such as Hornby *et al.* (1995), Ramjhun (1995) or Warin (1995). It is difficult to measure how responsible school staff are for the generation of policies, if the school policies are indeed little more than copies of, or implementation plans for, policies made elsewhere: the 'vision' is likely to be very 'blinkered'. Yet in the recent guidance on UK teaching professional standards, it is stated that in order to be established as a qualified teacher (that is, to pass the initial qualification and the 'induction' year), candidates must 'contribute to the development, implementation and evaluation of the policies and practice of their workplace' (TDA 2006b, p. 6, with TDA 2006a, an earlier draft, having required this also of initial qualification), whilst 'excellent' teachers should '[b]e prepared to take a leading role in developing workplace policies' (TDA 2006b, p. 6).

Perhaps the clearest analysis of such uncertainties over the exercise of power, as here, is that of Lukes (1974, 2005). For Lukes, simply studying who wins in conflicts is a 'one-dimensional' view and may not take account of more hidden forms of power, leading to over-optimistic views of power distribution such as those of Dahl. Dahl (1961, and see also 1989, 2005) most famously studied the political conflicts in New Haven, Connecticut, and concluded that power was spread relatively evenly, and in a way best described as 'pluralism' (a form of democracy, as also in Dahl 1989). Lukes notes that power may be exerted by setting the agenda (this is a 'two-dimensional' view of power), so that it appears as if power is spread, but it could instead be concentrated in the hands of a small group of agenda-setters. To the extent that school or local government policies are nominally created at those levels, but are set to a clear agenda developed nationally, policy-making can no longer be said to be devolved. Examples of national policies being set to an international agenda, such as those on special educational needs quoted above, may even suggest a globalization of policy-making, as stressed by those analysing the 'McDonaldization' of education policy (Wilkinson 2006, and see also Ritzer 2004). To research such policy-making decisions, people at different levels may be asked what they would like to 'put on the agenda', and to the extent that this differs from the substantive agenda, they can be described as having less power.

Lukes does however add a 'three-dimensional' view of power, where people may not realize that power is being exerted over them, due to the ability of others to prevent people from disagreeing with decisions, rather as in Marx's view of false consciousness, or Huxley's *Brave New World*. Much harder to investigate, such an exercise of power may be discovered when people apparently 'awake from their dream', as in the period following the 1989 collapse of communist rule in Central and Eastern Europe, when the apparently high degree of support for communism and the apparently low degree of religious belief seemed to swap overnight. Within educational policy-making, there are some examples of attempts to 'awaken' people from false dreams. Neill (1985) attempted to show that the need for adults within the school, local or national government, to set policies on curriculum or behaviour in schools was unnecessary, as pupils and adults could together determine how the school should be organized. Meanwhile, Illich (1971, 1974, whose work parallels that of Freire and religious traditions of liberation theology, as in Chater 2000) attempted to demonstrate that schooling was itself unnecessary, as 'for most men [*sic*] the right to learn is curtailed by the obligation to attend school' (Illich 1971, p. vii, also quoted above in ch. 4), and the 'major illusion on which the school system rests is that most learning is the result of teaching' (Illich 1971, p. 12). Referring to such illusions is not the same, of course, as demonstrating their veracity. Religious education provides a valuable source of evidence for the possibility of active non-illusory decision-making. The process of determining an Agreed Syllabus is a regular process within the UK educational system involving active agreement by participants who might not be expected to agree (as described in Chapter 8 above).

Taking account of the difficulties of determining the power over policy-making, it is still worth describing how policy-making may be distributed. There are three models of power distribution of educational policy-making described here. Each is presented alongside a religious tradition, not to suggest that religion influences policy (even if it does), but to help explain the significance of vision in policy-making and, thereby, the impact of policy – educational or religious – on individual people and communities. The three models are based on three distinct if overlapping contexts. One, the micro level, being that of pupils, school staff and the local community; a second, the meso level, being that of schools and local government; the third, the macro level, being that of central government and global organizations.

Model 1: centralized-unified systems

Within religious traditions, vision may be restricted and centralized. Some are said to have an acknowledged special access to or understanding of the will of God/gods or the truth (such as priests within Christianity or the ten Gurus within Sikhism), or to be messengers of God (such as prophets – often attributed with *visions*). Religious policy – the principles and plans of the tradition – may be received or developed by a single person, as described in biblical accounts of Moses receiving the law, or the Buddha becoming enlightened. Such a single point of reference may be institutionalized in policy-making. An example of this is can be given from the Roman Catholic church, which has an institutional structure and authority system that works through a single person (the Holy Father, the Pope), whose authority and insights are said to be derived from God, and who is the 'perpetual and visible principle and foundation of unity of both the bishops and of the faithful' (www.vatican.va/holy_father/). The Holy Father is responsible for local systems of authority (the bishops and the priesthood) who are attributed with their own, if subsidiary, access and understanding. There is a hierarchy of texts, from the Bible through to authoritative documents from the central human figure in the institution. In some systems, foundational texts seem to have a greater authority in policy-making than an individual person, as with some Christian approaches to particular versions of the Christian Bible, or Muslim approaches to the Qur'an. Within Sikhism, the central authority might be deemed the Guru Granth Sahib, the collection of writings of other Gurus and the wisdom of other writers, which itself is given the authority of a 'Guru', derived from God who is also called the True Guru.

Centralized policy control may have similar characteristics. Unique central access to authority, by 'visionary' central government, may involve the attribution of access to special understanding (i.e. a unique ability to understand the needs of the nation or of the education system), and may expect such understanding to be implemented locally by authority figures (perhaps principals/headteachers) who have a significant but critically limited 'vision' or understanding. The authority might be held in a document of approved wisdom, perhaps a curriculum or policy document that is said to determine the boundaries of all debate on education. Examples of model 1 policy-making with respect to religious education include those national confessional religious education policies, as in the Northern Irish Core Syllabus (made up of 'the Revelation of God', 'the Christian Church' and 'Christian Morality', www.eftre.net/), most schools in Belgium (www.eftre.net/), or the Kingdom of Saudi Arabia (Al-Buraidi 2006, and the requirement that '[a]ll public school children receive religious instruction that conforms with the official version of Islam', en.wikipedia.org/wiki/Status_of_religious_freedom_in_Saudi_Arabia). Other model 1 examples might be taken to be those national policies that largely outlaw religious education, as in the USA or France. In both cases – that is, whether religious education of one kind is required, or religious education of all kinds is disallowed – the national decision is attributed to a clear national policy, in the US, France and the Kingdom of Saudi Arabia with reference to the national constitution or Shari'a law.

Model 2: pluralist-decentralized systems

Some other religious traditions acknowledge the same idea of special access to God/gods or the truth or understanding, expressed in terms of vision, but have no acknowledgement of a single authority but many dispersed authorities, such as gurus in the Hindu tradition or ordained ministers in Nonconformist Protestant Christian traditions – with 'vision' prevalent in charismatic movements in many religious traditions. Each person may express allegiance to a single guru or minister, but there is no overarching institutionalized authority for all people, and the system might be called pluralist. Although authoritative documents may be referred to, there may be localized interpretations and reinterpretations, and additional documents, all of which can have different degrees of authority.

Pluralistic, localized educational policy may have similar characteristics. There are various ways of organizing education, and these will be quite different in different localities and even in separate schools. However, all might have a 'guru', a person to whom allegiance is given, whether this is a principal/headteacher or an influential superintendent or director of education. Of course, such systems are open to Lukes' (2005) critique of apparently pluralist systems, as there is a tendency of governments to promote a rhetoric of local control whilst imposing national control. Within religious education, there are several approaches that could be described as model 2 systems. Within Austria, for example, 'every religious community is treated equally' and 'schools offer (Roman) Catholic religious education, Protestant religious education and in some schools even [*sic*] Islamic RE', with religious groups being responsible for the training of teachers in these areas (www.eftre.net/). Germany, too, has a dispersed model, but with each part of the country having a clear and distinctive approach – with multi-religious and interreligious religious education common in cities such as Berlin and Hamburg, and single-religion and more confessional religious education common elsewhere (see Schreiner *et al.* 2002 and www.eftre.net/).

Model 3: wholly-dispersed egalitarian systems

There is a third set of religious traditions, which describe some people as enlightened or wise, but without giving them authority other than, perhaps, the ability to show others the path to enlightenment or wisdom. If there is vision, then it is not used by others. Every individual can go along the same path, although only some, if any, will gain enlightenment. Examples of this may be the Society of Friends (Quakers, the eventual religious 'home' of Macmurray), Congregationalist and Unitarian Christian traditions, or many Buddhist traditions.

The absence of clear education policy at either national or local level, other than a determination of the broad aim of education, with the intention of helping others become educated, might have similar characteristics. For religious education, the long history in the UK of local agreement on religious education syllabuses, involving a committee made up of representatives of a wide range of both religious, non-religious and professional groups, is an interesting example of the way that 'religious education is rooted in local communities' (Hull 1998, p. 1). However, criticisms of the process include Grimmitt who says that 'despite the existence of legislation requiring . . . agreed syllabuses to reflect local concerns and circumstances, the production of the model syllabuses [i.e. SCAA 1994a, b] came very near to establishing, if not in name but in practice, a national RE curriculum' (Grimmitt 2000, p. 14, and see also Zamorski 2000, and more the more recent national framework, QCA 2004).

Models 1, 2 and 3 and national education systems

Models 1 and 2 are exemplified by a number of national approaches to education policy. In France and Saudi Arabia, there are long histories of model 1 centralized policy on education affecting all aspects of the work of schools, whilst in Germany and the USA, more model 2 approaches are evident, with German Länder and US states having radically distinct policies on education, and national interventions more often being in the form of 'projects' rather than 'policies'. The UK, interestingly, appears to have moved from model 2 to model 1 in the last 20 years. It surprises some younger writers about UK education policy, when it is pointed out that until the late 1980s, there was very little national schools policy: no national policy on the curriculum (other than a requirement to have religious education), no national policy on assessment (other than a promotion of exams at the ages of 16 and 18), no national policy on pedagogy, no national policy on the quality of schools and how to assure that quality. Since the late 1980s, policies on all these issues have developed, although they have been patchily implemented across the different parts of the UK. Broadly, central government policy has recently dominated the English schools system, and has had a slightly smaller effect in Wales, and a considerably smaller effect in Scotland and Northern Ireland.

It is tempting to link the degree of centralization to religious patterns. A powerful argument might be made about the Roman Catholic-dominated, centralist, French approach to educational policy, where the centralized nature of religion influences an avowedly secular state. In contrast are the Protestant-influenced, localized, German and US systems, where education policy is dominated by local systems, with no serious attempt to impose a single national system. Sitting between these extremes is the mixed approach to education policy of the UK, with more centralized policy control in those areas where the influence of the established church (the Church of England) is greatest, and less centralized policy control in the more Protestant- and Nonconformist-dominated Wales, Scotland and Northern Ireland.

Tempting as those links are, their mere existence is not the whole story, and there may in any case be counter-examples, such as dispersed, relatively localized, approaches to educational policy in countries with centralized religious traditions (such as the Republic of Ireland, for which see www.education.ie/), and *vice versa* (such as Norway, for which see Royal Ministry of Church, Education and Research, 1994). The importance of the links is therefore also in making *use* of the religious traditions in order to understand the purposes of the educational policy, and in order to attempt to change that policy. For example, to influence education policy in France might require a focus on influencing central powers, or using subtle and perhaps 'dangerous' local subversion, whilst influencing education policy in the USA or Germany might involve more open independent dialogue and argument (see DelFattore 2004 for the USA and Rüppell and Schreiner 2003 for Germany), building up alliances of groups at local, regional or national levels. As the UK has elements of both traditions, examples from the UK are particularly good at illustrating the importance of such strategies. Exemplification of model 3 approaches to education policy-making are harder to come by, but are implied by some working for the voice of pupils, such as Flutter and Rudduck (2004) and Chapman *et al.* (1995). Flutter and Rudduck focus on the need for schools to climb up the 'Hart Ladder of Participation' (as described in Chapter 5 above, from Flutter and Rudduck 2004, p. 16, and see also Rudduck and Flutter 2004, Alderson 2000, and the Arnstein ladder of participation in Ward 1982, pp. 65–6). As mentioned earlier in this chapter, the development of Agreed

Syllabuses for religious education might be given as examples of model 3 approaches, and more generally work on dialogue in religious education and on ethnographic research in religious education (i.e. Chapters 7 above, and 14 below) are part of religious education's contribution to dispersed and participative education.

The impact of policy models on leadership and followership

The existence and level of determination of policy will impact on leadership and followership at school level.

Leadership and followership in model 1 systems

Under model 1, with centralized policy-making, school-level leadership might be assumed to be limited or purely symbolic. For example, in the UK, central influence on pedagogy has led to much less local leadership on pedagogy, and at the same time an increase in the development of what can only be described as symbolic school-level policies on teaching and learning. The views of Hoyle and Wallace are particularly apt. 'Central government expectations are enshrined in legislation, some quantified as targets ... [and e]ven where local diversity is promoted, central requirements make it clear what staff must do ... [so a]ny vision or mission statement and associated plan must be consistent with the aspiration to meet these expectations and requirements if they are to satisfy OFSTED inspectors' (Hoyle and Wallace 2005, p. 139). As schools have enough information with which to operationalize central government expectation, 'we wonder whether the implicit goals of vision-building are, at most, operationally to offer a locus for key-words acting as reminders to staff and members of the local community, and instrumentally to provide a rhetorical statement for OFSTED inspections' (Hoyle and Wallace 2005, p. 140). Hence, '[v]ision-building does work as a symbolic device for reassuring outsiders that staff are working in the best interests of the students and in compliance with national requirements', but is in large part simply a waste of time, a distraction for 'staff who already know what they have to do' (Hoyle and Wallace 2005, p. 141).

In effect, school-level leaders and followers in model 1 systems are all followers, perhaps suffering from what Bottery describes as feeling 'relatively powerless' and 'demoralised' (Bottery 2000, p. 223) or even suffering from 'professional impotence' (quoted in Hoyle and Wallace 2005, p. 173). As Moore *et al.* say, it seems that

> the concept of leadership has undergone a discursive shift, away from 'authentic' leadership based on educational values and strong personal and professional commitment, towards 'contrived' leadership in which the idea of the headteacher as leader is 'sold' to the headteacher and the school's teaching staff as a way of disguising or sweetening an actual *lack* of genuine leadership possibilities inherent in the extent of central government control. (Moore *et al.* 2002, p. 179)

Government knows best, and school-level staff are pushed into being either nominal 'disciples' or substantive 'rebels', as in Cooper and Higgott (1991), and, once again, in Moore *et al.* (2002) who note that the

> conscious association of academic and institutional leadership with the notion of the headteacher's personal, guiding vision appears to provide, at least in the headteachers' own minds, one possibility for political *resistance* (albeit a localized, 'subversive' form of resistance), that enables fundamental, individually held values – often associated with a belief in and pursuit of some version of the comprehensive ideal – to endure, while major organizational changes are taking place in the institution as a direct result of universally applicable reforms and/or changes in the nature and relations of national and local markets. (Moore *et al.* 2002, p. 183)

If the central government is truly democratic, then it might indeed prove appropriate for school-level 'leaders' to join the nominal followers in being, genuinely, 'followers' and true disciples. However, it would still take away from the possibility of leadership within schools, and would therefore still be in danger of pathologizing, rather than developing a healthy attitude towards, authority. Mitscherlich (1993) describes this in terms of the dangers of a 'sibling society' (as in Bly's introduction, p. xiv). Meanwhile, a limit on central powers, even apparently 'democratic' central powers, is argued for by Macmurray, for whom democracy is the 'denial of the omnicompetence of government' (quoted in Kirkpatrick 2005, p. 79). Buber also wrote of the necessary limits on 'I–It' government, as '[t]he state must cease to be a *machine machinarum* which "strangles the individuality of small associations" and must become intead a *communitas communitatum* – a union of communities within which the proper autonomous life of each community can unfold' (Friedman 2002, p. 249). Similarly, the long tradition of anarchist thought has denied the legitimacy of centralized states whilst recognizing local governance, as in Proudhon's account (from 1851) of the appropriate organization of school and higher education. He asks '[w]hy should not lower instruction be centralized in each district, in each province, and a portion of the funds destined for it be applied to the support of higher schools that are thought necessary, of which the teaching staff should be chosen from that of the lower schools' (Proudhon 2004, p. 274). This therefore leads on to model 2 and model 3 systems.

Leadership and followership in model 2 systems

Within model 2 pluralist systems, there is likely to be a locally-determined division of labour with respect to leadership and followership. Policy will be determined at local as well as national and global levels, with a philosophical-political framework perhaps closest to that of John Stuart Mill's liberal market system. Mill stresses the need for individual development, as '[i]n proportion to the development of his [*sic*] individuality, each person becomes more valuable to himself, and is, therefore, capable of being more valuable to others' (Mill 1974, p. 127), leading to a balance of 'local liberties' and national political freedom, supported by citizenship training as described in Chapter 10 above (from Mill 1974, p. 181). For Mill, leadership is clearly widely distributed, and followership is seen as a transitional stage in personal development. Each follower might be described as an 'apprentice' leader, as described in Madera 2000 (referring delightfully to the game of 'follow-the-leader'). This appears to be the 'transformational' and 'progressive' system promoted by the National College of School Leadership (NCSL), where leadership is based on learning theories. Policy questions include how to deal with followers who do not want to be leaders, and how change in *national* policy can be implemented in a truly 'apprenticeship' model: i.e. how to avoid the merely symbolic school-level policy-development, as in model 1 and as in Lukes' (2005) critique of Dahl's pluralist analysis.

Leadership and followership in model 3 systems

Within model 3 wholly-dispersed egalitarian systems, there is likely to be the possibility of leadership and followership at local level, and less leadership at national or global level. It might in that sense fulfil the wishes of Hoyle and Wallace for 'less leadership' (Hoyle and Wallace 2005, p. 9), as they 'take an explicitly negative normative stance towards what we judge to be a deleterious consequence of excessive leadership and management: unintentionally inhibiting the educational improvements that they are intended to foster' (Hoyle and Wallace 2005, p. 17). In the same way, Macmurray objected to much management, despite – or perhaps as a result of – his extensive and successful experience as a manager. 'We are becoming more and more technically minded: gradually we are falling victims to the illusion that all problems can be solved by proper organisation', he says, but '[t]o think thus in education is to pervert education' as '[i]t is not an engineering job': '[i]t is personal and human' (Macmurray, 1968, pp. 154–5).

There is a tradition of objection to leadership and management, to government of all kinds, from systematic political writings to comic operetta. In 1892, Kropotkin published *The Conquest of Bread* (Kropotkin 1995), describing mutuality as a natural characteristic of people, in contrast to the popular contemporary Social Darwinist descriptions of people, as 'it is government that represses our natural tendency for cooperation' (Rheingold 2002, p. 39, and see also Ward 1982, p. 18, on 'a society which organises itself without authority'). For Kropotkin, '[t]he history of the last fifty years furnishes a living proof that representative government is impotent to discharge all the functions we have sought to assign to it' (Kropotkin 1995, p. 39). Meanwhile, in the same year of 1892, the Gilbert and Sullivan operetta *Iolanthe* was premiered. That has a powerful comic description of the need for the British House of Lords (the upper house of parliament, referred to as the House of Peers) to refrain from thinking:

> When Wellington thrashed Bonaparte,
>   As every child can tell,

The House of Peers, throughout the war,

Did nothing in particular,

   And did it very well:

Yet Britain set the world ablaze

In good King George's glorious days! (Bradley 1996, p. 417)

In the absence of governmental leadership, for whatever reason, there is the possibility of school-level leadership. How this should be organized, and whether school leadership can be morally justified despite the absence of school-level democracy, remains a vital question. Schools that are hierarchical learning communities can perhaps be egalitarian (see Stern 2002), if such schools are inclusive learning communities, with followers having 'respectable' positions, and leaders able to demonstrate 'magnanimity'. Although such respect and magnanimity are also possible in model 2 systems, the tendency of model 2 systems is to school-level leadership succumbing to national or global pressures, as described by Bottery 2004 (e.g. ch. 9, and Wilkinson 2006), and as stressed by Macmurray in his attack on schools or any communities having external aims. 'The exact difference between society and community and the proper relation between them are best recognised by reference to the intentions involved', as '[t]he intention involved in society lies beyond the nexus of relation which it establishes', whilst '[i]n community it does not' (Macmurray 1968, p. 58).

Macmurray's idea of a school as a learning community therefore excludes the possibility that education should have examination results as its prime aim, let alone economic benefits (as described in Chapter 4 above). If leaders in model 3 systems have 'visions', they are in danger of trying to determine school goals in such a way that followers are limited to helping the leader achieve that goal, and becoming 'disciples' as in model 1 systems. This is the view of Bennis (1994), and is positively recommended by those promoting 'charismatic' leadership, such as Kleinsmith and Everts-Rogers (2000), and Conger and Kanunga (1998), and strongly criticized by Stroup (2004). Where leaders in model 3 system refrain from visioning, there is the possibility of recognizing immanence or what Hoyle and Wallace refer to as 'temperate' leadership, 'concerned with developing – without over-institutionalizing – ideas, techniques and interactions emerging from practice' (Hoyle and Wallace 2005, p. 191). This is in contrast to 'top-down' leadership and management, and Hoyle and Wallace refer to a range of literature on emergence, such as March, Wieck, Gron and Wenger, and on the role of emergence in complexity theory (Hoyle and Wallace 2005, pp. 191–2). Although they used arguments for emergence within an argument for 'irony', it has a much stronger philosophical and religious tradition, also recognized in the psychological literature. 'Because of the enormous risk of deception – particularly self-deception – education can never be complete', says Mitscherlich (1993, p. 13). Schooling may end but education does not, so being 'educated' means having retained a 'youthful receptiveness to the new and the unknown': '[o]ne does not know the truth about oneself, one seeks it, and to the end of one's life the search remains unsatisfied' (Mitscherlich 1993, p. 13). Education must involve uncertainty, they continue, as '[d]ogmatic certainty is the end of education (not excluding religious education)' (Mitscherlich 1993, p. 14).

Models 1, 2 and 3 leadership and followership

In summary, model 1 systems require followership or pseudo-leadership at school level, model 2 systems require a balance of leadership and followership with dangers of reverting to model 1 or to unaccountable charismatic versions of model 3, and model 3 systems require a school- or community-level leadership and followership emerging from the school community itself, with dangers of the fragmentation of national education systems. The model 3 approach is well described by Bhindi and Duignan, notwithstanding their reference to this as 'visionary', and their denial of hierarchy, as they

> argue for *authentic leadership* based on: *authenticity*, which entails the discovery of the authentic self through meaningful relationships within organizational structures and processes that support core, significant value; *intentionality*, which implies visionary leadership that takes its energy and direction from the good intentions of current organizational members who put their intellects, hearts and souls into shaping a vision for the future; a renewed commitment to *spirituality*, which calls for the rediscovery of the spirit within each person and a celebration of the shared meaning and purpose of relationship; a *sensibility* to the feelings, aspirations and needs of others, with special reference to the multicultural settings in which many leaders operate and in the light of the increasing globalizing trends in life and work. (Bhindi and Duignan 1997, p. 119)

Their conclusion is that 'many in our organizations are no longer prepared to be impelled by leadership charisma, status, or hierarchy or to be compelled into compliance by coercion, deceit or economic threat' (Bhindi and Duignan 1997, p. 119).

Researching the impact of policy

There are two aspects of power, addressed by the research described here, that will illuminate not only power, but the impact of policy more broadly. One is a concern with the continuing attempt to refer to political systems as democratic that are patently undemocratic, or to redefine democracy to mean its opposite, or to be a general term for all the virtues (as in Dewey's definition of democracy as 'the idea of community life itself', quoted in Barber 1984, p. 117, and see also Dewey 1916). Within education research, numerous authors write of a need for schools to be 'democratic'. For example Blase and Anderson on a 'vision of leadership' that is 'open, honest, collaborative, inclusive and democratic' (Blase and Anderson 1995, p. viii), or Bottery on educational management being such that 'measures of democracy' can be introduced (Bottery 1992, p. 186), or Furlong's 'new democratic project' and 'democratic professionalism' (Furlong *et al.* 2000, pp. 177 and 175 respectively), or Gordon on the possibility of achieving democracy in a single school (Gordon 1986), or Fielding on '*dialogic democracy*' (Fielding 1999, p. 82). The other is a concern at the absence of a serious moral justification for leadership in systems that are not democratic. A research exercise that unexpectedly illuminated both these concerns was carried out by the author with trainee teachers (and available in Stern 2001), who were describing what they thought of the schools they had been working in, and how those schools might be more 'ideal'. One of the statements they had to play with was 'most managers in the school act as if they are superior to people below them in the hierarchy'. One respondent in one of the groups identified the statement as true of an 'ideal' version of that person's school. Were they really saying that 'acting superior' was a good quality for managers to have in a school, and one that would be present even in an ideal version of that same school? This small empirical puzzle was to prove a rich source of further analysis and critique. The eventual explanation turned on the possibility of a leader having the quality of 'magnanimity' (as defined by Aristotle 1976, p. 153), if and only if that leader also had all the other virtues associated with a good leader. Such magnanimity is an uncommon virtue. Aristotle is very clear about those who act superior but lack other positive leadership qualities, and about those who refuse to act superior when they do indeed have the other leadership qualities: the former exhibit 'vanity', the latter undue humility or 'pusillanimity' (Aristotle 1976, p. 105).

The concept of magnanimity therefore provides an explanatory framework for a number of aspects of leadership. It was complemented, in Aristotle's work, by an attempt to provide a positive moral justification for non-democratic leadership. Aristotle attempts this by looking at the intentions of leaders. There are three basic political forms, each one having a 'proper' and a 'deviant' form. Rule by one person is either a monarchy (good) or tyranny (bad). Rule by a small group is either aristocracy (good) or oligarchy (bad). Rule by the citizens as a whole is either polity (good) or democracy (bad, though not considered as bad as either tyranny or oligarchy). What distinguished the proper from the deviant forms was not, therefore, the distribution of power within the system, as power could be distributed in each of the three ways, and in each way might be considered proper or deviant. The distinguishing features, in each of the three distributive systems, were the intentions of the leaders. A good leader *intends* the benefit of the led, they 'work for the people'; deviant leaders work for their own benefit or (though this is rather left to the imagination) for some external benefit or for no benefit at all. Aristotle's way of describing this uses familial terms. A good leader looks after the led like good parents look after their children: '[t]he association of a father with his sons has the form of monarchy, because he is concerned for the welfare of his children' (Aristotle 1976, p. 276). Intentions are identified, in turn, by the *friendly* nature of the relationship between leader and led.

> [I]n a tyranny there is little or no friendship. For where there is nothing in common between ruler and ruled there is no friendship either, just as there is no justice. Their relation is like that ... of master to slave. (Aristotle 1976, p. 278, and see also Buber

2002a, p. 138, on how '[a] great and full relation between man and man [*sic*] ... is much more rarely found in the totalitarian collective than in any historically earlier form of society; much more rarely also in the authoritarian party that in any earlier form of free association'.)

Even the warrior-led people of Britain a thousand years after Aristotle lived, saw the wisdom and the moral weight of a leader who aimed for the benefit of the led. The highest compliment offered Beowulf is that 'he worked for the people' (Heaney 1999). For Macmurray, in the twentieth century, intentions are also vital to equality (not democracy), as 'equality is intentional: it is an aspect of the mutuality of the relation' (Macmurray 1991b, p. 158), and any unity in a society 'is not merely matter of fact, but matter of intention' (Macmurray 1991b, p. 127). For Aristotle, and many writers since, the key performance indicators of effective political systems were the (effectively enacted) intentions of the leaders, the relationships between leaders and led, and the framework of justice or equity that made this all possible (see Stern 2002).

The professional standards expected of new teachers in the UK do refer (in various, currently draft, forms) to the intentions of the teachers, as they should '[h]ave high expectations of children and young people and a commitment to ensuring that they can achieve their full educational potential and to establishing fair, respectful, trusting, supportive and constructive relationships with them' (TDA 2006b). The 'advanced skills teachers' are expected to have those same high expectations and are also expected to 'have an important part to play in leading learning', 'take a lead and play a significant part in developing and implementing the policies and practices of their workplace', and 'act as role model in order to promote collective responsibility, and commitment to policies and practices in different educational contexts/workplaces' (TDA 2006a). Using Aristotle's terminology, leaders might be expected to fulfil a 'magnanimous' final 'crown of the standards' standard, along these lines: 'They regard themselves as worthy of great things, provided that they *are* worthy of them; they worry about few things, are not excitable, and are not highly strung'.

It would be possible to argue, as Barber does, that the presence of 'strong' democracy makes leadership unnecessary. However, his argument retains what are called 'transitional' leaders for whom 'to be successful is to make oneself superfluous' (Barber 1984, p. 239), and this is a good description of cyclical rather than dyadic teacher-learner relationships in apprenticeship models of learning. He also envisages the need to retain 'facilitating' and 'moral' leaders. Artificially stretching 'democracy' to refer to schooling under current legislation is something like the 'contrived collegiality' (from Hargreaves, as outlined in Hoyle and Wallace 2005, pp. 125–6). Instead of avoiding the term 'leadership', therefore, it would be possible to retain much of Barber's argument and retain leadership (in these forms) whilst discarding the need to use Barber's version of the term 'democracy'. This would at least have the advantage of avoiding the disjunction between an apparently 'democratic' school with patently 'undemocratic' legal underpinnings of schooling. Such a re-formed version of Barber's view – that is, of model 3 magnanimous leadership in a participative egalitarian school community – would imply a relatively small impact of national-level policy on leadership, but would recognize the need for holistic, principled, leadership at school level that would be an example of genuinely communal policy-making.

Conclusion: enlightened policy

So, what is the impact of policy on leadership and followership? The absence of policy can leave action unprincipled and disorganized, although that situation might in some circumstances also be liberating and empowering. The presence of visionary policy, whether local or national, is liable to disempower followers and many nominal leaders either through the influence of false rhetoric or true charisma. In Buber's novel *Gog und Magog*, he writes about the dangers of vision even in a purely religious context:

> Jaacob Yitzchak was called the 'Seer' because in truth he 'saw'. It was told that, when he was born, he had been able to see from world's end to world's end. ... The child who 'saw', however, was so dismayed by the flood of evil which he beheld engulfing the earth, that he besought the gift to be taken from him and his vision to be restricted to a narrower span. (Buber 1999, p. 4, also quoted, in a different translation, in Friedman 2002, p. 176)

Strong national- and international-level policy-making (as in model 1) can be disguised by a rhetoric of local vision, and tends to disempower followers and nominal leaders. It is that kind of policy rejected by Lee in the quotation heading this chapter, who says that '[s]ome ... would love the government to have a clear policy ..., whatever its content, so that they could pay homage to it ... [whilst o]thers, of whom I am one, would prefer the government consciously decide not to have policies on a whole range of life, including lifelong learning' (Lee 2005).

A model 2 mixture of local and national policy can provide opportunities for a variety of leadership and followership roles at all levels, although the very lack of consistency may itself be problematic. Locally-determined, model 3, policy will enable the development of magnanimous leadership, in the best circumstances, with an egalitarian approach to followership, as in Sennett's view of equality. He sees that people believe 'that by treating one another as equals we affirm mutual respect', but studies how it is possible to 'convey mutual regard and recognition' between people who are intractably unequal (Sennett 2003, p. xv). Being unequal in some ways – including power inequalities or inequalities in talent – does not imply inequality in every way. The possibility of equality of some kinds in a society that is unequal in some ways, is the conclusion of Stern (not the present author), for whom 'the realisation of an equalitarian society may be far removed', but 'an equalitarian and co-operative attitude can be, not only worked for, but practised to a considerable extent in any society' (Stern 1971, p. 525). Sennett's approach to such equality is based on autonomy, or 'accepting in others what one does not understand about them', so '[t]he grant of autonomy dignifies the weak or the outsider; to make this grant to others in turn strengthens one's own character' (Sennett 2003, p. 262, and see also Lukes 2005 pp. 84–5 on 'dignified dependency').

Whereas vision can 'blind' through misdirecting leaders and misleading all, policy – principled, coordinated, planning – is part of a communal opportunity for respectful leadership and followership in schools. Within the curriculum, as exemplified by religious education, there are opportunities for developing dialogue in an inclusive school properly informed by research. Such enlightened policy and enlightened schooling will of necessity stretch beyond the school, by enabling schooling to 'mediate between the family and the larger world of adult life' (Macmurray 1968, p. 35).

Chapter 13

Learning beyond school: worldly homework

work which might be completed comfortably in a short school period may linger fitfully throughout the evening.

(Great Britain Board of Education 1936)

Introduction: schools, homes, families and worlds

Throughout this book, and especially in Chapter 4, the argument has been made for schools being considered as learning communities, where pupils learn to live human lives properly. The argument has also been made, especially in Chapters 7 and 8, for dialogue beyond the school with religious and other communities and other schools. That is, schools are to be learning communities, but not at the expense of learning in other communities. It is the engagement with religious education that best illustrates the need to go beyond the school, for the school to fulfil its own purposes, as the study of religion cannot be carried out without drawing on activities, experiences, feelings and ways of living that take place outside the school community. A religious education classroom without voices from other communities would be like a music classroom that was forever silent, or an art lesson with the lights off. Religious education comes alive with connection beyond the classroom, as music comes alive with sound and art with vision – notwithstanding the restricted vision or hearing or community connections of some of those taking part in the lessons.

Schools must be places of learning; schools are damaging if they are claimed to be the only places of learning. That is the very strong message of Lave and Wenger, who see schools as something of a distraction when it comes to learning, as 'the organization of schooling as an educational form is predicated on claims that knowledge can be decontextualized, and yet schools themselves as social institutions and as places of learning constitute very specific contexts' (Lave and Wenger 1991, p. 39, quoted more fully in Chapter 4 above). The relationship between schools and the rest of the world is determined in part by the curriculum and its drawing on texts and artefacts from around the world and throughout history (as discussed in Chapters 6–11 above, including the communicative possibilities introduced in recent years by computers). The relationship is also determined by connections with families (as in Hornby 2000, Munn 1993, Vincent 2000, Stern 2003), and the possibility of school work being extended beyond the school through homework (whose history is summarized in Hallam 2004, pp. 1–4). Those curriculum and family relationships and that homework can be improved.

Loving and hating homework

Homework, for these purposes, is learning 'that is relevant to teachers' curricular objectives ... which takes place outwith formal classroom teaching ... which is primarily the responsibility of the learner himself/herself' (MacBeath and Turner 1990). Some pupils ask why they have to do homework (as described in Stern 1997, 2006a), but they have the wrong question: the peculiar thing is schoolwork, not homework. To learn, people do not always need teachers – certainly not in the sense people now think of teachers. Through most of history, people learned from their families, amateurs as teachers, and from their peers and their colleagues. Homework, or at least learning outside the influence of a professional teacher, is therefore ancient and venerable. However, school-set homework is more recent, and is disliked by many, with frequent attempts to abolish it altogether. Indeed, one survey suggested that 50 per cent of children enjoyed school, but only 2 per cent enjoyed homework (from Macfarlane, quoted in Macbeath and Turner 1990). Homework can be seen as an unpleasant chore, a test only of the power of schools over pupils, rightly hated (as also in Stern 2006a, p. 3). There are at least four kinds of reason for everyone – teachers, pupils, families – hating homework. Homework takes time, and takes all the 'nicest' times, when you want to be watching television or playing computer games or sleeping. Homework creates mistrust amongst teachers, pupils and their families. Homework is an administrative nightmare of bits of paper and instructions and lists and mark books and deadlines. And homework is associated with the giving and receiving of punishments.

On the other hand, there are also many reasons for valuing homework (as in Stern 2006a). Homework can be what learning is at its best: grabbing hold of the world and making it make sense for you. How many adults still have, hidden away, some piece of work done years ago at school – a project on the Incas, or a story for the school magazine? Of all the 'kept' pieces of work, most were completed largely or entirely at home. In college and university education, the most remembered products are the dissertations done in the library and in college rooms, not the notes taken in lectures, seminars and tutorials. Are you more fluent in the language you learnt in the classroom, or the language you learnt at home, aged nothing, or on holiday? There is a good basis for promoting homework, then, as the most exciting, memorable, side of education. It is what we love most about our school days. It is the way in which we actively demonstrate what we know, rather than passively responding, in class, to a teacher's request for one-word answers. Pupils who can complete homework are learning independently, and are applying classwork beyond the classroom. Often enough, homework is a chance to do something distinctive and original, a chance to show off what you know about a topic that is a real interest of yours. Some children do not get much of a chance to talk and work creatively with friends and family: homework can encourage such work. More than that, it can show pupils that the school 'recognizes' their homes and communities, and can show family members that the school has, or should have, relevance to their lives.

Amongst all the reasons for loving and hating homework, the process of setting and completing homework is likely to be effective to the extent that the homework is useful (i.e. expands the amount of time pupils spend learning), is relevant (i.e. applicable to pupils' lives, especially given the context in which it is likely to be completed), and is able to make use of the fact that it is homework (i.e. captures the world beyond the school, and 'exploits' the people and other resources of the communities beyond the classroom). This is described in terms of a threefold model of homework of 'expansion', 'application' and 'capture' (Stern 2006a, pp. 17–18). That model has been informed by, and is particularly significant for, work on religious education, and more broadly on the relationship between schools and religions.

Expansion homework: schooling beyond school, using computers

Firstly, we could use homework to 'expand' the 15,000 hours of schooling currently endured by children. This is based on the idea that there are not enough hours in the school day to complete all the learning needed. The 'expansion' model of homework includes 'finishing off' and related 'just do a bit more' homework tasks, the worst kinds of homework, unnecessarily stressful and inefficient. Yet at its best it is a worthwhile addition to school. Homework can allow schools to 'spill out' into the rest of the world, raising the profile of school learning. Although homework can do much more than simply expand school, some forms of expansion homework can make learning more personal and significant for pupils. Simple examples of such expansion homework in religious education (from Stern 2006a, pp. 13, 33, 38, and Stern 2000a) include ways of giving each pupil a distinct, personal, task. Instead of all pupils producing an advent calendar, to illustrate issues related to Christmas, each pupil might produce an illustration for a different day, for a whole-class calendar. Pupils might be asked to develop questions that could best be asked of a key religious figure from the past, in preparation for a role-play 'hot seating' exercise in class. Making use of the internet to study a moral issue, each pupil might be given the web address of a different campaign group on an issue and be asked to summarize the group's position, for a 'positional' display and debate in class. Computers are generally helpful for expanding schooling, too. Becta, the British agency responsible for computers in schools, says that

> [i]n the literature, the term 'home–school' work is sometimes substituted for 'homework' to reflect the fact that students may be able to continue work at home which they started in the classroom. There are various technologies which can support

this. The main ones are portable computers, wireless networks, school intranets and online curriculum materials. (Becta 2003a)

Factors for effective computer use include 'an audit of home computer ownership and use', measures in place 'to ensure out of school access to ICT [information and communication technology] for all', '[t]echnical support ... available out of school hours', and the 'aims and objectives of having home–school links ... agreed and understood by all' (Becta 2003a). Computers can help in more distinctive ways, not least the fact – attested to by parents as much as teachers – that computers can for the time being motivate people (as in Becta 2003b on motivation and Becta 2003a on home–school links more generally). An otherwise rather dull task might be able to be completed at home on a computer, simply because the computer itself provides sufficient interest for the pupil. More creatively, computers can provide the support needed for expansion homework to be effective, including resources related to religions and also specific support materials from the school, such as resources on the school website, discussion groups and expert help. Becta (2003a) also describes research on home–school work in general, including the move from 'traditional' homework to wider issues of home–community relationships. They investigated '[e]lectronic communication between school staff, parents and students', '[r]emote access from home to school records and curriculum content', and '[a]llowing learning to take place in the home as an extension of the school environment'. This idea brings the argument back to the significance of expansion itself. Schooling is not to be limited by school hours or school buildings, any more than a 'church' can be restricted to the building of that name. Schools are positively described in terms of learning communities; they expand beyond themselves as part of their bridging role between family and wider society.

Application homework: the meaning of schooling
for the rest of the world

Secondly, homework could be used in such a way that the 15,000 hours of schooling could be 'applied' to the rest of the child's world. This model implies that school subjects need to be relevant, and school learning consists of a set of 'apprenticeships' in the world, with the pupils understanding the value of school learning and the value of their world, through homework. Whereas expansion homework implies a spilling over of schooling, application homework implies a more active engagement of schooling with the rest of the world. Amongst the examples of application homework in religious education (from Stern 2006a, pp. 43–4, 49, 53, and Stern 2000a) are interviewing two people who have different views on a religious topic being studied in religious education, planning for a birth ceremony or a wedding of someone from a specified religious tradition, analysing television soap operas to see who breaks which of the Ten Commandments or the Five Precepts or the Seven Deadly Sins and what the consequences are for those characters, or contemplating quietly on an issue for a specified time. Schooling in this sense provides models to be taken out of school and used. For religious education, the clear risk is that this would mean making pupils more religious – a problem for non-confessional religious education. However, even those promoting non-confessional religious education must expect the subject to have some impact on the lives of pupils, and application homework can be, precisely, the test of those effects. In many religious education syllabuses, the effects are described not in terms of religiosity, but in terms of 'moral education'.

Moral education has a distinguished place in schooling (see Bailey 2000 and Gardner *et al.* 2000), and modelling – applying models to different situations – is a common approach to the subject, and one that has been greatly developed in recent years with the help of computers. Philosophers and religious teachers have used models of situations for thousands of years: what would you do if ..., what would the world be like if ..., what are the consequences of ...? Some might describe modelling as 'playing games', with play also having a long educational history such as Schiller in the late eighteenth century on the 'play-drive': 'man only plays when he is in the fullest sense of the word a human being, and he is only fully a human being when he plays' (Schiller 1967, letter 15). Hence, modelling and gaming – and now, computer gaming – can be exploited to support moral education just as it can support other forms of education (literacy for Marsh in Monteith 2002, various subjects for McFarlane *et al.* 2002). Both individual and social/online gaming, completed outside lessons for homework, are increasingly able to simulate all kinds of moral situations. The Sims family of games (www.thesims.co.uk) is the most prominent example, able to model and play with complex societies (and see also www.womengamers.com for a gendered approach to gaming). One example of modelling is given by a remarkably simple and unpleasant online 'Death Clock' (deathclock.com/), which asks some questions, works out the respondent's life expectancy, and tells them when they are most likely to die. Despite its unpleasantness, teachers and pupils who have used it generally respond enthusiastically, and its impact on moral education can be remarkable.

Other examples of moral modelling that can be seen as applying school work to the rest of life include investigating the situation of a tied labourer, a modern 'slave'. The sensitive Anti-Slavery Society site (www.antislavery.org/) provides case studies of young people who are currently working as tied labourers. Their situations can be used as the basis of much moral education. Pupils can also consider what the world would be like if everyone used the resources that each pupil used. There is a modelling exercise where respondents can work out their 'footprints' on the world, using the 'measure your impact on the planet' exercise at www.rprogress.org/ (or www.myfootprint.org/). Having completed that, pupils can work out what they are going to do to change their 'footprint', and make a set of promises to themselves for the future. Pupils could also investigate the Ecoquiz on the Religious Education and Environment Programme website (www.reep.org.uk), which provides a helpful stimulus to moral and political debate on this issue.

To consider the consequences of sin and the ethics of punishment for homework, pupils might consider the morality of a quite different punishment system, with an older English system comprehensively modelled at the historic Old Bailey website. The Old Bailey, the most famous criminal court in England, has put all their records from 1674 to 1834 online (at www.oldbaileyonline.org/), providing a wonderful engaging archive of materials for the study of crime and punishment. As transcripts are given of the proceedings of over 100,000 trials, and descriptions of the verdicts and punishments, pupils can easily work on individual cases, for example completing incomplete information such as deciding what the verdict or punishment is likely to be, prior to seeing it, or deciding on the justice in legal or religious terms of particular proceedings, or arguing for or against particular defendants, on the basis of information available to them. The crimes include a range of sexual offences, and the punishments include various sentences that would be considered cruel today: they are sufficiently disturbing to suggest teachers check with the school policies prior to using the site, and that the site be used with pupils older than 14 or perhaps 16. However, using only the Old Bailey website, pupils can investigate religious offences. These are described (at www.oldbaileyonline.org/history/crime/crimes.html# religiousoffences) as of four kinds: recusancy (related to Catholicism), 'pretending to have divine powers', 'blasphemy' and 'witchcraft'. By searching for such cases (search for 'religious offences' under 'specific criminal act'), pupils can analyse any of dozens of such crimes, including the account of the trial of Lodowick Muggleton, leader of the Muggletonians – an anti-Trinitarian group that continued until the mid-twentieth century. Using the Old Bailey website and also archives of current legal proceedings, pupils can also compare eighteenth and twenty-first century approaches. For example, pupils might wish to compare transportation in the eighteenth century with policies on deportation in the twenty-first century. Current legal policies can be found at the UK's Department of Constitutional Affairs website (www.dca.gov.uk), which is in turn linked to the UK's Criminal Justice System (at www.cjsonline.gov.uk/) and sentencing guidelines (at www.sentencing-guidelines.gov.uk/). Further archives of criminal cases for particular areas can be found in local and national newspapers (www.onlinenewspapers.com/), and further information at Amnesty (www.amnesty.org or www.amnesty.org.uk) or RE-XS (re-xs.ucsm.ac.uk).

There is a sense, gained by many teachers and pupils, of being allowed to see the whole world, through various forms of computing. This is not simply a matter of having access to a lot of information, although the information available is voluminous, or of being able to communicate easily and cheaply with people and groups all around the world, but of being a part of a distinctive, worldwide, virtual community. Those who use computers also commonly experience awe and wonder – the opportunities can take one's breath away. The virtual, worldwide, community to which people may feel they belong, is rather US-dominated, English-language-dominated, although even these characteristics appear to be changing. Yet it can still be a special experience. Helping pupils to develop the sense of 'one-worldness' might be done in a number of ways. Some distinctive, computer-based, ways of seeing the whole world include the use of 'seeing' sites like the UK's Met Office (www.meto.gov.uk/ with good pictures under 'satellite') or Google Earth (earth.google.com), and 'camera' sites (like the EarthCam site at www.earthcam.com/ with a 'religion' section, containing many religious 'views', under the advanced search heading, or try www. armchair-travel.com/). The Religious Education and Environment Programme (REEP) has a carefully constructed set of approaches to 'the world' as environment with religious significance (at www.reep.org). A teacher could also try stories from around the world from newspapers (e.g. www.onlinenewspapers.com/). For these and other sites, pupils will need tasks – generally based around simple tasks such as finding out similarities and differences between different parts of the world, or between parts of the world and the world as a whole. There are many forms of religious broadcasting that attempt to represent the views of religious and other world views, to give a perspective on the day that should be of interest to those studying religion, such as the well-established BBC Radio 4 *Thought for the Day* (www.bbc.co.uk/radio4/religion/). A view on the day that is regarded by some as a 'God's eye view' is the Daily Hukamnama (from www.sikhnet.com/hukam). This is regarded by Sikhs as that day's 'command of God', the 'instructions' for all people around the world. A Sikh might expect to act differently during the day, depending on that day's Hukamnama. Pupils could work out how their lives would be different, that day, if or because they are Sikhs and believe the Hukamnama is indeed the command of God. This could then be extended to an analysis of the impact of the Hukamnama on the class or whole school as a learning community.

Some of the work described here, using computers, can also be completed in an adapted form without computers. The critical lesson learned is that school work on religious and moral issues can be 'effected' beyond school, so that schooling becomes more applied. How the world beyond school can, in turn, be effected within the school, is the subject of the third form of homework.

Capture homework: families, communities and religions brought in to the curriculum

Thirdly, homework could be used to ensure that the remaining 125,000 hours of childhood be made use of in school: homework 'captures' the child's world for the schoolwork. This may be based on the idea of 'exploiting' homes, a sort of recycling of home 'stuff' in school. Homework can 'catch people out' learning when they least expect it: in their homes. Homework can also help pupils become more human. Pupils learn how to be human in school (that is what personal, social, cultural and spiritual development mean), and they do this by working within the school community. School communities are half-way houses, between families and broader social groups. Homework can therefore capture aspects of other communities, in order to help pupils and the staff within the school. Schooling helps to make, or make more possible, a community of communities in and beyond school. In these ways, homework creates more inclusive schooling. This final model of homework completes the picture of the relationship between school and non-school. Here, non-school talks back to school. There is a dialogue between schools, families and other communities. The idea that homework can be 'about' homes should be of no surprise to those working in religious education. The growth of Christian 'home church' movements (under names such as 'home churches', 'house churches' and 'house fellowships', also grouped under 'new churches', for which see www.religioustolerance.org/chr_hous.htm and www.home-church.org/ and www.newchurches.com/), along with longstanding home-based religious traditions in Hindu and Sikh communities, as in all religions, should make the 'capture' of homes that much more significant for religious education than for other subjects. Of course, homes are by their nature private, and 'capture' work should not be intrusive (as noted for example in Bastiani 1997). Yet there are many valuable opportunities for homework to capture the world beyond the school.

Pupils may complete detailed interviews with adults from their home or neighbourhood about what religion means to them or about key concepts to be studied in religious education, or they might have the task of making a choice of a suitable present for a key religious figure from the products available in a shop they and their family visits that week (from Stern 2006a, pp. 62, 63, 68–9, and Stern 2000a). To continue the theme of shopping, as all pupils are involved through their homes in shopping of some kind, it is worth investigating the consequences of religions having a range of views on ethical issues relevant to shopping. These may include food patterns related to kashrut, halal and vegetarian food, clothing related to animal skins, but also the purity of cloths and trading issues, technology related to approved and disapproved machines and uses, and books related to allowed and disallowed versions of sacred and secular texts. There are also company and country boycotts, associated with religious, ethical and political issues. Pupils could investigate 'real' shops or, as most goods and services can now be found online, pupils could use computers to investigate their own shopping patterns and those of their homes or families, and investigate the consequences of following a different – religious or ethical – way of life. Specialist websites are often related to animal rights issues but also link into trading issues. These include Ethical Wares (www.ethicalwares.com/), Get Ethical (www.getethical.com/), the Vegetarian Shoe Shop (www.vegetarian-shoes.co.uk/), along with specialist religious sites such as those of Hindu and Christian vegetarians (www.hindunet.org/vegetarian/ and www.jesusveg.com/). Mainstream supermarket sites can also be used to compare availability and prices of goods suitable for different traditions (for example, search for 'kosher' or 'vegetarian' or 'fair trade' on www.sainsburystoyou.com), as can pressure groups such as the Vegetarian Society (www.veg.org).

Capturing the world beyond the school, for work within the school, promotes independent learning, and there is a wide range of research on how computers, too, may enhance independent learning. This has been enshrined in UK government guidance with suggestions that '[i]ncreased capability in the use of ICT promotes initiative and independent learning, with pupils being able to make informed judgements about when and where to use ICT to best effect, and to consider its implications for home and work both now and in the future' (DfEE and QCA 1999). It is also complemented by research evidence that, for example, '[t]here appear to be significant learning and social gains when pupils act as peer mentors for other children during activities involving the use of digital media' (Burden and Kuechel 2004, p. 12), as in the computer-based independent learning described by Ipgrave (2001, 2003). There are substantive communal and social changes, resulting from changes in computer use, that schools must recognize, even though they should avoid the idea that all computer-based work is necessarily 'better' or is uniquely novel. As Sacks says, '[i]nformation technology ... is more than a technology: it has a profound impact on the democratization of human dignity', and '[t]here is a story to be told about personal computers, modems, e-mail and the Internet that is, in its way, both spiritual and political and a source of genuine hope' (Sacks 2003, p. 125).

On the other hand, '[i]n promoting a more remote and individualistic style of religious practice, the coming of the Internet has contributed further to the privatization of religion that has been so much a feature of the modern period. ... [and] may well contribute to increasing religious syncretism, just as its rapid communications systems further accelerate the process of globalization' (Beckerlegge 2001b, pp. 258–9). Beckerlegge's conclusion is that

> The Internet has already begun to reshape religious institutions, and ... may undermine inherited ideas about the roles of religious officiants and the duties of religious adherents. ... For the Brahmins of the digital age, the Internet has provided the imagery and metaphors for a new style of theologizing or presentation of the faith. ... [Yet] it is the expectations engendered by the capacity of the Internet and computer technology to transcend finally the inherent limitations of human existence that arguably will have the most profound effect upon religion in the cyberfuture. (Beckerlegge 2001b, p. 259)

Many people are making communities using computers. In the US and UK, people write more emails, and many more text messages, than letters – and it is not just young people, as the people who make the greatest use of the Internet, of those with access, are those over 60. Growing online religious communities are well described by Beckerlegge (ch. 5 in Beckerlegge 2001b). There is also the possibility of communication between religious education teachers (such as www.rpi-virtuell.net/), and between pupils. When relationships of all kinds are being made with computers, schools need computers to make and to understand people, relationships and communities. Ways of helping pupils to build real relationships with others, include setting up email peer tutoring systems, with older pupils, or pupils with particular skills, acting as 'mentors' to younger pupils, or as academic experts in particular fields. Beyond the school, taking part in national or international links can also help build relationships, if and only if those links are positive and focused on significant and appropriate issues. Peer tutoring systems between university students and school students are possible, and there could be a system whereby a pool of local or national or international 'experts' could respond to questions of pupils, as in the *All Experts* site (at www.allexperts.com/). That could be based on the principles that expertise is more widely spread than might be expected, and that acting as an expert itself motivates one to be more of an expert. Online technology is available such that a single religious education class, never mind a single school or local authority, can easily build up a website of its collective knowledge and understanding. Such a site can then be a 'notice board' of interesting and useful information, photographs of places visited, audio clips of visiting speakers, examples of valuable pieces of research completed by pupils or teachers, answers to commonly-asked questions. It can also contain information about syllabuses and exams, as appropriate.

Treating all the members of the class or school or local community as experts, able to contribute to the site under the editorial control of teachers, makes for a serious concern with the idea that all pupils should be experts, in their own way, in some aspects of religious education. Encouraging contributions from members of families of pupils, local religious communities and pupils or teachers from link schools in other parts of the country or other parts of the world, should all add to the sense of spreading expertise. Pupils elsewhere in the school or in other schools, or in other parts of the country or other countries, may be able to access the site, and both appreciate the expertise demonstrated and wish to contribute their own expertise. Ethical issues, with respect to privacy and the risk of causing or eliciting inappropriate responses, suggest that such a site should be open only to those willing to agree to conditions of acceptable use (with specific religious issues tackled in Houston 1998). Password-protecting a site is technically easy, and most schools will already have access to virtual learning environments or intranets that could be used. Making expertise a dimension of homework has the benefit of raising the status of the home and family, as well as of homework and schooling. It captures communities.

A further example of capture homework, in this case without using computing, is worth describing here. It was originally developed by Marie Stern in a London special school to help children understand the number 6,000,000, a number referred to in lessons on the Shoah (and reported in Stern 2006a, p. 73). In class, pupils are given a sheet covered in 10,000 dots. Starting towards the end of the lesson, to be completed for homework, individual pupils, or if possible groups of two or three friends, should label each dot with the name of a person they know, personally, who is not a member of that class. They can label with initials and arrows, and should start with the top left-hand corner of the page of dots, labelling dots close together. The people named may be friends or family or neighbours, past and present, as long as they are personally known to the pupils: stars from television do not count. Handing the homework in, the sheets can be displayed: few pupils will have been able to label more than 100 dots (and it is not a competition, in any case). The teacher should then get the pupils to help roll out five rolls of paper, each roll consisting of 20 sheets of A3 paper with each sheet having six times 10,000 dots on it. (These dimensions have been carefully practised in many school settings.) The 'roll out' (in a large classroom, or better still in a corridor or hall) will reveal exactly six million dots. This must only be done after the homework task of labelling: the pupils will understand large numbers, and will understand 6,000,000 in a way that they did not before. So will teachers. It may seem like a simple set of class and homework tasks, but it has given more pupils and teachers sleepless nights – upset at the thought of the large number – whether it is applied to the Shoah, deaths in wars, or the analysis of poverty. Large numbers are worth knowing, personally; people are worth knowing, in large numbers. In a remarkably simple way, personal connections are expanded and given new meaning. The personal world of pupils is not only captured by the school: the school is able to set that in an historical context.

Conclusion: more than lingering fitfully

The work of school can be restricted to lingering fitfully in the world beyond school. This was the troubling conclusion of a report on homework published in 1936:

> Except in a few cases the children return home to work in the common living room. Often a meal is in more or less continuous session, the wireless booms and the family chatters. Against such odds, work which might be completed comfortably in a short school period may linger fitfully throughout the evening. (Great Britain Board of Education 1936)

To do more than linger fitfully, the work of schools should have a relationship with the world beyond school that reflects its proper nature. The way in which schools use homework and use computers, especially in religious education, is a sensitive indication of this relationship. To see schools as the only, or the prime, site for learning of all kinds, is likely to lead to homework being set as an expansion of schooling, with the help of computing, and homes treated as quasi-schools. Recognizing the wider world, beyond the home, and accessing that throughout the curriculum including using homework, in part through the use of computing, suggests a more embedded sense of schooling, but one that still sees schools as the prime site for learning 'applied' to the world beyond. It is 'application' and 'capture' homework that suggest another way of seeing schooling, with school as a site of learning, just as home and workplace are sites of learning, all using computing as appropriate to enhance learning that is variously situated in communities (the family, the school, some religious groups, friendship groups) and societies (the workplace, voluntary groups, political associations). Schools are linked to the other sites of learning through worldly homework, and schooling in that way does more than linger fitfully beyond the school. The purpose of the following, final, chapter is to see how research, a particular form of learning, can be embedded in schooling. The opportunities provided by religious education, for supporting schools as learning communities, are related to research in schools.

Chapter 14

Sincerity in research: people mattering

all *research is inherently 'interested'*

(Milley 2002, p. 48)

Introduction

The nature of schools and religions, the nature of religious education, and the nature of research in religious education, are closely connected. Those connections are made throughout this book. If 'learning is a way of being in the social world, not a way of knowing about it' (Hanks, in Lave and Wenger 1991, p. 24, quoted in Chapter 4 above), the same can be said of research, a form of learning. Religion is itself a way of being, an activity not simply an abstract 'belief'. In this final chapter, then, there is an attempt to bring together the various themes in schooling, religion, religious education and research.

- Within the study of humanity and community, issues have been identified related to how the self can exist in and through the 'between' of dialogue, how communities are distinguished from other social groups by how people treat each other, and how schooling must have as its first aim learning to be human through community.

- Within religious education, issues have been identified with respect to the proper understanding and use of sacred texts, the methods of developing dialogue within and between communities, the nature of and ways of achieving inclusion, the development of coherent pedagogy in religious education, and how religious education can properly contribute to political issues.

- Within research, issues have been identified with respect to interpretation and translation, how meaningful dialogue can be stimulated and captured, how to measure inclusion, understanding the relationship between what teachers do and what pupils learn, and understanding and measuring the impact beyond the school of religion and religious education.

There is clearly a relational theme running through all these issues. How do pupils relate to sacred texts and their use in religious communities, how do pupils relate to each other and to communities within and beyond school, how do pupils and teachers relate to each other, how do pupils and teachers of religious education relate to national and international social and political contexts, and how do religious education and research relate to each other? What connects all of research in religious education is how embedded research is in the everyday work of schools, and how sensitive research must be to the relationships and the ways of life that make up the whole school community. It is fitting, then, to conclude with a chapter on researching schools and religions. This focuses on two themes of sincerity and ethnography. Ethnography is well established in the research literature, sincerity is less established. Both illuminate schools and religion, and are illuminated, in turn, by practice in religious education.

Research and sincerity: more than not lying

Sincerity is not the answer to all the problems of religious education or research, but it is a valuable principle rarely addressed in the literature, and one that can help carry religious education and research, schools and religions through to a better future, a future of more than not lying. Much empirical research in religious education (as described for example in the excellent Francis *et al.* 1996) has followed social scientific methodologies, focusing on questioning in a way that avoids confusing (over-complex or unclear) or leading questions. If confusing questions generate confused answers, and leading questions bias the answers in the direction in which the questioner leads, researchers can simply avoid these types of questions. By avoiding misleading questions, it is thought that lying will be avoided and truth will emerge. Those involved in religion will understand how limited is 'avoiding lying' as an approach to research, and how much more is required for meaningful dialogue about religion. Reaching towards the truth, in religious education research or in the rest of life, requires more than not lying. The 'more' that is required may be described as 'sincerity'.

Within social science research, there are two major traditions, phenomenological or interpretive research, which generally makes use of more qualitative research methods, and positivistic research, which generally makes use of more quantitative research methods. Research projects have often gone beyond such 'false dichotomies', however (as in the account by Pring in Chapter 5 above), drawing on both traditions, despite those traditions being related to contrasting philosophies. The implications of 'sincerity' are therefore worth working through both traditions. And although sincerity is little studied in mainstream methodology textbooks, it is supported by philosophic heavyweights such as Wittgenstein, Macmurray and Habermas. Wittgenstein contrasts 'truthfulness' and 'sincerity', so that 'A dog cannot be a hypocrite, but neither can he be sincere' (Wittgenstein 1958, p. 229e). That is, people and dogs can be truthful, but only people can be sincere. As well as attempting to avoid some of the biases associated with particular research tools, then, religious education research should try to elicit a form of sincerity from respondents, something more than avoiding 'lying'. Macmurray, similarly, contrasts 'negative untruthfulness' (i.e. lying) and sincerity, with sincerity being 'much more than' avoiding lying. Sincerity 'is positively expressing what you do think and believe', and '[t]o refrain from expressing what you think or believe or know to someone, if it is to his advantage or to someone else's advantage that he should know it, is positive dishonesty', that is, 'dissimulation – the suppression of the truth' (Macmurray 1995b, p. 76). This is similar to the contrast in Habermas between 'truth' and 'truthfulness'. For him, 'any communicative utterance aimed at generating understanding and agreement implicitly raises four validity claims – that it is comprehensible, that it is factually correct or in principle possible (truth), that it is acceptable normatively (rightness), and that it is meant sincerely (truthfulness)' (Mingers 1999, p. 4).

More phenomenological research approaches focus on 'meaning-making', with the meaning often being seen as made by individuals, and in some circumstances by the researcher and the respondent together (as also described in Pring 2000, described in Chapter 5 above). Research methods used include participant observation when the researcher joins the group to be studied, the close analysis of conversations or texts, and in-depth interviews sometimes modelled on psychotherapeutic interviewing techniques (many of which are well described in Silverman 1997, and for studies of religion in McCutcheon 1999). This can lead to more individualistic meaning-making, as in Moustakas' description of heuristic research. 'Heuristics' is a term used in general research methodology for rather open investigation or discovery, sometimes by trial and error, and for Moustakas, heuristic research 'refers to a process of internal search through which one discovers the nature and meaning of experience and develops methods and procedures for further investigation and analysis' (Moustakas 1994, p. 17). In this model of research, '[t]he self of the researcher is present throughout the process and, while understanding the phenomenon with increasing depth, the researcher also experiences growing self-awareness and self-knowledge', so '[h]euristic processes incorporate creative self-processes and self-discoveries' (Moustakas 1994, p. 17). This is an approach that will have echoes for those in religious education concerned with the search for truth. He explains that researchers should be 'immersed' in the world being researched, and should pause and consider the meaning of their own lives, as 'knowledge does not end with moments of connectedness, understanding, and meaning' (Moustakas 1994, p. 65). 'No scientific discovery is ever complete ... [and t]his is the beauty of knowledge and discovery ... [that i]t keeps us forever awake, alive, and connected with what is and with what matters in life' (Moustakas 1994, p. 65).

That is a wonderful picture of research. However, the tendency to more individualistic meaning-making of this kind might yet trouble some researchers of religion. For example, personal involvement can cause difficulties, as described of the meetings with a Vodou priestess noted by MacCarthy Brown in McCutcheon 1999. Helpfully, the individualistic (and potentially over-personal) approach is contrasted by Silverman with the possibility of systematic analysis in qualitative research. He stresses the need 'to broaden our conception of qualitative research beyond issues of subjective "meaning" and towards issues of language, representation and social organization' (Silverman 1997, p. 1). He also notes his 'belief that a social *science*, which takes seriously the attempt to sort fact from fancy, remains a valid enterprise', as part of the 'search for ways of building links between social science traditions rather than dwelling in "armed camps" fighting internal battles' (Silverman 1997, p. 1, as also in Pring, quoted in Chapter 5 above). Ethnography can be building that bridge, by following the guidance of Silverman and also that of Moustakas, who himself refers back to Buber's 'explorations of dialogue and mutuality' (Moustakas 1994, p. 17). It is the return to issues of dialogue that reaffirms the need for *sincerity* in phenomenological research, and it is dialogue that can also bring back the broader community dynamics, vital in schools and in school-based research in religious education. The mutuality of relationships in community is underpinned by Macmurray's concern with schools as communities, affirming the humanity and integrity of pupils and teachers alike. Children are young people; older people have, often enough, 'betrayed the personal integrity of our childhood in becoming conformed to the fashion of this world' (Macmurray 1968, p. 18). In order to 'recover our integrity, we have to become as little children', and '[f]rom this perspective the task of the teacher appears no longer as an effort to achieve an integrity of character that is absent in the young animal; but rather to preserve the integrity of childhood through the process of its growth and maturity' (Macmurray 1968, p. 18).

More positivist approaches to research, in contrast to phenomenological approaches, can at times be stereotyped as entirely focused on 'scientific counting', creating systematic models of organizations, and ignoring all questions of meaning. Yet some of the more positivist research does indeed investigate meanings, and most certainly recognizes the difficulties of achieving neutrality. It is possible that sincerity can help enhance positivist research, and that is what is attempted here. To develop sincerity in research requires creating contexts in which respondents feel that their answers matter, and that the questioner wants and needs to know what they think for substantive reasons. This may require more dialogue and 'engagement', and less anonymity and pretended neutrality, than is usual in research. It can mean that research should routinely be set in the context of purposes related to the subject of research. For example, introducing research on school effectiveness to pupils, a researcher might ask the pupils whether they would like to help improve their school (the answer is almost inevitably 'yes'), and whether they know better than, say, their teachers, how to improve their school (the answer is generally also 'yes'). In such a context, and if the researcher is committed to reporting the research back to the pupils, the student council, and the staff, the pupils are likely to feel – correctly – an incentive to be sincere. The only people who might be excluded from accepting the assumption that school might be improved, say, would be those who believed school as a whole, or this school in particular, was wholly inadequate – for example, those who might support the 'deschooling' movement (as for example in Illich 1971, 1974) – and those who believed the school was perfect in every way. Such pupils are rare, and work by Rudduck and colleagues suggests that pupils have criticisms of schools (including schools with better and worse public 'reputations'), but that they share basic educational goals, so that '[b]ehind the public mask of nonchalance that some pupils wear to hide their anxiety about the future is a concern to succeed and some realisation of the consequences of not making the grade' (Rudduck *et al.* 1996, p. 3).

Researchers, too, will avoid the 'mask of nonchalance', by admitting their interest in the responses. In that way, sincerity creates a more honest relationship that is likely to involve more sincere responses from pupils. The apparent bias of the research – a bias towards finding out what matters – will itself be likely to enhance, rather than detract from, the value of the responses. 'Sincerity' as an approach to research can also be related to the stress on 'ownership' of research tools, highlighted in the methodology of Dalin and Rust. They say that '[o]rganization development assumes that school personnel should have a maximum degree of ownership in the renewal process', as '[r]esearch on change indicates that successful implementation is highly correlated with a sense of ownership of the ideas, the process and solutions found' (Dalin and Rust 1983, p. 175). In this way, ownership can be seen as a way of increasing the likelihood of sincerity. Developing the theme of ownership, sincerity can also be demonstrated by valuing the *products* of research: research results can be given back to those researched, for their own use. The sincerity involved in such approaches to research also has professional implications.

Sincerity in religious education research

Sincerity in religious education research has an impact on religious education classrooms when those classrooms involve pupils and teachers working together as researchers, as in ethnographic, interpretive, constructivist and various other religious education traditions. Classrooms aiming for 'more than not lying' will be learning communities, bound together in a rich dialogue of truths and human development. Religious education, a subject itself rich in dialogue, truths and human development, can lead the way to research-rich schooling. The six themes in religious education research identified for the Westhill Trust seminar series in 2004–5, and therefore addressed in Chapters 6 to 10 and later in the current chapter of this book, addressed current research in religious education. The various case studies and other activities described throughout this book illustrate different ways in which religious education research, and therefore religious education, might exemplify sincerity from across the 'false dichotomies' of phenomenological and positivistic traditions. It is helpful to give specific examples, explaining the relationship between the task and sincerity.

In Chapter 6 on sacred text, work on story-telling from the Bhagavad Gita is helped by the expectation of trying to understand the intentions of those who use the text in a religious context, and trying to understand the purposes to which pupils might put the text. The work would demonstrate less sincerity to the extent that pupils were given questions with simple, ready-made, right and wrong answers, or were given no time to consider the importance of the texts to their own lives, religious or not. Research on dialogue, like dialogue of all kinds, can be made more likely to be sincere if participants have something of importance to talk about. The work from Chapter 7 on what more can be done to promote religious harmony provides such a topic, a topic of especial significance in those periods when disharmony is all too common. Inclusion, the topic of Chapter 8, is investigated by inspection bodies such as Ofsted, and some of the guidance on inspection (such as Ofsted 2000a) suggests inspectors should talk to pupils about their feelings on inclusion. The involvement of pupils is to be welcomed, and research on inclusion in religious education should go even further. Work on the contrasting pairs of statement asks pupils and teachers to investigate in detail how inclusive the religious education curriculum is, with sincerity promoted by the self-reflective nature of the research. It can be further enhanced by explicitly framing the research as part of improvement-planning for the religious education department. In a similar way, on pedagogy, it was suggested in Chapter 9 that pupils be asked about their own subjects, and the responses are not guesses at the 'right answers', but answers to genuinely-meant questions about how teachers and pupils typically speak in lessons. Human rights, values and citizenships are increasingly researched in religious education across the world. Making research more sincere can be about making the questions and answers current and relevant to the lives of the pupils, as in the United Nations-style debate on a current issue.

Ethnography and religious education: they see us in a very funny way!

The sixth of the themes of the Westhill Seminars was ethnography, a valuable set of case studies of research methodology in religious education. Ethnography has at its heart the need to understand not only the people being studied, on their own terms, but also the researchers completing the study, and the relationships between researchers and researched. It is not simply that people can have an 'ethnographic approach to life', attempting to understand people and communicate this understanding sensitively to others. It is that the ethnographic researcher is not, and should not attempt to be, a separate, impersonal and neutral observer of life, looking at 'interesting objects of study'. Buber (1958) describes how a person can treat the other as an object, as 'it', or can treat the other as a subject, as 'thou'. Buber's contrast between 'I–it' and 'I–thou' relationships is used to understand people and to understand social and political structures. His is a good basis for the work of this book, as it also applies to teachers, pupils and researchers, most especially ethnographic researchers. Starting with some definitions, ethnography is etymologically derived from 'people-writing' or 'people-drawing', with 'people' perhaps meaning race or nation. So ethnography is related to ethnology (for example investigating tea ceremonies), and to anthropology, which in the past often involved investigating isolated and pre-literate communities, though it later developed into social anthropology often in urban settings. 'Ethnography' refers to immersive fieldwork in a real or a virtual community, and to the report of the fieldwork, which may be in print or a documentary or a film. It is an empirical study consisting largely of more-or-less participant observation, and semi-structured or unstructured interviewing allowing the interviewee some 'agency'. It is described by Pring as referring 'to that kind of research which takes seriously the perspectives and the interactions of the members of the social groups being studied', 'based on the premise that social reality cannot be understood except through the rules which structure the relations between members of the group and which make it possible for each to interpret the actions, gestures and words of others' (Pring 2000, p. 104).

This issue of agency is an important ethical and political issue. One of the leading ethnographic researchers working in religious education is Nesbitt, who describes researching young Hindu homes (reported in Jackson and Nesbitt 1993, and in the Westhill Seminars), and the potential problems of power, of having the power to interpret and use material gained from people. Increasingly, therefore, the subjects of research are being treated as active participants, with some editorial input. Such 'deep listening', and empowering people, can be an attitude to life as well as to research. People can have an 'ethnographic' approach to life, although they can also choose to reject that, as people and as researchers. The aims of ethnography are to understand human behaviour at ever-increasing depth, from the point of view of those studied, and to communicate this deepening understanding sensitively to others. When ethnographic research is completed for religious education, as it is by Nesbitt and others at the Warwick Religions and Education Research Unit (www.warwick.ac.uk/wie/WRERU), there are therefore benefits to religious education teaching and learning, and to research in religious education.

It is also, in contrast, important to be aware of some of the dangers of small-scale ethnographic studies. The dangers include the possibility of being superficial (simply looking for 'easy to see' characteristics), 'essentializing' an aspect of religion (making something that is incidental into something that is central to the religious life), homogenizing a 'religion' (assuming all those of a religion are like the people studied), or creating artificial boundaries between religions (by making differences between individuals into universal differences). A simple example given by Nesbitt is her self-questioning, when studying Hindu children, asking why she was picking out the child's use of a *puja* corner, to describe life at home, whilst ignoring the child spending time watching soap operas on the television. A classroom example, from Stern, is of a group of children watching a video of a Muslim wedding in Bangladesh, the wedding of family members of one of the class. When the class was asked to say what they had learned from watching the video, the most striking 'lesson' was described by one pupil (not from Bangladesh), who said with real surprise in his voice 'I'd no idea they had mopeds in Bangladesh!' Some of the advantages and challenges of the ethnographic study of religion are analysed and exemplified in the work of various writers, including Nesbitt (especially Nesbitt 2004, and other related work in Jackson and Nesbitt 1993, Nesbitt 2001, 2003, 2005 and Nesbitt and Kaur 1998), Searle-Chatterjee (2000), Searle-Chatterjee *et al.* (2000), Ballard (1994), Baumann (1996, 1999) and Geaves (Geaves 1998, and see also Geaves *et al.* 2004).

Ethnography and religious education are in turn connected to pluralism. Skeie (1995) talks about pluralism as a commitment to an affirmative response to diversity or plurality. Plurality is a significant aspect of post- or late-modernity, while pluralism is our response to this, according to Skeie. And there is an acknowledgement of religious and cultural plurality, which has driven much recent religious education. Intercultural education, as exemplified in Nesbitt's recent book (Nesbitt 2004), is a phrase used more in French than English, with 'intercultural' helpfully bypassing some of the conflict between multicultural and anti-racist movements. This can therefore connect the study of religion (as in Sutcliffe 2004) and religious education. People should ask themselves whether they, in universities or schools, can be more like ethnographers in how they work and teach and interact in schools. This is relevant to the whole school ethos, not just to religious education. It may boil down to something pretty close to 'respect'.

Pupils as researchers can construct a 'respect map' of their own school. If work in religious education has included how people identify themselves as (for example) an atheist, a Buddhist, a Christian, a Hindu, a Jew, a Humanist, a Muslim, a New Age follower, or a Sikh, pupils (in pairs or small groups) could become researchers concerned with one of those 'labels' (see also Jackson 1990 on children as ethnographers). The questions and topics described by Nesbitt ('guidelines for teachers' in Nesbitt 2004, pp. 154–66) may be helpful as preparation for pupils and teachers alike, as would her subtle analysis of identity (Nesbitt 2004, ch. 10). Each group of pupils can be given a map of the school, with the rooms appropriately labelled with the subjects or activities they host. The pupils should interview other pupils and staff, asking about where in the school 'atheists' (or whichever group is being studied) would be most respected, and why. For example, pupils might say that 'atheists' are most respected in science laboratories, and in the staffroom, or that Jews are most respected in religious education rooms and in English rooms. The analysis of the respect maps of members of all the groups can provide a subtle picture of the social organization of the school, how different subjects and activities of the school are regarded by pupils, and how much pupils understand about these issues. Other 'respect maps' can be completed for boys and girls, or for members of different social groups. The value, for religious education, of starting with those self-identified with religious categories, is that it can provide a basis for much further religious education, clearly connected to the lives of the pupils as lived in their own school.

Ethnography, Muslim diversity and religious education

Using ethnography can not only help teachers and pupils to understand the people being studied, it can also help researchers to see how they in turn are understood by those studied. This is particularly well illustrated by the research of Smalley (as reported in Smalley 2005, and in the Westhill Seminars, and see also Grove and Smalley 2003), on teaching about and learning from Muslims, in part in order to understand Islamophobia in the classroom. Smalley completed ethnographic work with two Muslim communities in Peterborough, and it is worth describing some of the processes of that research, as an example of some of the opportunities for ethnographic research with clear implications for religious education.

Peterborough in the south of England had two distinct Muslim communities, representing a huge diversity in terms of ethnicity, language, reasons for being in Britain, religion, and of course individual, personal, differences. There were interviews with 24 parents and further research with their children, with the sample coming from each of the two groups. One group was from Pakistani background families who were mostly labour migrants, Sunni Muslims, from a rural background and with varied educational backgrounds. These interviewees mostly had an expectation of marrying and doing business with other British people from Pakistani backgrounds. The second group were from African Asian background families, originally refugees, Shi'a Muslims (Khoja Shi'a Ithna'asheri) with urban backgrounds. They mostly had an expectation of marrying and doing business with a wide range of people from Britain, East Africa, India, Canada, the USA and Dubai. Smalley looked across two generations: how did parents bring up children and how did this compare with how they were brought up? It is helpful to describe some examples of research findings, along with their implications for religious education. As one respondent said of other people in the UK, 'they see us in a very funny way!'

One piece of research involved participant observation at a mosque during *Muharram* (related to the death of Hussein, the grandson of the Prophet), stressing suffering and martyrdom and moral issues for the contemporary world such as remorse and mercy. Preaching on one occasion was by a woman on the theme of Islam as 'all or nothing', on the death of Hussein, with breast-beating and, later, cheerful socializing. Later preaching also involved the congregation being drawn 'to a pitch of frenzied weeping', which 'ended as quickly as it had begun'. Even small children were involved with active roles to play and written work, taking them back to the routes of Shi'a Islam and the morals of Karbala. For teaching religious education content authentically, this work would bring to life characteristics of Sunni and Shi'a Islam. It could also help teachers to convey something of the power and purpose of ritual, thus providing a more accessible view of what might otherwise seem inexplicable. It could provide religious education with a view of the practice and experience of women and girls (which is not always easily available), and connections with the expressions of remorse in other traditions (such as Good Friday processions in southern Europe). In terms of the process of religious education, this work would provide a way of recording and communicating religion, and an insight into how this experience fits into a bigger picture and tensions between different experiences within a tradition.

A second theme of Smalley's research involved interviewing Muslim women about the *hijab*. Textbooks on research (such as Cohen *et al.* 2000) point out many of the difficulties of completing interviews, including problems with leading questions and with confidentiality. Researchers are divided over the advantages of being 'insiders' and 'outsiders' (with a superb set of articles on the topic in McCutcheon 1999). Smalley helped create a 'connection' with the interviewees by talking as a parent, herself. Responses to talking about *hijab* varied widely, itself an important lesson for anyone wishing to teach 'the right answer' (or scared of presenting 'the wrong answer') on such issues. One respondent said 'I just feel more comfortable in it now – I feel more confident', others talked about the importance of inward goodness not (just) outward appearances, others about only doing things when they are understood (for the right reasons). However, such paraphrasing of the accounts takes away from their power and interest. The full accounts and, even more, being involved in the interviews themselves, provide a much better sense of the individual life stories behind each decision.

Learning from home environments is a third theme of Smalley's research. This involved visits to homes in order to complete interviews, but the visits themselves provided further insights. For example, the pictures on the walls and the position of books around rooms all contributed to children's informal learning about Islam. The interviews took place, often, with children in other rooms or sitting with the mother, food being offered, and questions about schooling such as difficulties over homework. These 'ambient' characteristics, which could have been seen as distractions from the purpose of the interview, in fact helped retain a focus on people rather than on edicts and doctrines, and helped stress how people negotiate everyday life.

For religious education, then, it is important to understand the variety of experience that children from different backgrounds bring to a diverse school. Overall, the qualitative fieldwork, according to Smalley, 'gives polyphonic depth and richness – we hear many voices'. Ethnographic research can add *authenticity* to religious education, and can add personal – but not institutional – *authority* to religious education. Smalley points out that this is no simple matter, as authenticity may not be 'positive' in the way religious education teachers would expect. In Smalley 2005 the question is asked 'How can we be positive but realistic?', which is an extension of the same problem. It takes the argument back to the issues raised in Chapter 6 above, on controversy in religious education: religious education must be a gritty subject, and must not be a bland diet of 'niceness'. For Smalley, the answer to the question is in multiple views (i.e. seeing examples from the whole range of all traditions) and in active involvement (i.e. through ethnographic research and through dialogue within religious education classrooms).

An exercise described in detail in Stern 2006b is referred to as 'reverse ethnography'. As ethnography has already been described as deriving etymologically from 'people-writing' or 'people-drawing', it is an attempt at the reverse: an attempt to 'draw with people'. Most pupils and adults are familiar with photo-stories, where a kind of strip cartoon is not drawn but made up using a series of posed photographs. They have been popular in newspapers and magazines, and have been often used to illustrate social and moral problems or dilemmas. Pupils can create their own photo-stories. Such an activity has been made considerably easier in recent years, with the emergence of electronic cameras and the ease of editing pictures and text with the simplest of word-processors. Working in groups of four to six pupils, the pupils should be given a particular issue or dilemma related to their religious education lesson topic, and be asked to create a 12-photo photo-story to illustrate that issue. They will need to pose for, as well as photograph, the 12 scenes: hence, 'drawing with people'. They will also need to write the captions to each of the 12 scenes. An example of a topic, related to Smalley's research, could be a discussion in a Muslim family about *hijab*. Pupils creating photo-stories are often motivated by the task itself, as well as the topic. Further motivation might be added by an expectation that the photo-stories would be used to teach the topic to other pupils in the school.

Ethnographic research is by its nature small-scale research, developing complex accounts of the everyday lives of people rather than generalized accounts of society as a whole. It is the sharing of ethnographic accounts, the communication between ethnographic researchers, that can build up our understanding beyond that of the initial subjects of the study: indeed, 'it is the sharing of a common life which constitutes individual personality' (Macmurray 1993, p. 37). Such work can be shared around a school or a wider community making use of computer-based blogging (i.e. an Internet diary or 'weblog', with guidance on blogging from www.blogger.com and www.blogging-brits.co.uk). Schools would need to consider the ethics of what material it is appropriate to put on Intranet or Internet sites, and the consideration of online ethics is itself a valuable contribution to understanding religious education and to understanding research. The content of the blog would itself be intended to demonstrate the value of its ethnographic research. A class could create a blog for religious education, accessible to other classes in that school. The ethics of presenting research in this way should be discussed with the class and with those having a responsibility for the school's web policy (with general research ethics available from Cohen *et al.* 2000). The blog may helpfully start with reports on ethnographic research as described in this chapter, and might also move on to include reports on other work based on the various activities described elsewhere in this book, reports on visits to religious and other communities, and reports on visits from such communities – perhaps including answers to questions posed by pupils. It might also include work by local students of religion, members of local communities, and accounts of religious and other celebrations.

Conclusion: we live amidst unfinished business

Ethnography helps bring people together, based on an attempt to understand what things mean to people. People, in this approach, matter. That what people say matters, is also the basis of sincerity. The more sincerity there is in religious education research, the more value that research is likely to have, in itself and for religious education, schools and the wider communities in which they are set. There are those who will joke about sincerity, and trivialize its significance. There is a well-known quotation from Jean Giraudoux, a French diplomat and writer of the early twentieth century: 'The secret of success is sincerity. If you can fake that, you've got it made' (www.quotationspage.com/quote/ 481.html). Joking apart, an approach to religious education and research that embodies sincerity is one that could help enrich and enliven an already rich and vibrant subject. Teaching religious education, with teachers and pupils as researchers in the classroom, can bring people and communities together. Now, just as in every other period of history, this is a worthwhile and much needed task.

There is plenty to be done. Religious education contributes not only to pupils understanding the world, but to how teachers and researchers understand education as a whole. This is the answer to Jackson's challenge, described in the preface to this book (and in Jackson 2004, ch. 9), to put research in religious education in the mainstream of education research. Religions and schools have much in common: all live in mystery, and all deal with change and emerging truth. As Hick says, '[w]e live amidst unfinished business; but we must trust that continuing dialogue will prove to be dialogue into truth' (Hick 1974, p. 155). Dialogue into truth cannot be completed alone, and the truth is not something just 'in the head'. 'Truth is not born from dialectic in the head of an individual person but "between people collectively searching for truth, in the process of their dialogic interaction"' (Friedman 2002, p. 361). Individuals, schools, communities and religions are brought together, personally and politically, by learning – systematically and thoughtfully by research – through imagining the real.

> It is only through our imaginative construction that we shall be able to own the full heritage of the experience we have acquired through living in time. And if we are to confirm the meaning, the value, of our own story, we must make an act of personal faith. In the end it is the storyteller who, like any novelist, commands the audience. Our sense of the meaning of our story – that is our contribution to life. (Salmon 1985, quoted in Frances 2005)

This is action philosophy. It is good to know: the point, however, is to change.

Bibliography

Abbott, C. (ed.) (2002) *Special Educational Needs and the Internet: Issues for the Inclusive Classroom*; London: RoutledgeFalmer.

Alderson, P. (2000) *Young Children's Rights: Exploring Beliefs, Principles and Practice*; London: Jessica Kingsley.

Alexander, R. J. (2004) *Towards Dialogic Teaching: Rethinking Classroom Talk*; Thirsk: Dialogos.

—— (2006) *Education as Dialogue: Moral and Pedagogical Choices for a Runaway World*; Thirsk: Hong Kong Institute of Education with Dialogos.

Ali, T. (2002) *The Clash of Fundamentalisms: Crusades, Jihads and Modernity*; London: Verso.

Alperson, P. (ed.) (2002) *Diversity and Community: An Interdisciplinary Reader*; Oxford: Blackwell.

Aristotle (1925) *The Nicomachean Ethics of Aristotle*; London: Oxford University Press.

—— (1962) *The Politics*; Harmondsworth: Penguin.

—— (1976) *Nichomachean Ethics*; London: Penguin.

Armstrong, K. (2000) *The Battle For God: Fundamentalism in Judaism, Christianity and Islam*; London: Harper Perennial.

The Assessment Reform Group (1999) *Assessment for Learning: Beyond the Black Box*; Cambridge: University of Cambridge School of Education.

Atlanta Symphony Orchestra and Chorus (1994) *A Vision of Heaven: Choral Masterpieces by Mozart, Beethoven, Mahler, Fauré* [also known as *Absolute Heaven – Essential Choral Masterpieces*]; Cleveland, Ohio: Telarc PTCD347.

Attia, A. (1994) *Musique Liturgique Juive*; Paris: CDM CMT 274 993.

Attridge, D. (2004) *The Singularity of Literature*; London: Routledge.

Atwood, M. (2003) *Negotiating With the Dead: A Writer On Writing*; London: Virago.

Bacharach, S. B. and Mundell, B. (eds) (1995) *Images of Schools: Structures and Roles in Organizational Behavior*; Thousand Oaks, California: Corwin.

Bacon, F. (2002) *Francis Bacon: The Major Works: Including* New Atlantis *and the* Essays; Oxford: Oxford University Press.

Bailey, R. (ed.) (2000) *Teaching Values and Citizenship across the Curriculum*; London: Kogan Page.

Bakhtin, M. M. (1981) *The Dialogic Imagination: Four Essays by M M Bakhtin: Edited by Michael Holquist, Translated by Caryl Emerson and Michael Holquist*; Austin, Texas: University of Texas Press.

Ball, S. J. (1987) *The Micro-Politics of the School: Towards a Theory of School Organization*; London: Routledge.

Ballard, R. (ed.) (1994) *Desh Pradesh: South Asian Experience in Britain*; London: C. Hurst & Co.

Barber, B. (1984) *Strong Democracy: Participatory Politics for a New Age*; Berkeley: University of California Press.

Barker, E. (ed.) (1982) *New Religious Movements: A Perspective for Understanding Society*; New York and Toronto: Edwin Mellen Press.

—— (1984) *The Making of a Moonie: Brainwashing or Choice?*; Oxford: Blackwell.

—— (1989) *New Religious Movements: A Practical Introduction*; London: HMSO.

Barth, R. S. (1990) *Improving Schools from Within: Teachers, Parents, and Principals Can Make the Difference*; San Francisco: Jossy-Bass.

Bastiani, J. (ed.) (1997) *Home–School Work in Multicultural Settings*; London: Fulton.

Baum, L. F. (novel), Langley, N., Ryerson, F. and Woolf, E. A. (screenplay) (1939) *The Wizard of Oz*; Los Angeles, Ca.: MGM (also from ww.imdb.com/title/tt0032138/quotes).

Baumann, G. (1996) *Contesting Culture: Discourses of Identity in Multi-Ethnic London*; Cambridge: Cambridge University Press.

—— (1999) *The Multicultural Riddle: Rethinking National, Ethnic and Religious Identities*; London: Routledge.

Baumfield, V. (2002) *Thinking Through Religious Education*; Cambridge: Chris Kington.

—— (2003) 'Democratic RE: Preparing Young People for Citizenship', *BJRE* 25:3, Summer 2003.

—— Bowness, C., Cush, D. and Miller, J. (1994) *A Third Perspective*; privately published.

Beadle, L. (ed.) (2006) *Steps in RE Onwards and Upwards: Addressing the Additional Support Needs of Students in Key Stage 3 (11–14 year olds) in RE*; Birmingham: RE Today Services.

Beane, J. A. (1995) 'Curriculum integration and the disciplines of knowledge', *Phi Delta Kappan*, 76:8, April 1995, pp. 616–22.

Beckerlegge, G. (ed.) (2001a) *The World Religions Reader* (2nd edition); London: Routledge/Open University.

—— (2001b) *From Sacred Text to Internet*; Aldershot, Berks: Ashgate and the Open University Press.

Bell, J. (1999) *Curriculum and Professional Development in RE: Syllabus Implementation Studies 1996–99: Research Report on the Implementation of the New Syllabus in LEA 1: 'Construction, Communication and Confidence'*; Norwich: University of East Anglia.

Benjamin, W. (1997) *One-Way Street and Other Writings*; London: Verso.

Benn, C. and Chitty, C. (1996) *Thirty Years On: Is comprehensive Education Alive and Well or Struggling to Survive?*; London: Fulton.

Bennis, W. (1994) 'Followership', from *An Invented Life: Reflections on Leadership and Change* (Chapter 11), www.cio.com/executive/edit/chapter11.html.

Bhattacharya, D. (collector) (1999) *Religious Chants from India: Sikh, Buddhist, Hindu*; East Grinstead, West Sussex: ARC Music EUCD 1537.

Bhindi, N. and Duignan, P. (1997) 'Leadership for a New Century: Authenticity, Intentionality, Spirituality and Sensibility', *Educational Management and Administration*, 25:2, pp. 117–32.

Biott, C. (1991) *Semi-Detached Teachers: Building Support and Advisory Relationships in Classrooms*; London: Falmer.

Black, P. and Wiliam, D. (1998a) 'Assessment and Classroom Learning', *Assessment in Education: Principles, Policy & Practice*, 5:1, March 1998, pp. 7–74.

—— (1998b) 'Inside the Black Box: Raising Standards Through Classroom Assessment', *Phi Delta Kappan*, 89:2, October 1998, pp. 139–48.

Blase, J. and Anderson, G. (1995) *The Micropolitics of Educational Leadership: From Control to Empowerment*; London: Cassell.

Blaylock, L. (1993) *The Implementation of Agreed Syllabuses of Religious Education: A Study in Leicestershire: Report to the Farmington Institute*; Oxford: Farmington Institute.

—— (2000) 'Teachers With Others Specialisms in RE: The "TWOS" Project', *REsource*, 22:2, Spring 2000.

—— (ed.) (2001a) *Listening to Children in Primary Religious Education*; Birmingham: PCfRE.

—— (ed.) (2001b) *Listening to young people in Secondary Education*; Birmingham: PCfRE.

—— (2004) 'Six Schools of Thought in RE', *Resource*, 27:1, Autumn 2004.

Bleakley, A. (2004) ' "Your creativity or mine?": a typology of creativities in higher education and the value of a pluralistic approach', *Teaching in Higher Education*, 9:4, October 2004, pp. 463–75.

Blue Murder (2002) *No One Stands Alone*; London: Topic TSCD537.

Boden, M. A. (2004) *The Creative Mind: Myths and Mechanisms* (2nd edition); London: Routledge.

Bolton, J. (1999) *An Investigation into the place of Paganism within RE*; Oxford: The Farmington Institute (also from http://www.farmington.ac.uk).

Bottery, M. (1992) *The Ethics of Educational Management: Personal, Social and Political Perspectives on School Organization*; London: Cassell.

—— (2000) *Education, Policy and Ethics*; London: Continuum.

—— (2004) *The Challenges of Educational Leadership*; London: Paul Chapman.

Bowker, J. (ed.) (1997) *The Oxford Dictionary of World Religions*; Oxford: Oxford University Press.

Bradley, I. (ed.) (1996) *The Complete Annotated Gilbert and Sullivan*; Oxford: Oxford University Press.

Brighouse, T. (2004) 'Everyone can walk on water', *Friday magazine, TES*, 4th June 2004, pp. 18–19.

Britannica CD, Version 1998 (Britannica) (1994–8) *Encyclopædia Britannica*; Chicago, Ill: Encyclopædia Britannica Inc.

British Educational Communications and Technology Agency (Becta) (2003a) *What the Research Says About ICT and Home-School Links*; Coventry: Becta (and from www.becta.org.uk/research).

—— (2003b) *What the Research Says About ICT and Motivation*; Coventry: Becta (and from http://www.becta.org.uk/research).

British Sociological Association (1995) *Statement of Ethical Practice*; Durham: British Sociological Association.

Brittan, S. (1997) 'Tony Blair's real guru', *New Statesman*, 2 July 1997, 126 Issues 4320, pp. 18–20.

Broadbent, L. and Brown, A. (eds) (2002) *Issues in Religious Education*; London: RoutledgeFalmer.

Brown, E. (1996) *Religious Education for All*; London: David Fulton.

—— (1999) *Loss, Change and Grief: An Educational Perspective*; London: Fulton.

Bryk, A. S. and Schneider, B. (2002) *Trust in Schools*; New York: Russell Sage Foundation.

Buber, M. (1958) *I and Thou: Translated by Ronald Gregor Smith: 2nd edition with a postscript by the author*; Edinburgh: T&T Clark.

—— (1965) *The Way of Man According to the Teaching of Hasidism*; London: Routledge.

—— (1999) *Gog and Magog: A Novel*; Syracuse, New York: Syracuse University Press.

—— (2002a) *Between Man and Man*; London: Routledge.

—— (2002b) *Meetings: Autobiographical Fragments* (3rd edition); London: Routledge.

Al-Buraidi, J. A. (2006) *An Empirical Study of the Perceptions of Male Teachers and Students of the Islamic Education Curriculum in Secondary Schools in the Kingdom of Saudi Arabia*; PhD thesis, University of Hull.

Burden, K. and Kuechel, T. (2004) *Evaluation Report of the Teaching and Learning With Digital Video Assets Pilot 2003–2004*; Coventry: Becta (and from http://www.becta.org.uk/page_documents/research/evaluation_dv_assets03.pdf).

Burke, C. and Grosvenor, I. (2003) *The School I'd Like: Children and Young People's Reflections on an Education for the 21st Century*; Abingdon, Oxon: RoutledgeFalmer.

Campaign for Real Education (2001) *Educational Philosophies*, www.cre.org.uk/philosophies.htm.

Canter, L. and Canter, M. (1992) *Lee Canter's Assertive Discipline: Positive Behavior Management for Today's Classroom*; Santa Monica, California: Lee Canter & Associates.

Carr, D. (2003) *Making Sense of Education: an Introduction to the Philosophy and Theory of Education and Teaching*; London: RoutledgeFalmer.

Carrington, B. and Troyna, B. (eds) (1988) *Children and Controversial Issues: Strategies for the Early and Middle Years of Schooling*; London: Falmer.

Chapman, J., Froumin, I. and Aspin, D. (eds) (1995) *Creating and Managing the Democratic School*; London: Falmer.

Chater, M. F. T. (2000) 'To Teach Is to Set Free: Liberation Theology and the Democratisation of the Citizenship Agenda', *British Journal of Religious Education*, 23:1, pp. 5–14.

Cherry, F. (1995) *The 'Stubborn Particulars' of Social Psychology: Essays on the Research Process*; London: Routledge.

Chödzin, S. and Kohn, A. (with illustrations by Marie Cameron) (1997) *The Barefoot Book of Buddhist Tales* [also published as *The Wisdom of the Crows and Other Stories*]; Bath: Barefoot Books.

Chryssides, G. (1991) *The Advent of Sun Myung Moon: the Origins, Beliefs and Practices of the Unification Church*; London: Macmillan.

—— (1994) 'New Religious Movements: Some problems of definition', *DISKUS International Journal of Religion* 2:2, available at www.uni-marburg.de/religionswissenschaft/journal/diskus/chryssides.html.

—— (1999) *Exploring new Religions*; London: Cassell.

—— (2000) 'Defining the New Spirituality', a paper presented at CESNUR 14th International Conference, Riga, Latvia, August 29–31, available at www.cesnur.org/conferences/riga2000/chryssides.htm.

—— (2003) 'Books on New Religious Movements', in *Resource*, 26:1, pp. 4–7.

Cohen, L., Manion, L. and Morrison, K. (2000) *Research Methods in Education* (5th edition); London: Routledge.

Conger, J. A. and Kanunga, R. N. (1998) *Charismatic Leadership in Organizations*; Thousand Oaks, California: Sage.

Cooling, T. (1994a) *A Christian Vision for State Education: Reflections on the Theology of Education*; London: SPCK.

—— (1994b) *Concept Cracking: Exploring Christian Beliefs in School*; Stapleford, Nottinghamshire: The Stapleford Centre (and http://www.stapleford-centre.org/).

Cooper, A. F. and Higgott, R. A. (1991) 'Bound to Follow? Leadership and Followership in the Gulf Conflict', *Political Science Quarterly*, 106: 3, Fall 1991, pp. 391 ff.

Cooper, R. (2001) 'The State We're In', *Free Associations*, 8:3.

Copley, C., Copley, T., Freathy, R., Lane, S. and Walshe, K. (2004) *On the Side of the Angels: The Third Report of the Biblos Project*; Exeter: University of Exeter.

Copley, T. (1998) *Echo of Angels: The First Report of the Biblos Project*; Exeter: Biblos Project, School of Education University of Exeter.

—— Lane, S., Savini, H. and Walshe, K. (2001) *Where Angels Fear To Tread: The Second Report of the Biblos Project*; Exeter: Biblos Project, School of Education University of Exeter.

—— and Walshe, K. (2002) *The Figure of Jesus in Religious Education*; Exeter: School of Education and Lifelong Learning, University of Exeter.

Costello, J. (1998a) [Comments to Julian Stern in conversations during The Life and Work of John Macmurray Conference, University of Aberdeen, March 1998]

—— (1998b) 'The Life and Thought of John Macmurray', in *The Life and Work of John Macmurray: Conference Proceedings, University of Aberdeen, March 1998*.

Costello, J. E. (2002) *John Macmurray: A Biography*; Edinburgh: Floris.

Craft, A., Jeffrey, B. and Leibling, M. (eds) (2001) *Creativity in Education*; London: Continuum.

Crick, B. (1998) *Education for Citizenship and the Teaching of Democracy in Schools: Final Report of the Advisory Group on Citizenship*; London: QCA.

—— (2004) 'Civic talk', *TES*, 5 March 2004.

Cupitt, D. (1991) *What is a Story?*; Norwich: SCM Press.

Cush, D. (1994) 'RE does not equal worship', *TES*, 23 September 1994.

Dahl, R. A. (1961) *Who Governs?: Democracy and Power in an American City*; New Haven, Connecticut: Yale University Press.

—— (1989) *Democracy and Its Critics*; New Haven, Connecticut: Yale University Press.

—— (2005) *Who Governs?: Democracy and Power in an American City (2nd edition)*; New Haven, Connecticut: Yale University Press.

Dalin, P., with Rolff, H.-G., in cooperation with Kleekamp, B. (1993) *Changing the School Culture*; London: Cassell.

—— and Rust, V. D. (1983) *Can Schools Learn?*; Windsor: NFER-Nelson.

Daniels, H. (ed.) (1993) *Charting the agenda: Educational activity after Vygotsky*; London: Routledge.

—— (ed.) (1996) *An Introduction to Vygotsky*; London: Routledge.

—— (2001) *Vygotsky and Pedagogy*; London: RoutledgeFalmer.

—— and Edwards, A. (eds) (2004) *The RoutledgeFalmer Reader in Psychology of Education*; London: RoutledgeFalmer.

Darwin, C. (1971) *The Origin of Species*; London: Dent.

Davie, G. (1994) *Religion in Britain since 1945: Believing without Belonging*; Oxford: Blackwell.

Delf, R. and East Sussex County Council Education Department, Communications and Member Support Team (1999) *Teaching Pupils with Autism and Asperger Syndrome: Guidelines for Schools*; Lewes, East Sussex: East Sussex County Council.

DelFattore, J. (2004) *The Fourth R: Conflicts Over Religion in America's Public Schools*; New Haven, Connecticut: Yale University Press.

Dennett, D. C. (1995) *Darwin's Dangerous Idea: evolution and the meanings of life*; London: Penguin.

Department for Education, Welsh Office (DfE, Welsh Office) (1994) *Code of Practice on the Identification and Assessment of Special Educational Needs*; London: DfE.

Department for Education and Employment (DfEE) (1999) *All Our Futures: the National Advisory Committee for Creativity, Culture and Education*; London: DfEE.

Department for Education and Employment and the Qualifications and Curriculum Authority (DfEE and QCA) (1999) *The National Curriculum for England*; London: HMSO.

Department for Education and Skills (DfES) (2004a) *Every Child Matters: Change for Children*; Nottingham: DfES (and www.everychildmatters.gov.uk).

—— (2004b) *Every Child Matters: Next Steps*; Nottingham: DfES.

Department of Education and Science (DES) (1988) *Education Reform Act*; London: HMSO.

—— (1989) *Discipline in Schools: Report of the Committee of Enquiry chaired by Lord Elton*; London: HMSO.

Dewey, J. (1916) *Democracy and Education: An Introduction to the Philosophy of Education*; New York: The Free Press.

Dodd, T., Hartshorn, B., Due, B., Gunnarsson, G., Vedelsby, M. and MacAdam, R. (2002) *Intercultural Matters: Islam and European Education: Issues of Relevance for Teachers*; Castelo Branco, Portugal: Escola Superior de Educaçã, Instituto Politécnico de Castelo Branco.

Donald, J. and Rattansi, A. (eds) (1992) *Race, Culture and Difference*; London: Sage.

Dryden, W. (ed.) (1984) *Individual Therapy in Britain*; Milton Keynes: Open University Press.

Dunne, J. (1997) *Back to the Rough Ground: Practical Judgment and the Lure of Technique*; Notre Dame, Indiana: University of Notre Dame Press.

Durkheim, E. (1973) *Emile Durkheim on Morality and Society: Selected Writings: Edited and with an Introduction by Robert N Bellah*; Chicago: University of Chicago Press.

—— (1982) *The Rules of Sociological Method: And Selected Texts on Sociology and its Method: Edited with an Introduction by Steven Lukes: Translated by W D Halls*; Basingstoke: Macmillan.

Eco, U. (ed.) (2004) *On Beauty*; London: Secker & Warburg.

Empson, W. (1961) *Seven Types of Ambiguity* (3rd edition); Harmondsworth: Penguin.

Engle, T. and Hall, R. (executive producers) (2001) *Early Recordings of the Copper Family of Rottingdean*; London: Topic TSCD534.

Epstein, D. (2002) 'Re-Theorising Friendship in Educational Settings'; *Discourse: Studies in the Cultural Politics of Education*, 23:2, August 2002, pp. 149–51.

Erricker, C. (2001) *Teach Yourself Buddhism* (2nd edition); London: Hodder.

—— and Erricker, J. (2000) *Reconstructing Religious, Spiritual and Moral Education*; London: RoutledgeFarmer.

Fageant, J. and Blaylock, L. (eds) (1998) *Faith in the Future: An Anthology of pupils' writing from the National RE Festival Questionnaire*; Birmingham: PCfRE.

Fergusson, D. and Dower, N. (eds) (2002) *John Macmurray: Critical Perspectives*; New York: Lang.

Fielding, M. (1999) 'Communities of Learners: Myth: Schools Are Communities', in O'Hagan, B. (ed.) (1999) *Modern Educational Myths*; London: Kogan Page, pp. 67–87.

—— (2000) 'Community, Philosophy and Education Policy: Against Effectiveness Ideology and the Immiseration of Contemporary Schooling', *Journal of Education Policy*, 15:4, 2000, pp. 397–415.

—— (2001) 'Learning Organisation or Learning Community? A Critique of Senge', *Reason in Practice*, 1:2, 2001.

Flutter, J. and Rudduck, J. (2004) *Consulting Pupils: What's In It for Schools?*; London: RoutledgeFalmer.

Fowler, J. W. (1981) *Stages of Faith: The Psychology of Human Development and the Quest for Meaning;* San Francisco: Harper.

Frances, M. (2005) 'Dr Phillida Salmon 1933–2005', *European Personal Construct Association news* (www.epca-net.org/index.php?option = com_content&task = view&id = 23&Itemid = 2).

Francis, L. J., Kay, W. K., and Campbell, W. S. (eds) (1996) *Research in Religious Education*; Leominster, Herefordshire: Gracewing.

Freire, P. (1993) *Pedagogy of the Oppressed*; Harmondsworth: Penguin.

Friedman, M. (1999) 'The Interhuman and What is Common to All: Martin Buber and Sociology', *Journal for the Theory of Social Behaviour*, 29:4, pp. 403–17.

Friedman, M. S. (2002) *Martin Buber: The Life of Dialogue* (4th edition); London: Routledge.

Furlong, J., Barton, L., Miles, S., Whiting, C. and Whitty, G. (2000) *Teacher Education in Transition: Re-forming Professionalism?*; Buckingham: Open University Press.

Furlong, J. and Oancea, A. (2005) *Assessing Quality in Applied and Practice-based Educational Research: A Framework for Discussion*; Oxford: Oxford University Department of Educational Studies and the ESRC.

Gardner, H. (1993) *Multiple Intelligences: The Theory in Practice*; Basic Books.

Gardner, R., Cairns, J. and Lawton, D. (eds) (2000) *Education for Values: Morals, Ethics and Citizenship in Contemporary Teaching*; London: Kogan Page.

Gates, B. (1989) *RE: Supply of Teachers for the 1990s*; Lancaster: RE Council.

—— (1991) *What Conspired against RE Teacher Supply?*; Lancaster: RE Council.

—— (1994) *Time for Religious Education and Teachers to Match: A Digest of Under-provision*; Lancaster, RE Council.

Gearon, L. (ed.) (2002a) *Human Rights and Religion: A Reader*; Brighton: Sussex Academic Press.

—— (2002b) Human Rights and Religious Education: Some Postcolonial Perspectives', *British Journal of Religious Education* 24:2, Spring 2002, pp. 140–51.

—— (ed.) (2003a) *Learning to Teach Citizenship in the Secondary School*; London: Routledge.

—— (2003b) *The Human Rights Handbook: A Global Perspective for Education*; Stoke-on-Trent: Trentham.

—— (2004) *Citizenship Through Secondary Religious Education*; London: RoutledgeFalmer.

—— (2005) 'The Teaching of Human Rights in Religious Education: The Case of Genocide', in Bates, D. (ed.) (2005) *Education, Religion and Society: Essays in Honour of John M Hull*; London: Routledge.

Geaves, R. (1998) 'The Borders between Religions: A Challenge to the World Religions Approach to Religious Education', *British Journal of Religious Education*, 21:1, pp. 20–31.

—— Gabriel, T., Haddad, Y. and Idleman Smith, J. (2004) *Islam and the West Post September 11th*; Aldershot: Ashgate.

Ghosh, P. P., Khan, U. A. H. J., Khan, U. B. and Banerjee, P. N. (1987) *Morning To Midnight Ragas: Afternoon Ragas*; Calcutta: RPG CDNF150279.

Glatzer, N. N. and Mendes-Flohr, P. (eds) (1991) *The Letters of Martin Buber: A Life of Dialogue*; Syracuse, New York: Syracuse University Press.

Gordon, T. (1986) *Democracy in One School? Progressive Education and Restructuring*; London: Falmer.

Gould, S. J. (1977) *Ever Since Darwin: Reflections in Natural History*; Harmondsworth: Penguin.

Great Britain Board of Education (1936) *Homework (Educational Pamphlets, No. 110)*; London: HMSO.

Greene, G. (screenplay) (1949) *The Third Man*.

Grice, P. (1997) *The Use of Music and Video Resources in Religious Education: The Farmington Reports* (www.farmington.ac.uk/library/reports/tt/tt9.html).

Grimmitt, M. (1987) *Religious Education and Human Development*; Great Wakering, Essex: McCrimmon.

—— (ed.) (2000) *Pedagogies of Religious Education: Case Studies in the Development of Good Pedagogic Practice*; Great Wakering, Essex: McCrimmons.

Grove, J. and Smalley, S. (2003) *Diversity and Inclusion and Religious Education: A Good Practice Guide*; AREIAC www.areiac.org.uk/.

Habermas, J. (1999) 'From Kant to Hegel and Back again – The Move Towards Detranscendentalization', *European Journal of Philosophy*, 7:2, pp. 129–57.

Hallam, S. (2004) *Homework: The Evidence: Bedford Way Papers*; London: Institute of Education.

Hammond, J., Hay, D., Leech, A., Moxon, J., Netto, B., Robson, K. and Straughier, G. (1990) *New Methods in RE Teaching: An Experiential Approach*; London: Oliver & Boyd.

Sheikh Hamza Shakkur and Ensemble Al-Kindi (2000) *Les Derviches Tourneurs de Damas (The Whirling Dervishes of Damascus)*; Paris: Le Chant Du Monde, CMT574112324.

Hargreaves, D. H. (1967) *Social Relations in a Secondary School;* London: Routledge.

———— (1972) *Interpersonal Relations and Education;* London: Routledge & Kegan Paul.

—— (1982) *The Challenge For The Comprehensive School: Culture, Curriculum and Community*; London: Routledge & Kegan Paul.

—— (1996) 'Teaching as a Research-based Profession: Possibilities and Prospects', The Teacher Training Agency Annual Lecture, London, Teacher Training Agency.

Hargreaves, D. H. and Hopkins, D. (1991) *The Epowered School: The Management and Practice of Development Planning*; London: Cassell.

Harris, A., Bennett, N., and Preedy, M. (eds) (1997) *Organizational effectiveness and improvement in education*; Buckingham: Open University Press.

Hay, D. (1998) 'Relational Consciousness in Children: Empirical Support for Macmurray's Perspective', in *The Life and Work of John Macmurray: Conference Proceedings*, University of Aberdeen, March 1998.

—— with Nye, R. (1998) *The Spirit of the Child*; London: Harper Collins.

Heaney, S. (trans) (1999) *Beowulf: A New Translation*; London: Faber.

Hegel, G. W. F. (1988) *Lectures on the Philosophy of Religion: One-Volume Edition: The Lectures of 1827*: Edited by Peter C Hodgson; Translated by R F Brown, P. C Hodgson and J M Stewart, with the assistance of H S Harris; Berkeley, Los Angeles: University of California Press.

Her Majesty's Inspectorate (HMI) (1989) *The Influence of Agreed Syllabuses on Teaching and Learning in Religious Education in Three Local Authorities*; London: HMSO.

Hick, J. (ed.) (1974) *Truth and Dialogue: The Relationship Between World Religions*; London: Sheldon.

—— (1991) *An Interpretation of Religion*; London: Macmillan.

Higher Education Funding Council for England (Hefce) (2005) *Guidance to panels: January 2005: Ref RAE 01/2005*; Higher Education Funding Council for England, Scottish Higher Education Funding Council, Higher Education Funding Council for Wales, Department for Employment and Learning Northern Ireland, online at http://www.rae.ac.uk/pubs/2005/01/ and from http://www.hefce.ac.uk/research/.

Hillman, J. (1990) *The Essential James Hillman: A Blue Fire: Introduced and Edited by Thomas Moore in Collaboration with the Author*; London: Routledge.

Hodgkin, R. A. (1997) 'Making Space for Meaning', *Oxford Review of Education*, 23:3, September 1997, pp. 385–99.

Hogg, J. (introduction by Douglas Gifford) (1978) *The Private Memoirs And Confessions Of A Justified Sinner: Written By Himself: With A Detail Of Curious Traditionary Facts And Other Evidence By The Editor*; London: Folio.

Hölderlin, F. (1990) *Hyperion and Selected Poems: Edited by Eric L Santner*; New York: Continuum.

Holt, J. D. (2002) 'The Church of Jesus Christ of Latter-day Saints in the RE Classroom', *Resource*, 24:3, pp. 6–8.

—— (2004) 'Jehovah's Witnesses in the RE Classroom', *Resource*, 26:2, pp. 617–19.

Hornby, G. (2000) *Improving Parental Involvement*; London: Continuum.

—— Davis, G. and Taylor, G. (1995) *The Special Educational Needs Co-ordinator's Handbook: A Guide for Implementing the Code of Practice*; London: Routledge.

Houston, G. (1998) *Virtual Morality: Christian Ethics in the Computer Age*; Leicester: Apollos.

Howie, G. (ed.) (1968) *Aristotle on Education*; London: Collier-Macmillan.

Hoyle, E. and Wallace, M. (2005) *Educational Leadership: Ambiguity, Professionals and Managerialism*, London: Sage.

Hull, J. M. (1975) *School Worship: An Obituary*; Norwich: SCM Press.

—— (1998) *Utopian Whispers: Moral, Religious and Spiritual Values in Schools*; Norwich: RMEP.

—— (2003) *Many Religions – One World: an Educational Response to Religious Violence*; paper for research seminar, University of Birmingham School of Education, 2 October 2003.

—— (2004) 'Teaching as a trans-world activity', *Support for Learning*, 19:3, August 2004, pp. 103–6.

—— (2005) 'Religious Education in Germany and England: The Recent Work of Hans-Georg Ziebertz', *British Journal of Religious Education*, 27:1, January 2005, pp. 5–17.

Huxley, A. (1931) *Music At Night and Other Essays*; Edinburgh: Penguin in association with Chatto & Windus.

I'Anson, J. (2004) 'Mapping the Subject: Student Teachers, Location and the Understanding of Religion', *British Journal of Religious Education*, 26:1, March 2004, pp. 45–60.

Illich, I. D. (1971) *Deschooling Society*; London: Calder & Boyers.

—— (1974) *After Deschooling, What?*; London: Writers' and Readers' Publishing Cooperative.

Ipgrave, J. (1999) 'Issues in the Delivery of Religious Education to Muslim Pupils: Perspectives from the Classroom', *British Journal of Religious Education*, 21:3, Summer 1999, pp. 146–57.

—— (2001) *Pupil-To-Pupil Dialogue in the Classroom as a Tool for Religious Education: Warwick Religions and Education Research Unit Occasional Papers II*; Coventry: WRERU.

—— (2003) *Building e-Bridges: Inter-Faith Dialogue by E-Mail*; Birmingham: REToday Services.

—— (2004) 'Including pupils' faith background in primary religious education', *Support for Learning*, 19:3, August 2004, pp. 114–18.

Jackson, R. (1990) 'Children as Ethnographers', in Jackson, R. and Starkings, D. (eds) *The Junior RE Handbook*; Cheltenham: Stanley Thornes.

—— (1997) *Religious Education: An Interpretative Approach*; London: Hodder.

—— (1999) *Reflections on Research in Religious Education: Paper Presented at the CEM Research Committee Meeting*, 28 October 1999.

—— (ed.) (2003) *International Perspectives on Citizenship, Education and Religious Diversity*; London: RoutledgeFalmer.

—— (2004) *Rethinking Religious Education and Plurality: Issues in Diversity and Pedagogy*; London: RoutledgeFalmer.

—— (2006) 'New European Union Research on Religious Education', *Editorial, British Journal of Religious Education*, 28:2, March 2006, pp. 111–13.

—— and Nesbitt, E. (1993) *Hindu Children in Britain*; Stoke-on-Trent: Trentham.

Jin Long Eun (1996) *Buddhist Chants and Peace Music: Music for Reflection and Relaxation from the Far East*; Watford, Hertfordshire: Music Club MCCD 235.

Johnson, C. and Stern, L. J. (2005) 'Westhill Seminar 6: Ethnography, Pluralism and Religious Education', *Resource*, 28:1, Autumn 2005, pp. 3–6.

Keats, J. (1947) *The Letters of John Keats: Edited by Maurice Buxton Forman*; London: Oxford University Press.

Kelly, G. A. (1955) *The Psychology of Personal Constructs*; New York: Norton.

Kirkpatrick, F. G. (2005) *John Macmurray: Community Beyond Political Philosophy*; Lanham, Maryland: Rowman & Littlefield.

Kleinsmith, S. L. and Everts-Rogers, S. (2000) 'The Art of Followership: Educators who can carry out the leader's vision are vital to the system's effectiveness', *The School Administrator Web Edition*, September 2000 (www.aasa.org/publications/sa/2000_09/kleinsmith.htm).

The Klezmatics (2003) *Rise Up! Shteyt Oyf!*; Berlin: Piranha CD-PIR 1686.

—— and Chava Alberstein (1998) *The Well*; Danbury, Connecticut: Xenophile Xeno 4052.

Knowles, M. (1984) *Andragogy in Action: Applying Modern Principles of Adult Learning*; San Francisco, CA: Jossy-Bass.

Krisman, A. (2001) 'The Yin and Yang of RE and Special Needs: Teaching RE to Pupils With Special Needs Within a Multi-Faith Community', *SHAP: World Religions in Education: 2001/2001: Living Community*, 2001, pp. 83–4.

Kropotkin, P. (1995) *The Conquest of Bread and Other Writings*; Cambridge: Cambridge University Press.

Lacey, P. (2001) *Support Partnerships: Collaboration in Action*; London: Fulton.

Larkin, P. (1988) *Collected Poems: Edited with an Introduction by Anthony Thwaite*; London: The Marvell Press and Faber & Faber.

Lave, J. and Wenger, E. (1991) *Situated Learning: Legitimate Peripheral Participation*; Cambridge: Cambridge University Press.

Lee, S. (2005) *Higher Education Policy and Institutional Diversity under Labour 1997–2010*; Leeds: Leeds Metropolitan University, available at www.lmu.ac.uk/vco/reflect/jun05/cpse.pdf (also presented as a seminar to the Centre for Policy Studies in Education, Leeds University, 9 June 2005).

Leicester, M. (1992) 'Antiracism Versus the New Multiculturalism: Moving Beyond the Interminable Debate', in Lynch, J., Modgil, C. and Modgil, S. (eds) *Cultural Diversity and the Schools: Equity or Excellence? Education and Cultural Reproduction*; London: Falmer.

Lenga, R-A and Ogden, V. (2000) *Lost in Transit: Attainment deficit in pupil transition from Key Stage 2 to Key Stage 3*; London: Institute of Education, University of London.

Levinas, E. (1989) *The Levinas Reader: Edited by Seán Hand*; Oxford: Basil Blackwell.

Lockyer, A., Crick, B., and Annette, J. (2004) *Education for Democratic Citizenship: Issues of Theory and Practice*; Aldershot: Ashgate.

Lovelace, A. (2001) *Speaking for Ourselves: A REaSE Project Video*; Norwich: RMEP.

Lowndes, J. (1999) *The REaSE Project: Implementing a New Agreed Syllabus for Religious Education*; Havant: Hampshire County Council.

—— (2001) *Effective Staff Development: Improving Pupils' Achievement*; Havant: Hampshire County Council and Brunel University.

Lukes, S. (1974) *Power: A Radical View*; London: Macmillan.

—— (2005) *Power: A Radical View* (2nd edition); Basingstoke: Palgrave.

MacBeath, J. (1999) *Schools Must Speak For Themselves: The Case for School Self-Evaluation*; London: RoutledgeFalmer.

—— and Turner, M. (1990) *Learning out of School: Report of Research Study carried out at Jordanhill College*; Glasgow: Jordanhill College.

McCutcheon, R. T. (ed.) (1999) *The Insider/Outsider Problem in the Study of Religion: A Reader*; London: Cassell.

McDonald, J. P. (1989) 'When Outsiders Try to Change Schools From the Inside' in *Phi Delta Kappan*, 71:3, November 1989.

McFarlane, A., Sparrowhawk, A. and Heald, Y. (2002) *Report on the Educational Use of Games: An Exploration by TEEM of the Contribution Which Games Can Make to the Education Process*; Cambridge: TEEM (www.teem.org.uk).

MacIntyre, A. (1985) *After Virtue: a Study in Moral Theory* (2nd edition); London: Duckworth.

Mackley, J. (ed.) (2002) *Evil and Goodness*; Birmingham: Christian Education Publications.

Macmurray, J. (1968) *Lectures/Papers on Education*; Edinburgh: Edinburgh University Library, Special Collections Gen 2162/2.

—— (1979) *Ye Are My Friends and To Save From Fear*; London: Quaker Home Service.

—— (1991a) *The Self as Agent: Volume 1 of The Form of the Personal: Introduction by Stanley M Harrison*; London: Faber.

—— (1991b) *Persons in Relation: Volume 2 of The Form of the Personal: Introduction by Frank G Kirkpatrick*; London: Faber.

—— (1992) *Freedom in the Modern World*; New Jersey: Humanities Press.

—— (1993) *Conditions of Freedom*; New Jersey: Humanities Press.

—— (1995a) *Search for Reality in Religion*; London and Toronto: Quaker Home Service and the John Macmurray Society.

—— (1995b) *Reason and Emotion*; London: Faber.

—— (1996) *The Personal World: John Macmurray on Self and Society: Selected and Introduced by Philip Conford*; Edinburgh: Floris.

—— (2004) *John Macmurray: Selected Philosophical Writings: Edited and Introduced by Esther McIntosh*; Exeter: Imprint Academic.

Macpherson, C. B. (1962) *The Political Theory of Possessive Individualism: Hobbes to Locke*; Oxford: Clarendon Press.

Madera, P. (2000) 'Following and Leading', *Re:View*, 32:2, Summer 2000, pp. 51 ff.

Mamet, D. (1992) *Oleanna*; London: Methuen.

Marshall, P. (ed.) (2000) *Religious Freedom in the World: A Global Report on Freedom and Persecution*; London: Broadman and Holman.

Marx, K. and Engels, F. (1970) *The German Ideology: Students Edition*; London: Lawrence & Wishart.

May, S. (ed.) (1999) *Critical Multiculturalism: Rethinking Multicultural and Antiracist Education*; London: Falmer.

Mill, J. S. (1974) *On Liberty*; Harmondsworth: Penguin.

Milley, P. (2002) 'Imagining Good Organizations: Moral Orders or Moral Communities?', *Educational Management and Administration*, 30:1, pp. 47–64.

Mingers, J. (1999) *Critical Management Education: A Critical Issue (paper presented at the UK Systens Society Conference, July 1999)*.

Mitscherlich, A. (1993) *Society Without the Father: A Contribution to Social Psychology*; New York: HarperPerennial.

Modood, T. and Werbner, P. (eds) (1997) *The Politics of Multiculturalism in the New Europe: Racism, Identity and Community*; London: Zed Books.

Monteith, M. (ed.) (2002) *Teaching Primary Literacy With ICT*; Buckingham: Open University Press.

Moore, A., George, R. and Halpin, D. (2002) 'The Developing Role of the Headteacher in English Schools: Management, Leadership and Pragmatism', *Educational Management and Administration*, 30:2, pp. 175–88.

Moustakas, C. (1994) *Phenomenological Research Methods*; Beverley Hills, CA: Sage.

Munn, P. (ed.) (1993) *Parents and Schools: Customers, Managers or Partners?*; London: Routledge.

Murphy, P. (ed.) (1999) *Learners, Learning and Assessment*; London: Paul Chapman.

Myers, K. (2005) *Teachers Behaving Badly: Dilemmas for School Leaders*; London: RoutledgeFalmer.

Neill, A. S. (1985) *Summerhill: A Radical Approach to Child-Rearing*; Harmondsworth: Penguin.

Nesbitt, E. (2001) *Interfaith Pilgrims*, London: Quaker Books.

—— (2003) *Interfaith Pilgrims: Living Truths and Truthful Living*; London: Quaker Home Service.

—— (2004) *Intercultural Education: Ethnographic and Religious Approaches*; Brighton: Sussex Academic Press.

—— (2005) *Sikhism: A Very Short Introduction*; Oxford: Oxford University Press.

———— and Kaur, G. (1998) *Guru Nanak*; Calgary, Alberta: Bayeux Arts.

Newnes, C. (ed.), Burman, E., Mitchell, S. and Salmon, P. (co-eds) (1996) *Changes: An International Journal of Psychology and Psychotherapy: Special Issue: Tensions and dynamics in qualitative research*; 14:3, August 1996; Bognor Regis: John Wiley for the Psychology and Psychotherapy Association.

Newton, C. and Tarrant, T. (1992) *Managing Change in Schools: A Practical Handbook*; London: Routledge.

Noddings, N. (1984) *Caring: A Feminine approach to Ethics and Moral Education*; Berkeley: University of California Press.

—— (1993) *Education for Intelligent Belief or Unbelief*; New York: Teachers College Press.

—— (2003) *Happiness and Education*; Cambridge: Cambridge University Press.

Novak, J. D. (1998) *Learning, Creating, and Using Knowledge: Concept Maps As Facilitative Tools in Schools and Corporations*; Mawah, New Jersey: Lawrence Erlbaum.

Oakley, A. (1992) *Social Support and Motherhood: The Natural History of a Research Project*; Oxford: Basil Blackwell.

O'Brien, L. (2002) *Connecting with RE*; London: National Society.

O'Brien, T. (ed.) (2001) *Enabling Inclusion: Blue Skies – Dark Clouds*; London: The Stationery Office.

Oczkus, L. (2003) *Reciprocal Teaching at Work: Strategies for Improving Reading Comprehension*; Newark, Delaware: International Reading Association.

Office for Standards in Education (Ofsted) (1997) *The Impact of New Agreed Syllabuses on the Teaching and Learning of Religious Education*; London: The Stationery Office.

—— (2000a) *Evaluating Educational Inclusion: Guidance for Inspectors and Schools*; www.ofsted.gov.uk.

—— (2000b) *The Annual Report of Her Majesty's Chief Inspector of Schools: Standards and Quality in Education 1998/99*; London: The Stationery Office.

—— (2002) *The Annual Report of Her Majesty's Chief Inspector of Schools: 2000–2001: Standards and Quality in Education*; London: The Stationery Office.

—— (2003) *Inspecting Schools: Framework for Inspecting Schools*; London: Ofsted.

—— (2004) *An evaluation of the work of Standing Advisory Councils for Religious Education*; London: Ofsted, and www.ofsted.gov.uk.

O'Hanlon, C. (2003) *Education Inclusion as Action Research: An Interpretive Discourse*; Maidenhead: Open University Press.

Olson, C. (ed.) (2005) *Original Buddhist Sources: A Reader*; New Brunswick, New Jersey: Rutgers University Press.

Orchard, J. (2001) *Raising the Standard, Flying the Flag – Challenging Activities for all in RE at Key Stage 3*; London: National Society.

Padmasri and Adiccabandhu (1997) *The Monkey King and other tales: Teacher's Handbook*; Manchester: The Clear Vision Trust.

Parmar, N. (2001) *Using the Bhagavad Gita to Improve the Teaching of Hinduism at Key Stage 2*; Oxford: Farmington Institute (and http://www.farmington.ac.uk).

Patinkin, M. (1998) *Mamaloshen*; New York: Nonesuch.

Power, S. (2003) *A Problem from Hell: America and the Age of Genocide*; London: Flamingo.

Pring, R. (2000) *Philosophy of Educational Research*; London: Continuum.

—— (2004) *Philosophy of Education: Aims, Theory, Common Sense and Research*; London: Continuum.

Proudhon, P. J. (2004) *General Idea of the Revolution in the Nineteenth Century*; Honolulu, Hawaii: University Press of the Pacific.

Putnam, R. D. (2000) *Bowling Alone: The Collapse and Revival of American Community*; New York: Simon & Schuster.

Qualifications and Curriculum Authority (QCA) (2004) *Religious Education: The Non-Statutory National Framework*; London: QCA.

Ramjhun, A. F. (1995) *Implementing the Code of Practice for Children with Special Educational Needs: A Practical Guide*; London: Fulton.

Ranson, S. (2000) 'Recognizing the Pedagogy of Voice in a Learning Community', *Educational Management and Administration*, 28:3, pp. 263–79.

Rauchwerger, P. E. (1999) [Personal correspondence with Julian Stern, December 1999.]

Ravenette, T. (1999) *Personal Construct Theory in Educational Psychology: A Practitioner's View*; London: Whurr.

Read, G., Rudge, J., Teece, G. and Howarth, R. B. (1988) *How Do I Teach RE?: The Westhill Project RE 5–16* (2nd edition); Cheltenham: Stanley Thornes.

Rheingold, H. (2002) *Smart Mobs: The Next Social Revolution: Transforming Cultures and Communities in the Age of Instant Access*; Cambridge, Massachusetts: Perseus.

Ritzer, G. (2004) *The McDonaldization of Society: Revised New Century Edition*; Thousand Oaks, Ca: Sage.

Rorty, A. O. (ed.) (1998) *Philosophers on Education: New Historical Perspectives*; London: Routledge.

Rose, J. (1995) *Hindu Story and Symbol*; Isleworth: BFSS National RE Centre, Brunel University.

Roseneil, S. (2004) *Towards A More Friendly Society – Work, Care and Play in the 21st Century: Centre for Policy Studies in Education (CPSE) Seminar*, University of Leeds, 3 June 2004.

Rosengren, K. S., Johnson, C. N., and Harris, P. L (2000) *Imagining the Impossible: Magical, Scientific, and Religious Thinking in Children*; Cambridge: Cambridge University Press.

Royal Ministry of Church, Education and Research (1994) *Core Curriculum for Primary, Secondary and Adult Education in Norway*; Oslo: Akademika a/s, Box 8134 Dep, 0033 Oslo, Norway.

Rudduck, J., Chaplain, R., and Wallace, G. (eds) (1996) *School Improvement: What Can Pupils Tell Us?*; London: Fulton.

—— and Flutter, J. (2004) *How To Improve Your School: Giving Pupils A Voice*; London: Continuum.

Rudge, L. (1998) 'I Am Nothing: Does It Matter?': A Critique of Current Religious Education Policy and Practice on Behalf of the Silent Majority', *British Journal of Religious Education, 20:3, pp. 155–65*.

—— (2001) *Making RE Work: Principles to Practice in Curriculum and Professional Development: Summary Report 2001: Review, Design and Implementation*; Norwich: University of East Anglia.

Rumi (1995) *The Essential Rumi: Translated by Coleman Barks with John Moyne, A. J. Arberry and Reynold Nicholson*; Harmondsworth: Penguin.

Rüppell, G. and Schreiner, P. (eds) (2003) *Shared Learning in a Plural World: Ecumenical Approaches to Inter-Religious Education*; Münster: Comenius Institut.

Ruse, M. (1986) *Taking Darwin Seriously*; Oxford: Blackwell.

Ruthven, M. (2004) *Fundamentalism: The Search for Meaning*; Oxford: Oxford University Press.

Sacks, J. (2003) *The Dignity of Difference: How To Avoid the Clash of Civilizations* (2nd edition); London: Continuum.

Salmon, P. (ed.) (1980) *Coming to Know*; London: Routledge.

—— (1985) *Living in Time: A New Look at Personal Development*; London: Dent.

—— (1988) *Psychology for Teachers: An Alternative Approach*; London: Hutchinson Education.

—— 'Grids are all very well, but ...' *EPCA Newsletter*, 1994, p. 2.

—— (1995) *Psychology in the Classroom: Reconstructing Teachers and Learners*; London: Cassell.

—— (1998) *Life at School: Education and Psychology*; London: Constable.

—— (2000) *Being at the Receiving End: a Story of Brain Surgery*; offprint, also published in *Changes: An International Journal of Psychology and Psychotherapy*.

—— (2001) 'Using Multiple Voices in Autobiographical Writing', *EPCA Newsletter, 2001*.

—— (2004) 'The Schizococcus: An Interpersonal Perspective', *Personal Construct Theory and Practice*, 1, pp. 76–81, www.pcp-net.org/journal/pctp04/salmon04.html.

Sankey, D., Sullivan and Watson (1988) *At Home on Planet Earth*, Oxford: Basil Blackwell.

Schiller, F. (1967) *On the Aesthetic Education of Man in a Series of Letters* [*Briefe über die ästhetische Erziehung des Menschen, 1795*]; Oxford: Clarendon.

School Curriculum and Assessment Authority (SCAA) (1994a) *Model syllabuses for religious education: Model 1: Living Faiths Today*; London: SCAA.

—— (1994b) *Model syllabuses for religious education: Model 2: Questions and Teachings*; London: SCAA.

—— (1995) *Spiritual and Moral Development: SCAA Discussion Papers: No. 3*; London: SCAA.

Schreiner, P. (2001) 'Different Approaches – Common Aims?: Current Developments in Religious Education in Europe', *Paper delivered in Oslo, November 2001*; Münster: Comenius-Institut (and www.comenius.de).

—— (2005) 'Towards Holistic Education: A Challenge for Education Philosophy', *Paper delivered in Oslo, 9 September 2005*; Münster: Comenius-Institut (and www.comenius.de).

—— Spinder, H., Taylor, J. and Westerman, W. (eds) (2002) *Committed to Europe's Future: Contributions from Education and Religious Education: A Reader*; Münster, Germany: CoGREE (Coordinating Group for Religious Education in Europe) and the Comenius-Institut.

Schutz, A. (1976) *Collected Papers II: The Problem of Social Reality*; Martinus Nijhoff: The Hague.

Schweitzer, F. (2006) 'Let the Captives Speak for Themselves! More Dialogue Between Religious Education in England and Germany', *British Journal of Religious Education*, 28:2, March 2006, pp. 141–51.

Searle-Chatterjee, M. (2000) ' "World Religions" and "Ethnic Groups": Do these Paradigms Lend themselves to the Cause of Hindu Nationalism?', *Ethnic and Racial Studies*, 23:3, pp. 497–515.

—— Boulton, D., Harnor, M. (2000) *Community: Description, Debate and Dilemma*; Birmingham: Venture Press.

Sennett, R. (2003) *Respect in a World of Inequality*; London: Norton.

Shankar, R. (1997) *Chants of India*; New York: Angel Records 7243 8 55948 2 3.

Shiloah, A. (1976) 'The Dimension of Sound', in Parsons, D. (producer) (1997), *The Music of Islam*; Tucson, Arizona: Celestial Harmonies 13159–2. Originally from *The World of Islam: Faith, People, Culture*; London: Thames and Hudson.

Sikes, P. and Everington, J. (2001) 'Becoming an RE teacher: a Life History approach', *British Journal of Religious Education*, 24:1, pp. 8–20.

Silverman, D. (ed.) (1997) *Qualitative Research: Theory, Method and Practice*; London: Sage.

Simpson, J. A. (chief editor) (2005) *The Oxford English Dictionary: Third Edition*; Oxford: Oxford University Press, at www.oed.com and dictionary.oed.com/

Skeie, G. (1995) 'Plurality and Pluralism: A Challenge for Religious Education', *British Journal of Religious Education*, 17:2, pp. 84–91.

Smalley, S. (2005) 'Teaching about Islam and Learning about Muslims: Islamophobia in the Classroom', *REsource*, 27:2, pp. 4–7.

Smart, N. (1960) *A Dialogue of Religions*; London: SCM.

—— (1969) *The Religious Experience of Mankind*; London: Collins.

—— (1999) *World Philosophies*; London: Routledge.

Smith, G. (2005) *Children's Perspectives on Believing and Belonging*; London: National Children's Bureau for the Joseph Rowntree Foundation.

Smith, M. K. (2000) 'Martin Buber on Education', *The Encyclopedia of Informal Education*, www.infed.org/thinkers/et-buber.htm

Smith, S. (2003) 'Teaching in a World of Genocide', *Resource*, 25:2, Spring 2003, pp. 7–10.

Smith, W. C. (1978) *The Meaning and End of Religion*; London: SPCK.

Soglasie Male Voice Choir of St Petersburg, Conducted By Alexander Govorov (1995) *Authentic Russian Sacred Music*; London: IMP PCD 2030.

Somerville, C. (1999) [Personal correspondence with Julian Stern, December 1999.]

Soweto String Quartet (1994) *Zebra Crossing*; BMG 74321268652.

Spinoza, B. (1955) *The Ethics*; New York: Dover.

Stead, J. (2006) *The Listening School*; London: NSPCC.

Stern, A. (1971) 'Equality', *Proceedings of the XIVth International Congress of Philosophy, Vienna*, September 1968, pp. 520–26.

Stern, L. J. (1997) *Homework and Study Support: A Guide for Teachers and Parents*; London: David Fulton.

—— (1998) 'Overcoming Pianist Envy: Collaborative Work in Music and Religious Education'; paper accompanying presentation at St Gabriel's Trust national inset weekend, Sunningdale.

—— (1999) *Developing as a Teacher of History*; Cambridge: Chris Kington.

—— (2000a) 'Home: Not Alone … how to use computers for homework in RE', *RE Today*, 17:3, pp. 26–7.

—— (2000b) 'RE and School Effectiveness', *Resource*, 23:1, pp. 8–14, Autumn 2000.

—— (2001a) *Developing Schools as Learning Communities: Towards a Way of Understanding School Organisation, School Development, and Learning*; London: London University Institute of Education: PhD thesis.

—— (2001b) 'John Macmurray, Spirituality, Community and Real Schools' *International Journal of Children's Spirituality*, 6:1, April 2001, pp. 25–39.

—— (2001c) 'Being DIRECT With Primary Religious Education: Linking Primary RE to Local Communities', *Resource* 23:2, Spring 2001, pp. 11–15.

—— (2001d) 'Making a Community of a School: Being DIRECT with Primary School Religious Education and Local Communities', *SHAP: World Religions in Education: 2001/2001: Living Community*, 2001, pp. 56–9.

—— (2001e) 'Triangulating RE INSET: Effective Support for a New Agreed Syllabus', *Resource*, 24:1, Autumn 2001, pp. 15–19.

—— (2002) 'EMU Leadership: An Egalitarian Magnanimous Undemocratic Way for Schools', *International Journal of Children's Spirituality*, 7:2, August 2002, pp. 143–58.

—— (2003) *Involving Parents*; London: Continuum.

—— (2004) 'Marking time: using music to create inclusive Religious Education and inclusive schools', *Support for Learning*, 19:3, pp. 107–13.

—— (2006a) *Getting the Buggers to Do Their Homework*; London: Continuum.

—— (2006b) *Teaching Religious Education: Researchers in the Classroom*; London: Continuum.

—— and James, S. (2006) 'Every Person Matters: Enabling Spirituality Education for Nurses', *Journal of Clinical Nursing*, 15:7, July 2006, pp. 897–904.

Stern-Gillet, S. (1995) *Aristotle's Philosophy of Friendship*; Albany, NY: SUNY.

Stoll, L. and Myers, K. (eds) (1998) *No Quick Fixes: Perspectives on Schools in Difficulty*; London: Falmer.

Stroup, J. (2004) 'Evolving theories of "followership"', contributed on 22 September 2004 to Managing Leadership: An open discussion about what leadership in organizations really is – and how to manage it', at managingleadership.blogspot.com/2004/09/evolving-theories-of-followership.html.

Sutcliffe, S. J. (ed.) (2004) *Religion: Empirical Studies: A Collection to Mark the 50th Anniversary of the British Association for the Study of Religions*; Aldershot: Ashgate.

Sutherland, A. (2006) 'How I put my husband through the hoops', *Guardian*, 6 July 2006, pp. 8–9 (and www.guardianunlimited.co.uk/).

Sweet Honey In The Rock (1988) *Breaths: Greatest Hits*; London: Flying Fish COOKCD 008.

Tavener, J. (2000) *Fall and Resurrection*; Colchester, Essex: Chandos Chan 9800.

Teece, G. (2004) 'A perspective from NASACRE: The National Framework for RE – Potential Unleashed', *Resource*, 27:1 Autumn 2004, pp. 7–8.

Tekbilek, O. F. (1994) *Whirling*; Tucson, Arizona: Celestial Harmonies 13086 2.

Thompson, P. (2004a) *Whatever Happened to Religious Education?*; Cambridge: Lutterworth Press.

—— (2004b) 'Whose Confession? Which Tradition', *British Journal of Religious Education*, 26:1, pp. 61–72.

Tilley, S. (ed.) (2005) *Psychiatric and Mental Health Nursing: The Field of Knowledge*; Oxford: Blackwell.

Times Higher Educational Supplement (THES) (1997) 'Messages resonant in the midst of a score', *Times Higher Educational Supplement, 22 August 1997*.

Training and Development Agency for Schools (TDA) (2006a) *Draft standards for classroom teachers*; London: TDA.

—— (2006b) *Professional Standards for Teachers (draft)*; London: TDA.

Troyna, B. (1983) 'Multicultural Education: Just Another Brick in the Wall?', *New Community*, 10, pp. 424–8.

—— and Carrington, B. (1990) *Education, Racism and Reform*; London: Routledge.

United Nations Educational, Scientific and Cultural Organisation (UNESCO) (1994) *The Salamanca Statement and Framework for Action on Special Needs Education*; Paris: UNESCO (and www.unesco.org/education/educprog/sne/salamanc/covere.html).

University of Bristol Graduate School of Education Document Summary Service (University of Bristol) (1998) *Teachers' Legal Liabilities and Responsibilities (DfEE Circular 4/98: QTS Standards): The Bristol Guide*; Bristol: University of Bristol.

Veer, R. vd and Valsiner, J. (eds) (1994) *The Vygotsky Reader*; Oxford: Blackwell.

Vincent, C. (2000) *Including Parents?: Education, Citizenship and Parental Agency*; Buckingham: Open University Press.

Ward, C. (1982) *Anarchy in Action* (2nd edition); London: Freedom Press.

Warin, S. (1995) *Implementing the Code of Practice: Individual Education Plans*; Tamworth, Staffs: NASEN.

Warren, J. (1989) *Becoming Real: An Introduction to the Thought of John Macmurray*; York: Sessions Book Trust.

The Watersons *et al.* (1996) *The Season Round: Traditional Carols and Celebrations for the Whole Year*; London: Topic TSCD 700.

Wearmouth, J. (2000) *Special Educational Provision: Meeting the Challenges in Schools*; London: Hodder.

—— (ed.) (2001) *Special Educational Provision in the Context of Inclusion: Policy and Practice in Schools*; London: Fulton/Open University.

Weeden, P., Winter, J. and Broadfoot, P. (2002) *Assessment: What's In It For Schools?*; London: RoutledgeFalmer.

Wenger, E. (1998) *Communities of Practice: Learning, Meaning, and Identity*; Cambridge: Cambridge University Press.

Weston, D. (2003) 'Children Talking Online'; *RE Today, 21:1, Autumn 2003, pp. 30–31.*

White, J. (2000) *DIRECT: Dialogue, Inclusion, Relevancy, Esteem, Changing Dynamics, Togetherness: Croydon LEA REaSE Report for 1999–2000*; Isleworth: BFSS National RE Centre, Brunel University.

—— (2001) *BRIDGES – A Way Forward: REaSE Report*; Isleworth: BFSS National RE Centre, Brunel University.

Wilkinson, G. (2006) 'McSchools for McWorld? Mediating Global Pressures With a McDonaldizing Education Policy Response', *Cambridge Journal of Education, 36:1, March 2006, pp. 81–98.*

Willis, P. (1977) *Learning to Labour: How Working Class Kids Get Working Class Jobs*; Farnborough, Hants: Saxon House.

Wintersgill, B. (1995) 'The Case of the Missing Models: Exploding the Myths', *Resource, 18:1, Autumn 1995.*

Wittgenstein, L. (1958) *Philosophische Untersuchungen: Philosophical Investigations (second edition)*; Oxford: Blackwell.

Wolfendale, S. (ed.) (2002) *Parent Partnership Services for Special Educational Needs: Celebrations and Challenges*; London: David Fulton.

—— and Bastiani, J. (eds) (2000) *The Contribution of Parents to School Effectiveness*; London: David Fulton.

Wong, P. H. (2006) *A Conceptual Investigation into Spirituality and Conditions for Education in Spirituality, With Application to the Case of Hong Kong*; Hull: University of Hull: PhD thesis.

Wood, D. (1988) *How Children Think and Learn: The Social Contexts of Cognitive Development*; Oxford: Blackwell.

Wright, A. (1993) *Religious Education in the Secondary School: Prospects for Religious Literacy*; London: David Fulton.

—— (1997) 'Mishmash, Religionism and Theological Literacy: an Appreciation and Critique of Trevor Cooling's Hermeneutical Programme', *British Journal of Religious Education, 19:2, pp. 143–56.*

—— (1999) *Discerning the Spirit: Teaching Spirituality in the Religious Education Classroom*; Abingdon: Culham College Institute.

Yaron, K. (1993) 'Martin Buber (1878–1965)', *Prospects: the quarterly review of comparative education, Paris, UNESCO: International Bureau of Education, XXIII:1/2,* 1993, pp. 135–46, and www.ibe.unesco.org/International/Publications/Thinkers/ThinkersPdf/bubere.pdf.

The Yearly Meeting of the Religious Society of Friends (Quakers) in Britain (1999) *Quaker Faith & Practice* (2nd edition); Warwick: The Yearly Meeting of the Religious Society of Friends (Quakers) in Britain.

Yeats, W. B. (ed.) (1936) *The Oxford Book of Modern Verse: 1892–1935*; Oxford: Oxford University Press.

Yovel, Y. (1989a) *Spinoza and Other Heretics: The Marrano of Reason*; Princeton, New Jersey: Princeton University Press.

—— (1989b) *Spinoza and Other Heretics: The Adventures of Immanence*; Princeton, New Jersey: Princeton University Press.

Zaehner, R. C. (ed. and trans) (1992) *Hindu Scriptures*; London: Everyman.

Zamorski, B. (2000) *Making RE Work: Principles to Practice in Curriculum and Professional Development: Research Report: Implementation of the Agreed Syllabus in LEAs 4, 5 and 6*; Norwich: University of East Anglia.

Index

Index